NOLO *Your Legal Companion*

"In Nolo you can trust." —**THE NEW YORK TIMES**

Whether you have a simple question or a complex problem, turn to us at:

NOLO.COM

Your all-in-one legal resource

Need quick information about wills, patents, adoptions, starting a business—or anything else that's affected by the law? **Nolo.com** is packed with free articles, legal updates, resources and a complete catalog of our books and software.

NOLO NOW

Make your legal documents online

Creating a legal document has never been easier or more cost-effective! Featuring Nolo's Online Will, as well as online forms for LLC formation, incorporation, divorce, name change—and many more! Check it out at **http://nolonow.nolo.com**.

NOLO'S LAWYER DIRECTORY

Meet your new attorney

If you want advice from a qualified attorney, turn to Nolo's Lawyer Directory—the only directory that lets you see hundreds of in-depth attorney profiles so you can pick the one that's right for you. Find it at **http://lawyers.nolo.com**.

ALWAYS UP TO DATE

Sign up for NOLO'S LEGAL UPDATER

Old law is bad law. We'll email you when we publish an updated edition of this book—sign up for this free service at nolo.com/legalupdater.

Find the latest updates at NOLO.COM

Recognizing that the law can change even before you use this book, we post legal updates during the life of this edition at **nolo.com/updates**.

Is this edition the newest? ASK US!

To make sure that this is the most recent edition available, just give us a call at **800-728-3555**.

(Please note that we cannot offer legal advice.)

7th Edition

Leases & Rental Agreements

By Marcia Stewart
& Attorneys Ralph Warner & Janet Portman

SEVENTH EDITION	NOVEMBER 2007
Legal Researcher	TERRY McGINLEY
Cover Design	JALEH DOANE
Production	SARAH HINMAN
CD-ROM Preparation	ELLEN BITTER
Proofreading	ROBERT WELLS
Index	BAYSIDE INDEXING
Printing	CONSOLIDATED PRINTERS, INC.

International Standard Serial Number (ISSN) 1555-5291

ISBN-13: 978-1-4133-0692-7

ISBN-10: 1-4133-0692-6

For information on bulk purchases or corporate premium sales, please contact the Special Sales
Department. For academic sales or textbook adoptions, ask for Academic Sales. Call 800-955-4775
or write to Nolo at 950 Parker Street, Berkeley, CA 94710.

Acknowledgments

Special thanks to Mary Randolph, editor and friend extraordinaire, who contributed many valuable ideas to this book.

Many other Nolo colleagues and friends helped with this book. Special thanks to: Terry McGinley for her excellent legal research; Stan Jacobsen for his research assistance; Amy Ihara, Terri Hearsh, Toni Ihara, and Sarah Hinman for their creative and skillful book design; and Susan Putney and Jaleh Doane, who always make the book production process go so smoothly.

Table of Contents

1 Being a Successful Landlord

2 Preparing a Lease or Rental Agreement

Which Is Better, a Lease or a Rental Agreement? 8

Completing the Lease or Rental Agreement Form 10

Signing the Lease or Rental Agreement 43

3 Choosing Tenants: Your Most Important Decision

How to Advertise Rental Property 52

Renting Property That's Still Occupied 54

Accepting Rental Applications 54

Checking References, Credit History, and More 60

Avoiding Illegal Discrimination 67

Choosing—and Rejecting—an Applicant 68

Choosing a Tenant-Manager 73

Property Management Companies 74

4 Getting the Tenant Moved In

Inspect and Photograph the Unit 76

Send New Tenants a Move-In Letter 82

Cash Rent and Security Deposit Checks 85

Organize Your Tenant Records 85

Organize Income and Expenses for Schedule E 86

5 Changing or Ending a Tenancy

How to Modify Signed Rental Agreements and Leases 90

Ending a Month-to-Month Tenancy 91

How Fixed-Term Leases End 98

Returning Security Deposits When a Tenancy Ends 103

Appendixes

A State Landlord-Tenant Law Charts

State Landlord-Tenant Statutes 108

Notice Required to Change or Terminate a
Month-to-Month Tenancy 109

State Rent Rules 112

State Security Deposit Rules 114

Required Security Deposit Disclosures 120

States That Require Landlords to Pay Interest on Deposits 123

Attachment to Florida Leases and Rental Agreements
(Security Deposits) 124

State Laws on Landlord's Access to Rental Property 125

B How to Use the Landlord Rental Forms CD-ROM

Installing the Form Files Onto Your Computer 132

Using the Word Processing Files to Create Documents 133

Using Print-Only Files 134

Files Included on the CD-ROM 136

C Tear-Out Landlord Rental Forms

Leases and Rental Agreements and Lead Disclosures

Month-to-Month Residential Rental Agreement

Month-to-Month Residential Rental Agreement (Spanish version)

Fixed-Term Residential Lease

Fixed-Term Residential Lease (Spanish version)

Disclosure of Information on Lead-Based Paint or Lead-Based Paint Hazards

Disclosure of Information on Lead-Based Paint or Lead-Based Paint Hazards
(Spanish version)

Protect Your Family From Lead in Your Home Pamphlet

Protect Your Family From Lead in Your Home Pamphlet (Spanish version)

Screening and Choosing Tenants

Rental Application

Consent to Contact References and Perform Credit Check

Tenant References

Notice of Denial Based on Credit Report and Other Information

Notice of Conditional Acceptance Based on a Credit Report or Other Information

Moving in Tenants

Landlord-Tenant Checklist

Move-In Letter

Moving Out Tenants

Tenant's Notice of Intent to Move Out

Move-Out Letter

eGuide

Complying with Discrimination Laws (on CD-ROM only)

Index

Being a Successful Landlord

The rental agreement or lease that you and your tenant sign is the contractual basis of your relationship. Taken together with the landlord-tenant laws of your state—and, in a few areas, local and federal laws—it sets out almost all the legal rules you and your tenant must follow. Your rental agreement or lease is also an immensely practical document, full of crucial business details, such as how long the tenant can occupy your property and the amount of the rent.

Given their importance, there's no question that you need to create effective and legal rental agreements or leases with your tenants. This book shows you how, by providing clearly written, fair, and effective lease and rental agreement forms, along with clear explanations of each clause.

Our agreements are legally accurate and up to date, based on careful research of every state's landlord-tenant laws. They can be tailored to fit the details of your situation using the 50-state law charts in Appendix A. Throughout the book, we suggest ways to do this.

In addition to showing you how to prepare a lease or rental agreement, this book also covers key legal issues that landlords need to understand, including how to legally choose tenants and start a tenancy. It also highlights the legal and practical issues involved with changing or ending a tenancy. This book provides forms that supplement a lease and a rental agreement, including a rental application designed to help you choose the best tenant. Other forms, such as a Landlord-Tenant Checklist (used to document the condition of the rental unit at the beginning and end of the tenancy), will help you avoid legal problems with tenants, such as disputes over security deposits.

CD-ROM

The lease and rental agreement and other forms included in this book are on the Landlord Rental Forms CD. We also include tear-out versions of these forms in Appendix C at the back of the book. The CD-ROM also includes a special legal guide to complying with discrimination laws.

CAUTION

Who shouldn't use our lease or rental agreement? Don't use the forms in this book if you're renting out property that is subsidized by the government, such as the Section 8 program of the federal Department of Housing and Urban Development. You may need to use a special government-drafted lease. Also, our forms should not be used for renting out mobile homes, townhouses, hotels, or commercial property. If you are renting out your condominium or townhouse, use this book in conjunction with your homeowners' association's rules and regulations (called CC&Rs, or covenants, conditions, and restrictions). These CC&Rs may affect how you structure the terms and conditions of the rental and how your tenant uses the unit.

Other Nolo Books and Products for Landlords

A lease or rental agreement is only one part of a landlord-tenant legal relationship. For example, many state (and some federal and local) laws are also extremely important. A comprehensive explanation of these laws, and the practical steps rental property owners can take to comply with them (while at the same time running an efficient and profitable business), is covered in *Every Landlord's Legal Guide*, by Marcia Stewart, Ralph Warner, & Janet Portman (Nolo).

It covers most key laws affecting landlords in all 50 states, including your repair and maintenance responsibilities and your liability for crime and environmental hazards such as lead; rules and procedures for collecting and returning security deposits; antidiscrimination laws; privacy rules; employment laws affecting managers; how to resolve problems with tenants or begin the eviction process; and more. *Every Landlord's Legal Guide* includes over 20 legal forms on CD and in tear-out form.

Nolo's other landlord titles include:

- *Every Landlord's Guide to Finding Great Tenants*, by Janet Portman, a comprehensive guide to attracting, screening, and choosing the best tenants possible

- *Every Landlord's Tax Deduction Guide*, by Stephen Fishman, a detailed explanation of deductions and other tax write-offs available to landlords

- *The California Landlord's Law Book: Rights & Responsibilities*, by David Brown, Ralph Warner, & Janet Portman

- *The California Landlord's Law Book: Evictions*, by David Brown, and

- *LeaseWriter Plus Landlord Software*.

You can order these landlord titles from Nolo's website (www.nolo.com) or by phone (800-728-3555). You can also find Nolo books at bookstores and libraries.

Be sure to check out the Nolo website, which has lots of free information of interest to landlords, including legal updates. On the home page, choose Property and Money, then Landlords and Property Management.

11 Tips for Being a Successful Landlord

1. **Don't rent to anyone before checking their credit history, references, and background.** Haphazard screening too often results in problems—a tenant who pays the rent late or not at all, trashes your place, moves in undesirable friends, or worse.

2. **Avoid illegal discrimination.** Comply with all federal and state laws prohibiting discrimination on the basis of race or color, national origin, gender, age, familial status, or disability. (See Chapter 3 for an overview of the topic and the special legal guide "Complying With Discrimination Laws" on the Landlord Rental Forms CD.)

3. **Get all the important terms of the tenancy in writing.** Beginning with the rental application and lease or rental agreement, be sure to document important facts of your relationship with your tenants—including when and how you handle tenant complaints and repair problems, notice you must give to enter a tenant's apartment, and the like.

4. **Establish a clear, fair system of setting, collecting, holding, and returning security deposits.** Inspect and document the condition of the rental unit before the tenant moves in to avoid disputes over security deposits when the tenant moves out.

5. **Stay on top of repair and maintenance needs and make repairs when requested.** If the property is not kept in good repair, you'll alienate good tenants. And they may have the right to withhold rent, sue for any injuries caused by defective conditions, or move out without notice.

6. **Don't let your tenants and property be easy marks for a criminal.** You could well be liable for the tenant's losses. Landlords are sued more than any other group of business owners in the country. The average settlement paid by a landlord's insurance company is $600,000, and the average jury award is $1.2 million.

7. **Respect your tenants' privacy.** Notify tenants whenever you plan to enter their rental unit, and provide as much notice as possible, at least 24 hours or the minimum amount required by state law.

8. **Disclose environmental hazards such as lead.** Landlords are increasingly being held liable for tenant health problems resulting from exposure to environmental poisons in the rental premises.

9. **Choose and supervise your manager carefully.** If a manager commits a crime or is incompetent, you may be held financially responsible. Do a thorough background check and clearly spell out the manager's duties to help prevent problems down the road.

10. **Purchase enough liability and other property insurance.** A well-designed insurance program can protect your rental property from losses caused by everything from fire and storms to burglary, vandalism, and personal injury and discrimination lawsuits.

11. **Try to resolve disputes with tenants without lawyers and lawsuits.** If you have a conflict with a tenant over rent, repairs, your access to the rental unit, noise, or some other issue that doesn't immediately warrant an eviction, meet with the tenant to see if the problem can be resolved informally. If that doesn't work, consider mediation by a neutral third party, often available at little or no cost from a publicly funded program. If your dispute involves money and all attempts to reach agreement fail, try small claims court, where you can represent yourself. Use it to collect unpaid rent or to seek money for property damage after a tenant moves out and the deposit is exhausted.

Get a Little Help From Your Friends

Many landlords have discovered the value of belonging to a local or state association of rental property owners. These organizations range from small, volunteer-run groups to substantial city, county, or even statewide organizations with paid staff and lobbyists. Many offer a wide variety of support and services to their members, including the following:

- legal information and updates through newsletters, publications, seminars, and other means

- tenant-screening and credit check services

- training and practical advice on compliance with legal responsibilities

- a place to meet other rental property owners and exchange information and ideas, and

- referrals to knowledgeable and appropriately priced professionals, including attorneys, accountants, maintenance firms, and property management companies.

If you can't find an association of rental property owners in your phone book or online, ask other landlords for references. You can also contact the National Apartment Association (NAA), a national organization whose members include many individual state associations:

National Apartment Association
4300 Wilson Boulevard, Suite 400
Arlington, VA 22203
703-518-6141
www.naahq.org

The National Multi-Housing Council, a national organization of many of the country's largest landlords, may also be helpful:

National Multi-Housing Council
1850 M Street, NW, Suite 540
Washington, DC 20036
202-974-2300
www.nmhc.org

Preparing a Lease or Rental Agreement

Which Is Better, a Lease or a Rental Agreement? 8
    Month-to-Month Rental Agreement 8
    Fixed-Term Lease 8

Completing the Lease or Rental Agreement Form 10
    Clause 1. Identification of Landlord and Tenant...11
    Clause 2. Identification of Premises 11
    Clause 3. Limits on Use and Occupancy 14
    Clause 4. Term of the Tenancy 14
    Clause 5. Payment of Rent..17
    Clause 6. Late Charges 19
    Clause 7. Returned Check and Other Bank Charges...20
    Clause 8. Security Deposit...21
    Clause 9. Utilities...25
    Clause 10. Assignment and Subletting..25
    Clause 11. Tenant's Maintenance Responsibilities...27
    Clause 12. Repairs and Alterations by Tenant..29
    Clause 13. Violating Laws and Causing Disturbances...31
    Clause 14. Pets 32
    Clause 15. Landlord's Right to Access...33
    Clause 16. Extended Absences by Tenant..35
    Clause 17. Possession of the Premises..35
    Clause 18. Tenant Rules and Regulations..36
    Clause 19. Payment of Court Costs and Attorney Fees in a Lawsuit...................................37
    Clause 20. Disclosures..38
    Clause 21. Authority to Receive Legal Papers...41
    Clause 22. Additional Provisions..41
    Clause 23. Validity of Each Part..42
    Clause 24. Grounds for Termination of Tenancy..42
    Clause 25. Entire Agreement...43

Signing the Lease or Rental Agreement..43

This chapter provides step-by-step instructions on how to prepare a lease or rental agreement form. It discusses important issues that relate to your choices—as to both the type of document and the specific provisions—including any state, federal, and local laws that may apply.

SEE AN EXPERT

The lease and rental agreement forms are legally sound as designed. If you change important terms or make major changes, however, you may affect a form's legal validity. In this case, you may wish to have your work reviewed by an experienced landlords' lawyer.

Which Is Better, a Lease or a Rental Agreement?

One of the key decisions you need to make is whether to use a lease or a rental agreement. Often, but by no means always, your choice will depend on how long you want a tenant to stay. But, since other factors can also come into play, read what follows carefully before evaluating your own situation and making a decision.

Month-to-Month Rental Agreement

A written rental agreement provides for a tenancy for a short period of time. The law refers to these agreements as periodic or month-to-month tenancies, although it is often legally possible to base them on other time periods, as would be the case if the rent must be paid every two weeks. A month-to-month tenancy automatically renews each month—or other agreed-upon period— unless the landlord or tenant gives the other the proper amount of written notice (typically 30 days) and terminates the agreement.

Month-to-month rental agreements give landlords more flexibility than leases. You may increase the rent or change other terms of the tenancy on relatively short notice (subject to any restrictions of local rent control ordinances—see "Rent Control," below). And with proper notice, you may also end the tenancy at any time (again, subject to any rent control restrictions). (Chapter 5 discusses notice requirements to change or end a rental agreement.) Not surprisingly, many landlords prefer to rent month to month, particularly in urban areas with tight rental markets where new tenants are usually easily found and rents are trending upwards.

On the flip side, a month-to-month tenancy almost guarantees more tenant turnover. Tenants who may legally move out with only 30 days' notice may be more inclined to do so than tenants who make a longer commitment. Some landlords base their rental business strategy on painstakingly seeking high-quality, long-term renters. If you're one of those, or if you live in an area where it's difficult to fill vacancies, you will probably want tenants to commit for a longer period, such as a year. As discussed below, a fixed-term lease, especially when combined with tenant-friendly management policies, may encourage tenants to stay longer. However, it is no guarantee against turnover.

Fixed-Term Lease

A lease is a contract that obligates both you and the tenant for a set period of time—usually six months or a year, but sometimes longer. With a fixed-term lease, you can't raise the rent or change other terms of the tenancy until the lease runs out, unless the lease itself allows future changes or the tenant agrees in writing to the changes.

In addition, you usually can't ask a tenant to move out or prevail in an eviction lawsuit before the lease term expires unless the tenant fails to pay the rent or violates another significant term of the lease or the law, such as repeatedly making too much noise, damaging the rental unit, or selling drugs on your property. This restriction can sometimes be problematic if you end up with a tenant you would like to be rid of but don't have sufficient cause to evict.

To take but one example, if you wish to sell the property halfway into the lease, the existence of long-term tenants—especially if they are paying less than the market rate—may be a negative factor. The new owner usually purchases all the obligations of the previous owner, including the obligation to honor existing leases. Of course, the opposite can also be true: If you have good, long-term tenants paying a fair rent, the property may be very attractive to potential new owners.

At the end of the lease term, you have several options. You can:

- decline to renew the lease, except in the few areas where local rent control requirements prohibit it

- sign a new lease for a set period, or

- do nothing—which means, under the law of most states, your lease will usually turn into a month-to-month tenancy if you continue to accept monthly rent from the tenant.

(Chapter 5 discusses in more detail how fixed-term leases end.)

Although leases restrict your flexibility, there's often a big plus to having long-term tenants. Some tenants make a serious personal commitment when they enter into a long-term lease, in part because they think they'll be liable for several months' rent if they leave early. And people who plan to be with you over the long term are often more likely to respect your property and the rights of other tenants, making the management of your rental units far easier and more pleasant.

CAUTION

A lease guarantees less income security than you think. As experienced landlords know well, it's usually not hard for a determined tenant to break a lease and avoid paying all of the money theoretically owed for the unused portion of the lease term. A few states allow tenants to break a lease without penalty in specific circumstances, such as the need to move to a care facility. (In addition, tenants who enter military service are entitled to break a lease, as explained in "Special Rules for Tenants Who Enter Military Service" in Chapter 5.) And many states require landlords to "mitigate" (minimize) the loss they suffer as a result of a broken lease—meaning that if a tenant moves out early, you must try to find another suitable tenant at the same or a greater rent. If you rerent the unit immediately (or if a judge believes it could have been rerented with a reasonable effort), the lease-breaking tenant is off the hook—except, perhaps, for a small obligation to pay for the few days or weeks the unit was vacant plus any costs you incurred in rerenting it. (Chapter 5 discusses a landlord's responsibility to mitigate damages if the tenant leaves early.)

As mentioned, you'll probably prefer to use leases in areas where there is a high vacancy rate or it is difficult to find tenants for one season of the year. For example, if you are renting near a college that is in session for only nine months a year, or in a vacation area that is deserted for months, you are far better off with a year's lease. This is especially true if you have the market clout to charge a large deposit, so that a tenant who wants to leave early has an incentive to find someone to take over the tenancy.

TIP

Always put your agreement in writing. Oral leases or rental agreements are perfectly legal for month-to-month tenancies and for leases of a year or less in most states. While oral agreements are easy and informal, it is never wise to use one. As time passes, people's memories (even yours) have a funny habit of becoming unreliable. You can almost count on tenants claiming that you made, but didn't keep, certain oral promises—for example, to repaint their kitchen or to not increase the rent. Tenants may also forget their own key agreements, such as no subletting. And other issues—for example, how deposits may be used—probably aren't covered at all. Oral leases are especially dangerous, because they require that both parties accurately remember one important term—the length of the lease—over a considerable time. If something goes wrong with an oral rental agreement or lease, you and your tenants are all too likely to end up in court, arguing over who said what to whom, when, and in what context.

Completing the Lease or Rental Agreement Form

This section explains each clause in the lease and rental agreement forms that are provided in this book. Both forms cover the basic terms of the tenancy (such as the amount of rent and date due). Except for Clause 4, Term of the Tenancy, the lease and rental agreement forms are identical.

You may be tempted to simply tear out the form you use from the back of this book or print out the lease or rental agreement from the CD, and skip over detailed instructions. This would be a mistake. If there is one area of landlord-tenant law where details count, this is it. Make sure you really do have the information necessary to create a lease or a rental agreement that accurately reflects your business strategy and complies with all the laws of your state.

CD-ROM

The Landlord Rental Forms CD includes copies of the Month-to-Month Residential Rental Agreement and the Fixed-Term Residential Lease (in English and in Spanish). Appendix C includes blank tear-out versions of these forms. A filled-in sample rental agreement is shown at the end of this chapter.

How to Prepare Attachment Pages

Although we have tried to leave adequate blank space on the forms, it's possible that you may run out of room in completing a particular clause, or you may want to add a clause. Space is obviously no problem if you use the Landlord Rental Forms CD. But if you need to add anything to the tear-out copies of the lease or rental agreement, take the following steps:

1. At the first place that you run out of room, begin your entry and then write "Continued on Attachment 1." Similarly, if there is another place where you run out of room, add as much material as you can and then write "Continued on Attachment 2," and so on. Use a separate attachment each time you need more space.

2. Make your own attachment form, using a sheet of blank white paper. At the top of the form, fill in the proper number—that is, "Attachment 1" for the first attachment, and so on.

3. Begin each attachment with the number of the clause you're continuing or adding. Then add "a continuation of" if you're continuing a clause, or "an addition to" if you're adding a clause.

4. Type or print the additional information on the attachment.

5. Both you and each tenant should sign the page at the end of the added material.

6. Staple the attachment page to the lease or rental agreement.

Clause 1. Identification of Landlord and Tenant

This Agreement is entered into between

_____ (Tenant) and

_____ (Landlord).

Each Tenant is jointly and severally liable for the payment of rent and performance of all other terms of this Agreement.

Every lease or rental agreement must identify the tenant and the landlord or property owner—usually called the "parties" to the agreement. The term "Agreement" (a synonym for contract) refers to either the lease or the rental agreement.

Any competent adult—at least 18 years of age—may be a party to a lease or rental agreement. (A teenager under age 18 may also be a party to a lease if he or she has achieved legal adult status through court order, military service, or marriage.)

The last sentence of Clause 1 states that if you have more than one tenant, they (the cotenants) are all "jointly and severally" liable for paying rent and abiding by all the terms of the agreement. This essential bit of legalese simply means that each tenant is legally responsible for the whole rent and complying with the lease. This part of the clause gives you important rights; it means you can legally seek the entire rent from any one of the tenants should the others skip out or be unable to pay. A "jointly and severally liable" clause also gives you the right to evict all of the tenants even if just one has broken the terms of the lease—for example, by seriously damaging the property, or moving in an extra roommate or a dog, contrary to the lease or a rental agreement.

How to Fill In Clause 1:

Fill in the names of all tenants—adults who will live in the premises, including both members of a married couple. It's crucial that everyone who lives in your rental unit signs the lease or the rental agreement. This underscores your expectation that each individual is responsible for the rent, the use of the property, and all terms of the agreement. Also, make sure the tenant's name matches his or her legal documents, such as a driver's license. You may set a reasonable limit on the number of people per rental unit. (See "How Many Tenants to Allow," below.)

In the last blank, list the names of all landlords or property owners—that is, the names of every person who will be signing the lease or rental agreement. If you are using a business name, enter your name, followed by your business name.

> **EXAMPLE:** Joe Smith, doing business as Apple Lane Apartments

If more than one landlord or owner is signing the lease (such as husband and wife property owners), you may want to put both names on the lease, if both of you plan to actively participate in managing the property.

CROSS REFERENCE

Chapter 3 provides detailed advice on choosing tenants.

Clause 2. Identification of Premises

Subject to the terms and conditions in this Agreement, Landlord rents to Tenant, and Tenant rents from Landlord, for residential purposes only, the premises located at _____ (the premises), together with the following furnishings and appliances:

_____

_____ .

Rental of the premises also includes _____

_____ .

Clause 2 identifies the location of the property being rented (the premises) and provides details on furnishings and what's included with the rental. The words "for residential purposes only" are to prevent a tenant from using the property for conducting a business that might affect your insurance or violate zoning laws, or that might burden other tenants or neighbors.

How to Fill In Clause 2:

Fill in the street address of the unit or house you are renting. If there is an apartment or building number, specify that as well as the city and state.

Add as much detail as necessary to clarify what's included in the rental premises, such as kitchen appliances. If the rental unit has only a few basic furnishings, list them here:

> **EXAMPLE:** Double bed, night table, blue sofa, and round kitchen table and two matching chairs.

If the rental is fully furnished—for example, complete living room, dining room, and bedroom sets, plus a fully equipped kitchen (dinnerware, pots and pans, flatware, etc.), it makes sense to attach a separate room-by-room list to the lease or rental agreement. In this case, simply write in "The rental unit is fully furnished. See Attachment __ for a complete list of furnishings." Or you can provide information on furnishings on the Landlord-Tenant Checklist included in Chapter 4.

In some circumstances, you may want to elaborate on exactly what the premises include. For example, if the rental unit includes a parking space, storage in the garage or basement, or other use of the property, such as a gardening shed in the backyard or the use of a barn in rural areas, specifically include it in your description of the premises.

> **EXAMPLES:**
> - Parking space #5 in underground garage
> - Open parking in lot on west side of building
> - Storage unit #5 in basement
> - Storage space available on west side of garage

If your parking rules are quite detailed—for example, covering guest parking—you may want to include them in Clause 18 (Tenant Rules and Regulations) of your lease or rental agreement.

Possible Modifications to Clause 2:

If a particular part of the rental property that a tenant might reasonably assume to be included is not being rented, such as a garage or storage shed you wish to use yourself or rent to someone else, explicitly exclude it from your description of the premises. Simply add the following sentence, with details on what part of the property is excluded from the rental: "Rental of the premises excludes the following areas: _____ ."

Home Businesses on Rental Property

Over 20 million Americans run a business from their house or apartment. If a tenant wants you to modify Clause 2 to allow him to operate a business, you have some checking to do—even if you are inclined to say yes. For starters, you'll need to check local zoning laws for restrictions on home-based businesses, including the type of businesses allowed (if any), the amount of car and truck traffic the business can generate, outside signs, on-street parking, the number of employees, and the percentage of floor space devoted to the business. And if your rental is in a planned unit or a condominium development, check the CC&Rs of the homeowners' association.

You'll also want to consult your insurance company as to whether you'll need a different policy to cover the potential liability of tenants' employees or guests. In many situations, a home office for occasional use will not be a problem. But if the tenant wants to operate a business that involves people and deliveries coming and going, such as a therapy practice, jewelry importer, or small business consulting firm, you should seriously consider whether to expand or add coverage. You may also want to require that the tenant maintain certain types of liability insurance, so that you won't wind up paying if someone gets hurt on the rental property—for example, a business customer who trips and falls on the front steps.

Finally, be aware that if you allow a residence to be used as a commercial site, your property may need to meet the accessibility requirements of the federal Americans with Disabilities Act (ADA). For more information on the ADA, contact the U.S. Department of Justice, Disability Rights Section, Civil Rights Division, in Washington, DC, at 800-514-0301, or check their website at www.usdoj.gov/crt/drs/drshome.htm. You can also check the ADA home page at www.ada.gov.

CAUTION

You may not be able to restrict a child care home business. A tenant who wants to do child care in the rental may be entitled to do so, despite your general prohibition against businesses. In California and New York, for example, legislators and courts have declared a strong public policy in favor of home-based child care and have limited a landlord's ability to say no. (Cal. Health & Safety Code §1597.40; *Haberbaum v. Gotbaum*, 698 NYS 2d 406 (N.Y. City Civ. Ct. 1999).) If you're concerned about a tenant running a child care business in the apartment, check with your state's office of consumer protection (www.consumeraction.gov) for information on laws that cover in-home child care in residential properties.

If you ultimately decide to allow a tenant to run a business from your rental property, you may want to provide details in Clause 22 (Additional Provisions) of your lease or rental agreement.

Clause 3. Limits on Use and Occupancy

The premises are to be used only as a private residence for Tenant(s) listed in Clause 1 of this Agreement, and their minor children. Occupancy by guests for more than _____ is prohibited without Landlord's written consent and will be considered a breach of this Agreement.

Clause 3 specifies that the rental unit is only the residence of the tenants and their minor children. It lets the tenants know that they may not move anyone else in as a permanent resident without your consent. The value of this clause is that a tenant who tries to move in a relative or friend for a longer period has clearly violated a defined standard, which gives you grounds for eviction. (New York landlords, however, are subject to the "Roommates Law," N.Y. Real Prop. Law § 235-f, which allows tenants to move in relatives and other qualified individuals. The number of total occupants is still restricted, however, by local laws governing overcrowding.)

Clause 3 also allows you to set a time limit for guest stays. Even if you do not plan to strictly enforce restrictions on guests, this provision will be very handy if a tenant tries to move in a friend or relative for a month or two, calling that person a guest. It will give you the leverage you need to ask the guest to leave, request that the guest apply to become a tenant with an appropriate increase in rent or, if necessary, evict the tenant for violating this lease provision.

How to Fill In Clause 3:

Fill in the number of days you allow guests to stay over a given time period without your consent. We suggest you allow up to two consecutive weeks in any six-month period, but, of course, you may want to modify this based on your own experience.

 CAUTION

Don't discriminate against families with children. You can legally establish reasonable space-to-people ratios, but you cannot use overcrowding as an excuse for refusing to rent to tenants with children, especially if you would rent to the same number of adults. (See "How Many Tenants to Allow," below.) Discrimination against families with children is illegal, except in housing reserved for senior citizens only. Just as important as adopting a reasonable people-to-square foot standard in the first place is the maintenance of a consistent occupancy policy. If you allow three adults to live in a two-bedroom apartment, you had better let a couple with a child live in the same type of unit, or you are leaving yourself open to charges that you are illegally discriminating.

Clause 4. Term of the Tenancy

This clause sets out the key difference between a lease and a rental agreement: how long a rent-paying tenant is entitled to stay. The early part of this chapter discusses the pros and cons of leases and rental agreements.

Lease Provision

The term of the rental will begin on

_____, and end on

_____. If Tenant vacates before the term ends, Tenant will be liable for the balance of the rent for the remainder of the term.

This lease provision sets a definite date for the beginning and the expiration of the lease and obligates both the landlord and the tenant for a specific term.

Most leases run for one year. This makes sense, because it allows you to raise the rent at reasonably frequent intervals if market conditions allow. Leases may be shorter (six months) or longer (24 months). This, of course, is up to you and the tenants. A long period—two, three, or even five years—can be appropriate, for example, if you're renting out your own house because you're taking a two-year sabbatical or if you have agreed to allow a tenant to make major repairs or remodel your property at his expense.

How to Fill In Clause 4 (Lease):

In the blanks, fill in the starting date and the expiration date of the lease. The starting date is the date the tenant has the right to move in, such as the first of the month. This date does not have to be the date that you and the tenant sign the lease. The lease signing date is simply the date that you're both bound to the terms of the lease. If the tenant moves in before the regular rental period—such as the middle of the month and you want rent due on the first of every month—you will need to prorate the rent for the first partial month as explained in Clause 5 (Payment of Rent).

Rental Agreement Provision

The rental will begin on _____ , and continue on a month-to-month basis. Landlord may terminate the tenancy or modify the terms of this Agreement by giving the Tenant _____ days' written notice. Tenant may terminate the tenancy by giving the Landlord _____ days' written notice.

This rental agreement provides for a month-to-month tenancy and specifies how much written notice you must give a tenant to change or end a tenancy, and how much notice the tenant must provide you before moving out. (Chapter 5 discusses changing or ending a month-to-month rental agreement.)

How to Fill In Clause 4 (Rental Agreement):

In the first blank, fill in the date the tenancy will begin. The date the tenancy will begin is the date the tenant has the right to move in, such as the first of the month. This date does not have to be the date that you and the tenant sign the rental agreement. The agreement signing date is simply the date that you're both bound to the terms of the rental agreement. If the tenant moves in before the regular rental period—such as the middle of the month and you want rent due on the first of every month—you will need to prorate the rent for the first partial month as explained in Clause 5 (Payment of Rent).

In the next two blanks, fill in the amount of written notice you'll need to give tenants to end or change a tenancy and the amount of notice tenants must provide to end a tenancy. In most cases, to comply with the law of your state, this will be 30 days for both landlord and tenant in a month-to-month tenancy. (See the "Notice Required to Change or Terminate a Month-to-Month Tenancy" chart in Appendix A for a list of each state's notice requirements.)

Possible Modifications to Clause 4 (Rental Agreement):

This rental agreement is month to month, although you can change it to a different interval as long as you don't go below the minimum notice period required by your state's law. If you do, be aware that notice requirements to change or end a tenancy may also need to differ from those required for standard month-to-month rental agreements, since state law often requires that all key notice periods be the same.

How Many Tenants to Allow

Two kinds of laws affect the number of people who may live in a rental unit.

State and local health and safety codes typically set *maximum* limits on the number of tenants, based on the size of the unit and the number of bedrooms and bathrooms.

Even more important, the federal government has taken the lead in establishing *minimum* limits on the number of tenants, through passage of the Fair Housing Act (42 U.S. Code §§ 3601-3619, 3631) and by means of regulations from the Department of Housing and Urban Development (HUD). HUD generally considers a limit of two persons per bedroom a reasonable occupancy standard. Because the number of bedrooms is not the only factor—the size of the bedrooms and configuration of the rental unit are also considered—the federal test has become known as the "two per bedroom plus" standard. States and localities can set their own occupancy standards as long as they are more generous than the federal government's—that is, by allowing more people per rental unit.

The Fair Housing Act is designed primarily to disallow illegal discrimination against families with children, but it also allows you to establish your own "reasonable" restrictions on the number of people per rental unit—as long as your policy is truly tied to health and safety needs. In addition, you can adopt standards that are driven by a legitimate business reason or necessity, such as the capacities of the plumbing or electrical systems. Your personal preferences (such as a desire to reduce wear and tear by limiting the number of occupants or to ensure a quiet, uncrowded environment for upscale tenants), however, do not constitute a legitimate business reason. If your occupancy policy limits the number of tenants for any reason other than health, safety, and legitimate business needs, you risk charges that you are discriminating against families.

Figuring out whether your occupancy policy is legal is not always a simple matter. Furthermore, laws on occupancy limits often change. For more information, call HUD's Housing Discrimination Hotline at 800-669-9777, or check the HUD website at www.hud.gov. Check your local and state housing authority for other occupancy standards that may affect your rental property. The HUD website includes contact information for these agencies.

> **TIP**
>
> **New York landlords should check out the state's "Roommate Law."** New York landlords must comply with the "Unlawful Restrictions on Occupancy" law, commonly known as the Roommate Law. (N.Y. RPL § 235-f.) The Roommate Law prohibits New York landlords from limiting occupancy of a rental unit to just the tenant named on the lease or rental agreement. It permits tenants to share their rental units with their immediate family members, and, in many cases, with unrelated, nontenant occupants, too, so long as a tenant (or tenant's spouse) occupies the unit as a primary residence. The number of total occupants is still restricted, however, by local laws governing overcrowding.

RENT CONTROL

Your right to terminate or change the terms of a tenancy, even one from month to month, can be limited by a rent control ordinance. Check local rules for details.

Clause 5. Payment of Rent

Regular monthly rent.

Tenant will pay to Landlord a monthly rent of $ _____ , payable in advance on the first day of each month, except when that day falls on a weekend or legal holiday, in which case rent is due on the next business day. Rent will be paid in the following manner, unless Landlord designates otherwise:

Delivery of payment.

Rent will be paid:

☐ by mail, to _____

☐ in person, at _____

Form of payment.

Landlord will accept payment in these forms:

☐ personal check made payable to

_____

☐ cashier's check made payable to

_____

☐ credit card

☐ money order

☐ cash

Prorated first month's rent.

For the period from Tenant's move-in date, _____ , through the end of the month, Tenant will pay to Landlord the prorated monthly rent of $ _____ . This amount will be paid on or before the date the Tenant moves in.

This clause provides details on the amount of rent and when, where, and how it's paid. It requires the tenant to pay rent monthly on the first day of the month, unless the first day falls on a weekend

or a legal holiday, in which case rent is due on the next business day. (Extending the rent due date for holidays is legally required in some states and is a general rule in most.)

How to Fill In Clause 5:

Regular monthly rent. In the first blank, state the amount of monthly rent. Unless your premises are subject to a local rent control ordinance, you can legally charge as much rent as you want (or, more practically speaking, as much as a tenant will pay).

Delivery of payment. Next, specify to whom and where the rent is to be paid. If you accept payment by mail (most common), list the specific person (such as yourself) to whom rent checks will be mailed. Be sure the tenant knows the exact address, including the building or office name and suite number for mailing rent checks. If the tenant will pay rent in person, specify the address, such as your office or the manager's unit at the rental property. Be sure to specify the hours when rent can be paid in person, such as 9 a.m. to 5 p.m. weekdays and 9 a.m. to noon on Saturdays.

Form of payment. Note all the forms of payment you'll accept, such as personal check and money order. You can require that tenants pay rent only by check, or give them several options, such as personal check, money order, cashier's check, or credit card.

TIP

Looking for ways to ensure that rent payments are timely and reliable? Credit card and automatic debit are two common methods, especially for landlords with large numbers of rental units. If you accept credit cards, you must pay a fee—a percentage of the amount charged—for the privilege, but the cost may be worth it if accepting credit cards results in more on-time rent payments and less hassle for you and your tenants. In terms of automatic debit, you can get tenants' permission to have rent payments debited automatically each month from the tenants' bank accounts and transferred into your account. This may be a good option for tenants who are in the military. Many tenants will be leery of this idea, however, and it's not worth insisting on.

> ⚠ **CAUTION**
>
> **Don't accept cash unless you have no choice.** You face an increased risk of robbery if word gets out that you are taking in large amounts of cash once or twice a month. And if you accept cash knowing that the tenant earned it from an illegal act such as drug dealing, the government could seize the money from you under federal and state forfeiture laws. For both these reasons, we recommend that you insist that rent be paid by check, money order, or credit card. If you do accept cash, be sure to provide a written, dated receipt stating the tenant's name and the amount of rent paid. Such a receipt is required by law in a few states, and it's a good idea everywhere.

Prorated first month's rent. If the tenant moves in before the regular rental period—say in the middle of the month, and you want rent due on the first of every month—you can specify the prorated amount due for the first partial month. To figure out prorated rent, divide the monthly rent by 30 days and multiply by the number of days in the first (partial) rental period. That will avoid confusion about what you expect to be paid. Enter the move-in date, such as "June 21, 20xx," and the amount of prorated monthly rent.

EXAMPLE: Meg rents an apartment for $1,800 per month, with rent due on the first of the month. She moves in on June 21, so she should pay ten days' prorated rent of $600 when she moves in. ($1,800/30 = $60 x 10 days = $600.) Beginning with July 1, Meg's full $1,800 rent check is due on the first of the month.

If the tenant is moving in on the first of the month, or the same day rent is due, write "N/A" or "Not Applicable" in the section on prorated rent, or delete this section of the clause.

Possible Modifications to Clause 5:

Here are a few common ways to modify Clause 5:

Rent due date. You can establish a rent due date different from the first of the month, such as the day of the month on which the tenant moves in. For example, if the tenant moved in on July 10, rent would be due on that date, a system which of course saves the trouble of prorating the first month's rent.

Frequency of rent payments. You are not legally required to have your tenant pay rent on a monthly basis. You can modify the clause and require that the rent be paid twice a month, each week, or by whatever schedule suits you.

Rent Control

Communities in only five states—California, the District of Columbia, Maryland, New Jersey, and New York—have laws that limit the amount of rent landlords may charge and how and when rent may be increased. Typically, only a few cities or counties in each of these states have enacted local rent control ordinances (also called rent stabilization, maximum rent regulation, or a similar term), but often these are some of the state's largest cities—for example, San Francisco, Los Angeles, New York City, and Newark all have some form of rent control.

Rent control laws commonly regulate much more than rent. For example, owners of rent-controlled properties must often follow specific "just cause" eviction procedures. And local rent control ordinances may require that your lease or rental agreement include certain information—for example, the address of the local rent control board.

If you own rental property in a city that has rent control, you should always have a current copy of the ordinance and any regulations interpreting it. Check with your local rent control board or city manager's or mayor's office for more information on rent control, and modify our forms accordingly.

CROSS REFERENCE

See the following chapters for rent-related discussions:

- Collecting deposits and potential problems with calling a deposit the "last month's rent": Clause 8, this chapter
- The value of highlighting your rent rules in a move-in letter to new tenants, and collecting the first month's rent: Chapter 4

- Tenant's obligations to pay rent when breaking a lease: Chapter 5
- Legal citations for state rent rules: Appendix A.

Clause 6. Late Charges

If Tenant fails to pay the rent in full before the end of the _____ day after it's due, Tenant will pay Landlord a late charge as follows:

_____ .

Landlord does not waive the right to insist on payment of the rent in full on the date it is due.

It is your legal right in most states to charge a late fee if rent is not paid on time. This clause spells out details of your policy on late fees. Charging a late fee does not mean that you give up your right to insist that rent be paid on the due date. To bring this point home, Clause 6 states that you do not waive the right to insist on full payment of the rent on the date it is due. A late fee is simply one way to motivate tenants to pay rent on time.

A few states have statutes that put precise limits on the amount of late fees or when they can be collected. (See the Late Fees column in the "State Rent Rules" table in Appendix A before completing this clause.)

RENT CONTROL

Some rent control ordinances also regulate late fees. If you own rental units in a municipality with rent control, check the ordinances carefully.

But even if your state doesn't have specific rules restricting late fees, you are still bound by general legal principles (often expressed in court decisions) that prohibit unreasonably high fees. Unless your state imposes more specific statutory rules on late fees, you should be on safe ground if you adhere to these principles:

- The total late charge should not exceed 4%–5% of the rent. That's $40 to $50 on a $1,000 per month rental.

- If the late fee increases each day the rent is late, it should be moderate and have an upper limit. A late charge that increases without a maximum could be considered interest charged at an illegal ("usurious") rate. Although state usury laws don't directly apply to late charges, judges often use these laws as one guideline in judging whether a particular provision is reasonable. Most states set the maximum interest rate that may be charged for a debt at about 10% to 12%. A late charge that would generally be acceptable for a $1,000 per month rent would be a charge of $10 if rent is not paid by the end of the second business day after it is due, plus $5 for each additional day, up to a maximum of 5% of the monthly rental amount.

CAUTION

Don't try to disguise excessive late charges by giving a "discount" for early payment. One landlord we know concluded that he couldn't get away with charging a $100 late charge on an $850 rent payment, so, instead, he designed a rental agreement calling for a rent of $950 with a $100 discount if the rent was not more than three days late. Ingenious as this ploy sounds, it is unlikely to stand up in court in many states, unless the discount for timely payment is modest. Giving a relatively large discount is, in effect, the same as charging an excessive late fee, and a judge is likely to see it as such.

How to Fill In Clause 6:

In the first blank, specify how many days (if any) you will allow as a grace period before you charge a late fee. You don't have to give a grace period, but many landlords don't charge a late fee until the rent is two or three days late. If you don't allow any grace period, simply cross out the first blank

and the word "after," so that the first line reads "If Tenant fails to pay the rent in full before the end of the day it's due … ."

Next, fill in details on your late rent fee, such as the daily charge and any maximum fee.

Possible Modifications to Clause 6:

If you decide not to charge a late fee (something we consider highly unwise), you may simply delete this clause, or write the words "N/A" or "Not Applicable" on it.

Clause 7. Returned Check and Other Bank Charges

If any check offered by Tenant to Landlord in payment of rent or any other amount due under this Agreement is returned for lack of sufficient funds, a "stop payment," or any other reason, Tenant will pay Landlord a returned check charge of $ _____ .

As with late charges, any bounced-check charges you require must be reasonable. Generally, you should charge no more than the amount your bank charges you for a returned check, probably $10 to $20 per returned item, plus a few dollars for your trouble. Check with your state consumer protection agency for any restrictions on bounced-check charges. For a list of state consumer protection agencies, go to the Consumer Action Website maintained by the Federal Citizen Information Center at www.consumeraction.gov.

TIP

Don't tolerate repeated bad checks. If a tenant habitually pays rent late or gives you bad checks, give written notice demanding that the tenant pay the rent or move within a few days. How long the tenant is allowed to stay depends on state law; in most places, it's about three to 15 days. In most instances, the tenant who receives this kind of "pay rent or quit" notice pays up and reforms his ways, and that's the end of it. But, if the tenant doesn't pay the rent (or move), you can file an eviction lawsuit. An alternative is to serve the tenant with a 30-day notice to change Clause 5 of the lease or rental agreement to require payment with a money order or a verified credit card transaction.

How to Fill In Clause 7:

In the blank, fill in the amount of the returned check charge. If you won't accept checks, fill in "N/A" or "Not Applicable."

Clause 8. Security Deposit

On signing this Agreement, Tenant will pay to Landlord the sum of $ _____ as a security deposit. Tenant may not, without Landlord's prior written consent, apply this security deposit to the last month's rent or to any other sum due under this Agreement. Within _____ after Tenant has vacated the premises, returned keys, and provided Landlord with a forwarding address, Landlord will return the deposit in full or give Tenant an itemized written statement of the reasons for, and the dollar amount of, any of the security deposit retained by Landlord, along with a check for any deposit balance.

Most landlords quite sensibly ask for a security deposit before entrusting hundreds of thousands of dollars worth of real estate to a tenant. But it's easy to get into legal trouble over deposits, because they are strictly regulated by state law and, sometimes, also by city ordinance. The law of most states dictates how large a deposit you can require, how you can use it, when you must return it, and more. Several states require you to put deposits in a separate account and pay interest on them.

The use and return of security deposits is a frequent source of disputes between landlords and tenants. To avoid confusion and legal hassles, this clause is clear on the subject, including:

- the dollar amount of the deposit

- the fact that the deposit may not be used for the last month's rent without your prior approval, and
- when the deposit will be returned, along with an itemized statement of deductions.

This section discusses the basic information you need to complete Clause 8. Check the tables on security deposit rules in Appendix A for specific details that apply to your situation:

- "State Security Deposit Rules"
- "States That Require Landlords to Pay Interest on Deposits."

If, after reviewing these tables, you have any questions of what's allowed in your state, you should get a current copy of your state's security deposit statute or an up-to-date summary from a landlords' association. In addition, be sure to check local ordinances in all areas where you own property. Cities, particularly those with rent control, may have additional rules on security deposits, such as a limit on the amount you can charge or a requirement that you pay interest on deposits.

Basic State Rules on Security Deposits

All states allow you to collect a security deposit when a tenant moves in and hold it until the tenant leaves. The general purpose of a security deposit is to give the landlord a source of funds if a tenant fails to pay the rent when it is due or doesn't pay for damage to the rental unit. Rent you collect in advance for the first month is not considered part of the security deposit.

State laws typically control the amount you can charge and how and when you must return security deposits:

- Many states limit the amount you can collect as a deposit to a maximum of one or two months' rent. Sometimes, the limit in a particular state is higher for furnished units.

- Several states and cities (particularly those with rent control) require landlords to pay tenants interest on security deposits, and establish detailed requirements as to the interest rate that must be paid and when payments must be made. Some states require you to put deposits in a separate account, sometimes called a "trust" account, rather than mixing the funds with your personal or business accounts. In most states, however, you don't have to pay tenants interest on deposits or put them in a separate bank account. In other words, you can simply put the money in your pocket or bank account and use it, as long as you have it available when the tenant moves out.

- When a tenant moves out, you will have a set amount of time (usually from 14 to 30 days, depending on the state) to either return the tenant's entire deposit or provide an itemized statement of deductions and refund any deposit balance, including any interest that is required.

- You can generally withhold all or part of the deposit to pay for:

  - unpaid rent

  - repairing damage to the premises (except for "ordinary wear and tear") caused by the tenant, a family member, or a guest

  - cleaning necessary to restore the rental unit to its condition at the beginning of the tenancy (over and above "ordinary wear and tear"), and

  - restoring or replacing rental unit property taken by the tenant. States typically also allow you to use a deposit to cover the tenant's other obligations under the lease or rental agreement, which may include payment of utility charges.

- The laws of many states set heavy penalties for violation of security deposit statutes.

See Chapter 5 for a discussion of inspecting the rental unit and returning deposits when a tenant leaves.

Don't Charge Nonrefundable Fees

State laws are often muddled on the subject of whether charging nonrefundable deposits and fees is legal. Some specifically allow landlords to collect a fee that is not refundable—such as for pets, cleaning, or redecorating—as long as this is clearly stated in the lease or rental agreement. In addition, most states allow landlords to charge prospective tenants a nonrefundable fee for the cost of a credit report and related screening fees (discussed in Chapter 3).

But many states—and this is clearly the trend—have enacted security deposit statutes that specifically prohibit nonrefundable fees such as a fixed fee for cleaning drapes or carpets or for painting; all such fees are legally considered security deposits, no matter what they are labeled in the lease or rental agreement, and must be refundable. It is also illegal in many states to make the return of deposits contingent upon a tenant staying for a minimum period of time.

Generally, it's best to avoid the legal uncertainties and not try to collect any nonrefundable fees from tenants. In addition, most landlords have found that making all deposits refundable avoids many time-consuming arguments and even lawsuits with tenants. We believe it's much simpler just to consider the expenses these fees cover as part of your overhead and figure them into the rent, raising it, if necessary.

If you have a specific concern about a particular tenant—for example, you're afraid a tenant's pet will damage the carpets or furniture—just ask for a higher security deposit (but do check your state's maximum). That way, you're covered if the pet causes damage, and if it doesn't, the tenant won't have to shell out unnecessarily.

If, despite our advice, you want to charge a nonrefundable fee, check your state's law to find what (if any) kinds of nonrefundable fees are allowed. Then, make sure your lease or rental agreement is clear on the subject.

How Much Deposit Should You Charge?

Normally, the best advice is to charge as much as the market will bear, within any legal limits. The more the tenant has at stake, the better the chance your property will be respected. And, the larger the deposit, the more financial protection you will have if a tenant leaves owing you rent.

The market, however, often keeps the practical limit on deposits lower than the maximum allowed by law. Your common sense and your business sense need to work together in setting security deposits. Here are a number of considerations to keep in mind:

- **Charge the full limit in high-risk situations:** where there's a lot of tenant turnover, if the tenant has a pet and you're concerned about damage, or if the tenant's credit is shaky and you're worried about unpaid rent.

- **Consider the psychological advantage of a higher rent rather than a high deposit.** Many tenants would rather pay a slightly higher rent than an enormous deposit. Also, many acceptable, solvent tenants have a hard time coming up with several months' rent, especially if they are still in a rental unit and are awaiting the return of a previous security deposit.

- **Charge a bigger deposit for single-family homes.** Unlike multiunit residences, where close-by neighbors or a manager can spot, report, and quickly stop any destruction of the premises, the single-family home is somewhat of an island. The condition of the interior and even the exterior may be hard to assess, unless you live close by or can frequently check the condition of a single-family rental. And, of course, the cost of repairing damage to a house is likely to be higher than for an apartment.

- **Gain a marketing advantage by allowing a deposit to be paid in installments.** If rentals are plentiful in your area, with comparable units renting at about the same price, you might gain a competitive edge by allowing tenants to pay the deposit in several installments, rather than one lump sum.

TIP

Require renter's insurance as an alternative to a high security deposit. If you're worried about damage but don't think you can raise the deposit any higher, require renter's insurance. You can give your property an extra measure of protection by insisting that the tenant purchase renter's insurance, which may cover damage done by the tenant or guests. (See "Renter's Insurance" under Clause 11.)

Last Month's Rent

It's a common—but often unwise—practice to collect a sum of money called "last month's rent" from a tenant who's moving in. Landlords tend to treat this money as just another security deposit, and use it to cover not only the last month's rent, but also other expenses such as repairs or cleaning.

Problems can arise because some states restrict the use of money labeled as the "last month's rent" to its stated purpose: the rent for the tenant's last month of occupancy. If you use any of it to repair damage by the former tenant, you're violating the law. Also, using the "last month's rent" for cleaning and repairs may lead to a dispute with a tenant who feels that the last month's rent is taken care of and resents having to pay all or part of it. You would be better off if the tenant paid the last month's rent when it came due, leaving the entire security deposit available to cover any necessary cleaning and repairs.

Avoiding the term "last month's rent" also keeps things simpler if you raise the rent, but not the deposit, before the tenant's last month of occupancy. The problem arises when rent for the tenant's last month becomes due. Has the tenant already paid in full, or does he owe more because the monthly rent is now higher? Legally, there is often no clear answer. In practice, it's a hassle you are best to avoid by not labeling any part of the security deposit "last month's rent."

Clause 8 of the form agreements makes it clear that the tenant may not apply the security deposit to the last month's rent, without your prior written consent.

How to Fill In Clause 8:

Once you decide how much security deposit you can charge (see "State Security Deposit Rules" in Appendix A), fill in the amount in the first blank. Unless there's a lower limit, we suggest about two months as your rent deposit, assuming your potential tenants can afford that much. (See "How Much Deposit Should You Charge?," above.) In no case is it wise to charge much less than one month's rent.

Next, fill in the time period when you will return the deposit, also using the table "State Security Deposit Rules" in Appendix A. If there is no statutory deadline for returning the deposit, we recommend 14 to 21 days as a reasonable time to return a tenant's deposit. Establishing a fairly short period (even if the law of your state allows more time) will discourage anxious tenants from repeatedly bugging you or your manager for their deposit refund. (See the discussion of returning security deposits in Chapter 5.)

Possible Modifications to Clause 8:

The laws of several states require you to give tenants written information on various aspects of the security deposit, including where the security deposit is being held, interest payments, and the terms of and conditions under which the security deposit may be withheld. The chart in Appendix A, "Required Security Deposit Disclosures," lists specific clauses you should add to Clause 8.

Even if it's not required, you may want to provide additional details on security deposits in your lease or rental agreement. Here are optional clauses you may add to the end of Clause 8.

The security deposit will be held at:_____
_____(name and address of financial institution)_____.
Landlord will pay Tenant interest on all security deposits at the prevailing bank rate.

Landlord may withhold only that portion of Tenant's security deposit necessary to: (1) remedy any default by Tenant in the payment of rent; (2) repair damage to the premises, except for ordinary wear and tear caused by Tenant; (3) clean the premises, if necessary; and (4) compensate Landlord for any other losses as allowed by state law.

Clause 9. Utilities

Tenant will pay all utility charges, except for the following, which will be paid by Landlord:

_____

_____

This clause helps prevent misunderstandings as to who's responsible for paying utilities. Normally, landlords pay for garbage (and sometimes water, if there is a yard) to help make sure that the premises are well maintained. Tenants usually pay for other services, such as phone, gas, electricity, cable TV, and Internet access.

How to Fill In Clause 9:

In the blank, fill in the utilities you—not the tenants—will be responsible for paying. If you will not be paying for any utilities, simply write in "N/A" or "Not Applicable."

Disclose Shared Utility Arrangements

If there are not separate gas and electric meters for each unit, or a tenant's meter serves any areas outside his unit (such as a water heater used in common with other tenants or even a light bulb not under the tenant's control in a common area), you should disclose this in your lease or rental agreement. Simply add details to Clause 9, preparing an attachment page if necessary. This type of disclosure is required by law in some states, and is only fair in any case. The best solution is to put in a separate meter for the areas served outside the tenant's unit. If you don't do that, you should:

- pay for the utilities for the tenant's meter yourself by placing that utility in your name

- reduce the tenant's rent to compensate for payment of utility usage outside of her unit (this will probably cost you more in the long run than if you either added a new meter or simply paid for the utilities yourself), or

- sign a separate written agreement with the tenant, under which the tenant specifically agrees to pay for others' utilities, too.

Clause 10. Assignment and Subletting

Tenant will not sublet any part of the premises or assign this Agreement without the prior written consent of Landlord.

Clause 10 is an antisubletting clause, the breach of which is grounds for eviction. It prevents a tenant from subleasing during a vacation or renting out a room to someone unless you specifically agree.

Clause 10 is also designed to prevent assignments, a legal term that means your tenant transfers her tenancy to someone else. Practically, you need this clause to prevent your tenant from leaving in the middle of the month or lease term and moving in a replacement—maybe someone you wouldn't choose to rent to—without your consent.

By including Clause 10 in your lease or rental agreement, you have the option not to accept the person your tenant proposes to take over the lease. Under the law of most states, however, you should realize that if a tenant who wishes to leave early provides you with another suitable tenant, you can't both unreasonably refuse to rent to this person and hold the tenant financially liable for breaking the lease. Typically, state law requires that you must try to rerent the property reasonably quickly and subtract any rent you receive from the amount the original tenant owed you for the remainder of the agreed-upon rental period. Lawyers call this the mitigation-of-damages rule, a bit of legalese it's valuable to know.

How to Fill In Clause 10:

You don't need to add anything to this clause in most situations. There may be local laws, however, that do apply.

RESOURCE

For a related discussion of subleases, assignments, and the landlord's duty to mitigate damages, see Chapter 5. Also, Chapter 8 of *Every Landlord's Legal Guide*, by Marcia Stewart, Ralph Warner, & Janet Portman (Nolo), covers these topics in detail.

Common Terms

Tenant. Someone who has signed a lease or a rental agreement, or who has gained the status of a tenant because the landlord has accepted his presence on the property or has accepted rent from him.

Cotenants. Two or more tenants who rent the same property under the same lease or rental agreement, each 100% responsible for carrying out the agreement, including paying all the rent.

Subtenant. Someone who subleases (rents) all or part of the premises from a tenant and does not sign a lease or rental agreement with the landlord. A subtenant may either rent (sublet) an entire dwelling from a tenant who moves out temporarily—for example, for the summer—or rent one or more rooms from the tenant, who continues to live in the unit. The key to subtenant relationships is that the original tenant retains the primary relationship with the landlord and continues to exercise some control over the rental property, either by occupying part of the unit or by reserving the right to retake possession at a later date.

Assignment. The transfer by a tenant of all of his rights of tenancy to another tenant (the "assignee"). Unlike a subtenant, an assignee rents directly from the landlord.

Roommates. Two or more people, usually unrelated, living under the same roof and sharing rent and expenses. A roommate is usually a cotenant, but in some situations may be a subtenant.

Should You Allow a Sublet or Assignment?

As a general rule, your best bet when a tenant asks to sublease or assign is to simply insist that the tenancy terminate and a new one begin—with the proposed "subtenant" or "assignee" as the new tenant who signs a new lease or rental agreement. This gives you the most direct legal relationship with the substitute. There are a few situations, however, in which you may want to agree to a subtenancy or assignment.

You might, for example, want to accommodate—and keep—an exceptional, long-term tenant who has every intention of returning and whose judgment and integrity you have always trusted. If the proposed stand-in meets your normal tenant criteria, you may decide that it is worth the risk of a subtenancy or assignment in order to keep the original tenant.

Another good reason is a desire to have a sure source of funds in the background. This might come up if your original tenant is financially sound and trustworthy, but a proposed stand-in is less secure but acceptable in every other respect. By agreeing to a sublet or assignment, you have someone in the background (the original tenant) still responsible for the rent. The risk you incur by agreeing to set up a subtenancy or assignment and the hassle that comes with dealing with more than one person may be worth what you gain in keeping a sure and reliable source of funds on the hook.

Clause 11. Tenant's Maintenance Responsibilities

Tenant will: (1) keep the premises clean, sanitary, and in good condition and, upon termination of the tenancy, return the premises to Landlord in a condition identical to that which existed when Tenant took occupancy, except for ordinary wear and tear; (2) immediately notify Landlord of any defects or dangerous conditions in and about the premises of which Tenant becomes aware; and (3) reimburse Landlord, on demand by Landlord, for the cost of any repairs to the premises damaged by Tenant or Tenant's guests or business invitees through misuse or neglect.

Tenant has examined the premises, including appliances, fixtures, carpets, drapes, and paint, and has found them to be in good, safe, and clean condition and repair, except as noted in the Landlord-Tenant Checklist.

Clause 11 makes the tenant responsible for keeping the rental premises clean and sanitary. This clause also makes it clear that if the tenant damages the premises—for example, by breaking a window or scratching hardwood floors—it's his responsibility to pay for the damage.

It is the law in some states (and a wise practice in all) to notify tenants in writing of procedures for making complaint and repair requests. Clause 11 requires the tenant to alert you to defective or dangerous conditions.

Clause 11 also states that the tenant has examined the rental premises, including appliances, carpets, and paint, and found them to be safe and clean, except as noted in a separate form (the Landlord-Tenant Checklist, described in Chapter 4). Before the tenant moves in, you and the tenant should inspect the rental unit and fill out the Landlord-Tenant Checklist in Chapter 4, describing what is in the unit and noting any problems. Doing so will help you avoid disputes over security deposit deductions when the tenant moves out.

How to Fill In Clause 11:

You do not need to add anything to this clause.

Elements of a Good Maintenance and Repair System

As a general rule, landlords are legally required to offer livable premises when a tenant originally rents an apartment or rental unit and to maintain the premises throughout the rental term. If rental property is not kept in good repair, the tenant may have the right to repair the problem and deduct the cost from the rent, withhold rent, sue for any injuries caused by defective conditions, or move out without notice. Your best defense against rent withholding hassles and other disputes with tenants is to establish and communicate a clear, easy-to-follow procedure for tenants to ask for repairs and for you to document all complaints, respond quickly when complaints are made, and schedule annual safety inspections. And, if you employ a manager or management company, make sure they fully accept and implement your guidelines.

Follow these steps to avoid maintenance and repair problems with tenants:

1. Regularly look for dangerous conditions on the property and fix them promptly. Reduce risk exposure as much as possible—for example, by providing sufficient lighting in hallways, parking garages, and other common areas, strong locks on doors and windows, and safe stairs and handrails.

2. Scrupulously comply with all public health and safety codes. Your local building or housing authority and health or fire department can provide any information you need. Also, check state housing laws governing landlords' repair and maintenance responsibilities. (Appendix A includes citations for the major state laws affecting landlords. Check your statutes under headings such as Landlord Obligations to Maintain Premises.)

3. Clearly set out the tenant's responsibilities for repair and maintenance in your lease or rental agreement. (See Clauses 11, 12, and 13 of the agreements in this chapter.)

4. Use the written Landlord-Tenant Checklist form in Chapter 4 to check over the premises and fix any problems before new tenants move in.

5. Encourage tenants to immediately report plumbing, heating, weatherproofing, or other defects and safety or security problems—whether in the tenant's unit or in common areas such as hallways and parking garages.

6. Handle repairs (especially urgent ones, such as a broken door lock or lack of heat in winter) as soon as possible. Notify the tenant by phone and follow up in writing if repairs will take more than 48 hours, excluding weekends. Keep the tenant informed—for example, if you have problems scheduling a plumber, let your tenant know with a phone call or a note. For nonurgent repairs, be sure to give the tenant proper notice as required by state law. (See Clause 15 for details on notice required to enter rental premises.)

7. Keep a written log of all tenant complaints, including those made orally. Record your immediate and any follow-up responses (and subsequent tenant communications) and details as to how and when the problem was fixed, including reasons for any delay.

8. Twice a year, give your tenants a checklist on which to report any potential safety hazards or problems that might have been overlooked—for example, low water pressure in the shower, peeling paint, or noisy neighbors. This is also a good time to remind tenants of their repair and maintenance responsibilities. Respond promptly and in writing to all repair requests, keeping copies in your file.

9. Once a year, inspect all rental units for safety and maintenance problems, using the Landlord-Tenant Checklist as a guide. Make sure smoke detectors, heating and plumbing systems, and major appliances are, in fact, safe and in good working order. (Keep copies of the filled-in checklist in your file.)

10. Get a good liability insurance policy to cover injuries or losses suffered by others as the result of defective conditions on the property and lawyers' bills for defending personal injury suits.

Renter's Insurance

It is becoming increasingly popular, especially in high-end rentals, to require tenants to obtain renter's insurance. This insurance covers losses of the tenant's belongings as a result of fire or theft. Often called a "Tenant's Package Policy," renter's insurance also covers the tenant if his negligence causes injury to other people or property damage (to his property or to yours). Besides protecting the tenant from personal liability, renter's insurance benefits you, too: If damage caused by the tenant could be covered by either his insurance policy or yours—for example, the tenant accidentally starts a fire when he leaves the stove on—a claim made on the tenant's policy will affect his premiums, not yours.

If you decide to require insurance, insert a clause like the following at the end of your lease or rental agreement, under Clause 22, Additional Provisions. This will help assure that the tenant purchases and maintains a renter's insurance policy throughout his tenancy.

Renter's Insurance

Within ten days of the signing of this Agreement, Tenant will obtain renter's insurance and provide proof of purchase to Landlord. Tenant further agrees to maintain the policy throughout the duration of the tenancy, and to furnish proof of insurance on a
☐ yearly
☐ semiannual basis.

 RESOURCE

Several times in this book, we recommend *Every Landlord's Legal Guide* by Marcia Stewart, Ralph Warner, & Janet Portman (Nolo). It is especially useful for its detailed discussion of landlords' and tenants' rights and responsibilities for repair and maintenance under state and local laws and judicial decisions. It provides practical advice on how to stay on top of repair and maintenance needs and minimize financial losses and legal problems with tenants. It discusses tenants' rights if you do not meet your legal responsibilities and the pros and cons of delegating repairs and maintenance to the tenant. *Every Landlord's Legal Guide* also includes chapters on landlords' liability for tenant injuries from defective housing conditions, such as a broken step or defective wiring; liability for environmental hazards such as asbestos and lead; and responsibility to provide secure premises and protect tenants from assault or criminal activities, such as drug dealing.

Clause 12. Repairs and Alterations by Tenant

a. Except as provided by law or as authorized by the prior written consent of Landlord, Tenant will not make any repairs or alterations to the premises, including nailing holes in the walls or painting the rental unit.
b. Tenant will not, without Landlord's prior written consent, alter, rekey, or install any locks to the premises or install or alter any burglar alarm system. Tenant will provide Landlord with a key or keys capable of unlocking all such rekeyed or new locks as well as instructions on how to disarm any altered or new burglar alarm system.

Clause 12 makes it clear that the tenant may not make alterations and repairs without your consent, including painting the unit or nailing holes in the walls.

And, to make sure you can take advantage of your legal right of entry in an emergency situation, Clause 12 specifically forbids the tenant from rekeying the locks or installing a burglar alarm system without your consent. If you do grant permission, make sure your tenant gives you duplicate keys or the name and phone number of the alarm company or instructions on how to disarm the alarm system so that you can enter in case of emergency.

The "except as provided by law" language in Clause 12 is a reference to the fact that, in certain situations and in certain states, tenants have a narrowly defined right to alter or repair the premises, regardless of what you've said in the lease or rental agreement. Examples include:

- **Alterations by a disabled person, such as lowering countertops for a wheelchair-bound tenant.** Under the federal Fair Housing Act, a disabled person may modify her living space to the extent necessary to make the space safe and comfortable, as long as the modifications will not make the unit unacceptable to the next tenant, or if the disabled tenant agrees to undo the modification when she leaves. (42 U.S.C. § 3604(f)(3)(A).)

- **Use of the "repair and deduct" procedure.** In most states, tenants have the right to repair defects or damage that makes the premises uninhabitable or substantially interferes with the tenant's safe use or enjoyment of the premises. Usually, the tenant must first notify you of the problem and give you a reasonable amount of time to fix it.

- **Installation of satellite dishes and antennas.** Federal law gives tenants limited rights to install wireless antennas and small satellite dishes. (47 C.F.R. § 1.4000.)

- **Specific alterations allowed by state statutes.** Some states allow tenants to install energy conservation measures (like removable interior storm windows) or burglary prevention devices without the landlord's prior consent. Check your state statutes or call your local rental property association for more information on these types of laws.

How to Fill In Clause 12:

If you do not want the tenant to make any repairs without your permission, you do not need to add anything to this clause.

You may, however, want to go further and specifically prohibit certain repairs or alterations by adding details in Clause 22 (Additional Provisions). For example, you may want to make it clear that any "fixtures"—a legal term that describes any addition that is attached to the structure, such as bolted-in bookcases or built-in dishwashers—are your property and may not be removed by the tenant without your permission.

If you do authorize the tenant to make any repairs, provide enough detail so that the tenant knows exactly what is expected, how much repairs can cost, and who will pay. For example, if you decide to allow the tenant to take over the repair of any broken windows, routine plumbing jobs, or landscaping, give specific descriptions and limits to the tasks.

> **CAUTION**
>
> **Do not delegate to a tenant your responsibility for major maintenance of essential services.** The duty to repair and maintain heating, plumbing, and electrical and structural systems (the roof, for example) is yours. Absent unusual circumstances, and even then only after carefully checking state law, it's a mistake to try to delegate this responsibility to the tenant. Many courts have held that landlords cannot delegate to a tenant the responsibility for keeping the premises fit for habitation, fearing that the tenant will rarely be in the position, either practically or financially, to do the kinds of repairs that are often needed to bring a structure up to par.

Clause 13. Violating Laws and Causing Disturbances

Tenant is entitled to quiet enjoyment of the premises. Tenant and guests or invitees will not use the premises or adjacent areas in such a way as to: (1) violate any law or ordinance, including laws prohibiting the use, possession, or sale of illegal drugs; (2) commit waste (severe property damage); or (3) create a nuisance by annoying, disturbing, inconveniencing, or interfering with the quiet enjoyment and peace and quiet of any other tenant or nearby resident.

This type of clause is found in most form leases and rental agreements. Although it contains some legal jargon, it's probably best to leave it as is, since courts have much experience in working with these terms. As courts define it, the "covenant of quiet enjoyment" amounts to an implied promise that you will not act (or fail to act) in a way that interferes with or destroys the ability of the tenant to use the rented premises.

Examples of violations of the covenant of quiet enjoyment include:

- allowing garbage to pile up
- tolerating a major rodent infestation, or
- failing to control a tenant whose constant loud music makes it impossible for other tenants to sleep.

If you want more specific rules—for example, no loud music played after midnight—add them to Clause 18: Tenant Rules and Regulations, or to Clause 22: Additional Provisions.

How to Fill In Clause 13:

You do not need to add anything to this clause.

Waste and Nuisance: What Are They?

In legalese, committing **waste** means causing severe damage to real estate, including a house or an apartment unit—damage that goes way beyond ordinary wear and tear. Punching holes in walls, pulling out sinks and fixtures and knocking down doors are examples of waste.

Nuisance means behavior that prevents neighbors from fully enjoying the use of their homes. Continuous loud noise and foul odors are examples of legal nuisances that may disturb nearby neighbors and affect their "quiet enjoyment" of the premises. So, too, are selling drugs or engaging in other illegal activities that greatly disturb neighbors.

How to Prevent Illegal Tenant Activity

There are several practical steps you can take, both to avoid trouble among your tenants and, in the event that hostilities do erupt, to limit your exposure to lawsuits:

- Screen tenants carefully and choose tenants who are likely to be law-abiding and peaceful citizens. (Chapter 3 recommends a comprehensive system for screening prospective tenants, including checking out references from past landlords and employers.)

- Establish a system to respond to tenants' complaints and concerns about other tenants, especially those involving drug dealing on the rental property.

- Make it clear that you will not tolerate tenants' disruptive behavior. An explicit lease or rental agreement provision such as Clause 13 prohibiting drug dealing and illegal activity is the most effective way to make this point. If a tenant does cause trouble, act swiftly. Some situations, such as drug dealing, call for prompt efforts to evict the troublemaker. Your failure to evict drug-dealing tenants can result in lawsuits from tenants injured or annoyed by drug dealers, and local, state, or federal authorities may choose to levy stiff fines for allowing the illegal activity to continue. In extreme cases, you may actually lose your property to the government under public nuisance abatement laws and forfeiture laws.

Clause 14. Pets

No animal, bird, or other pet will be kept on the premises, even temporarily, except properly trained service animals needed by blind, deaf, or disabled persons and _____

_____

under the following conditions:

_____

_____ .

This clause is designed to prevent tenants from keeping pets without your written permission. This is not necessarily to say that you will want to apply a flat "no pets" rule. (Many landlords, in fact, report that pet-owning tenants are more appreciative, stable, and responsible than the norm.) But it does provide you with a legal mechanism designed to keep your premises from being waist-deep in Irish wolfhounds. Without this sort of provision, particularly if you use a longer-term lease that can't be terminated early save for a clear violation of one of its provisions, there's little to prevent your tenant from keeping dangerous or nonhousebroken pets on your property, except for city ordinances prohibiting tigers and the like.

You have the right to prohibit all pets, or to restrict the types of pets you allow, with the exception of trained dogs used by blind, deaf, or physically or mentally disabled people.

How to Fill in Clause 14:

If you do not allow pets, put the word "None" in the blanks.

If you allow pets, be sure to identify the type and number of pets in the first blank—for example, "one cat" or "one dog under 20 pounds." It's also wise to spell out your pet rules in the second blank.

EXAMPLE: Tenant must keep the grounds and street free of all animal waste. Tenant's pet must be well-behaved and under Tenant's control at all times and will not pose a threat or apparent threat to the safety of other tenants, their guests, or other people on or near the premises.

Your tenant rules and regulations may be another place to spell out your pet rules—in which case, add this language in the second blank: Tenant must comply with pet rules included in the Tenant Rules and Regulations (Clause 18) attached to this agreement.

Renting to Pet Owners

Open Door, an ambitious program of the San Francisco Society for the Prevention of Cruelty to Animals (SPCA), seeks to show landlords how to make renting to pet-owning tenants a satisfying and profitable experience. The SPCA offers landlords:

- checklists to help screen pet-owning tenants
- pet policies to add to standard leases and rental agreements, and
- free mediation if landlords and tenants have pet-related problems after moving in.

For more information, contact the San Francisco SPCA at 2500 16th St., San Francisco, CA 94103, 415-554-3000, or check its website at www.sfspca. org/opendoor. Also, see *Every Dog's Legal Guide*, by Mary Randolph (Nolo), for more information on renting to pet owners.

Should You Require a Separate Security Deposit for Pets?

Some landlords allow pets but require the tenant to pay a separate deposit to cover any damage caused by the pet. The laws of a few states specifically allow separate, nonrefundable pet deposits. In others, charging a designated pet deposit is legal only if the total amount you charge for deposits does not exceed the state maximum for all deposits. (See Clause 8 for details on security deposits.)

Even where allowed, separate pet deposits can often be a bad idea, because they limit how you can use that part of the security deposit. For example, if the pet is well-behaved but the tenant trashes your unit, you can't use the pet portion of the deposit to clean up after the human. If you want to protect your property from damage done by a pet, you are probably better off charging a slightly higher rent or security deposit to start with (assuming you are not restricted by rent control or the upper security deposit limits).

> **CAUTION**
>
> It is illegal to charge an extra pet deposit for people with trained guide dogs, signal dogs, or service dogs.

Clause 15. Landlord's Right to Access

Landlord or Landlord's agents may enter the premises in the event of an emergency, to make repairs or improvements, or to show the premises to prospective buyers or tenants. Landlord may also enter the premises to conduct an annual inspection to check for safety or maintenance problems. Except in cases of emergency, Tenant's abandonment of the premises, court order, or where it is impractical to do so, Landlord shall give Tenant _____ notice before entering.

The tenant's duty to pay rent is typically conditioned on your having fulfilled your legal responsibility to properly repair and maintain the premises. This means that, of necessity, you have a legal responsibility to keep fairly close tabs on the condition of the property. For this reason, and because it makes good sense to allow landlords reasonable access to their property, nearly every state clearly recognizes the right of a landlord to legally enter rented premises while a tenant is still in residence under certain broad circumstances, such as to deal with an emergency and when the tenant gives permission.

Many states have access laws specifying the circumstances under which landlords may legally enter rented premises. Most access laws allow landlords to enter rental units to make repairs and inspect the property and to show property to prospective tenants and purchasers. (See "General Rules of Entry," below.) State access laws typically specify the amount of notice required for such entry—usually 24 hours (unless it is impractical to do so—for example, in cases of emergency). A few states simply require the landlord to provide "reasonable" notice, often presumed to be 24 hours.

Clause 15 makes it clear to the tenant that you have a legal right of access to the property to make repairs or to show the premises for sale or rental, provided you give the tenant reasonable notice. (The table "State Laws on Landlord's Access to Rental Property" in Appendix A provides details on a landlord's right to entry and notice requirements.)

How to Fill In Clause 15:

In the blank, indicate the amount of notice you will provide the tenant before entering—at least the minimum required in your state. If your state law simply requires "reasonable" notice or has no notice requirement, we suggest you provide at least 24 hours' notice.

General Rules of Entry

Here are the general circumstances under which landlords may legally enter rented premises. Except in cases of emergency, or where it is impractical to do so, you generally must enter only at reasonable times, and you must give at least the amount and type of notice required in your state.

Emergency. In all states, you can enter rental property to respond to a true emergency —such as a gas leak.

To make repairs or inspect the property. By law, many states allow you and your repairperson to enter the tenant's home to make necessary or agreed-upon repairs, decorations, alterations, or improvements, and to supply necessary or agreed-upon services—for example, when you need to fix a broken oven.

To show property. Most states with access laws allow a landlord to enter rented property to show it to prospective tenants toward the end of the tenancy or to prospective purchasers if the landlord wishes to sell the property. (See Chapter 3 for advice on renting property that's still occupied.)

With the permission of the tenant. You can always enter rental property, even without notice, if the tenant agrees.

Entry after the tenant has moved out. To state the obvious, you may enter the premises after the tenant has completely moved out—regardless of whether the tenant left voluntarily after giving back the key or involuntarily as a result of an eviction lawsuit. In addition, if you believe the tenant has abandoned the property—that is, skipped out without giving any notice or returning the key— you may legally enter.

Clause 16. Extended Absences by Tenant

Tenant will notify Landlord in advance if Tenant will be away from the premises for _____ or more consecutive days. During such absence, Landlord may enter the premises at times reasonably necessary to maintain the property and inspect for needed repairs.

Several states give landlords the specific legal right to enter the rental unit during a tenant's extended absence to maintain the property as necessary and to inspect for damage and needed repairs. Extended absence is often defined as seven days or more. For example, if you live in a cold-weather place and temperatures take a dive, it makes sense to check the pipes in rental units (to make sure they haven't burst) when the tenant is away for winter vacation.

While many states do not address this issue, either by statute or court decision, you should be on safe legal ground to enter rental property during a tenant's extended absence, as long as you have a genuine reason to enter to protect the property from damage. You should enter only if something really needs to be done—that is, something the tenant would do if he were home, as part of his obligation to keep the property clean, safe, and in good repair.

To protect yourself, include Clause 16, which requires that the tenant notify you when they will be gone for an extended time and alerts the tenant of your intent to enter the premises during these times, if necessary.

How to Fill In Clause 16:

In the blank, fill in the time frame that you think is reasonable to provide the tenant advance notice of entry. Ten or 14 days is common.

Clause 17. Possession of the Premises

a. *Tenant's failure to take possession.*
   If, after signing this Agreement, Tenant fails to take possession of the premises, Tenant will still be responsible for paying rent and complying with all other terms of this Agreement.

b. *Landlord's failure to deliver possession.*
   If Landlord is unable to deliver possession of the premises to Tenant for any reason not within Landlord's control, including, but not limited to, partial or complete destruction of the premises, Tenant will have the right to terminate this Agreement upon proper notice as required by law. In such event, Landlord's liability to Tenant will be limited to the return of all sums previously paid by Tenant to Landlord.

The first part of this clause (Part a) explains that a tenant who chooses not to move in (take possession) after signing the lease or rental agreement will still be required to pay rent and satisfy other conditions of the agreement. This does not mean, however, that you can sit back and expect to collect rent for the entire lease or rental agreement term. (As we explain in Chapter 5, you generally must take reasonably prompt steps to re-rent the premises, and you must credit the rent you collect against the first tenant's rent obligation.)

The second part of the clause (Part b) protects you if you're unable, for reasons beyond your control, to turn over possession after having signed the agreement or lease—for example, if a fire spreads from next door and destroys the premises. It limits your financial liability to the new tenant to the return of any prepaid rent and security deposits (the "sums previously paid" in the language of the clause).

! **CAUTION**

Clause 17 may not limit your liability if you cannot deliver possession because the old tenant is still on the premises—even if he is the subject of an eviction that you ultimately win. When a holdover tenant prevents the new tenant from moving in, landlords are often sued by the new tenant for not only the return of any prepaid rent and security deposits, but also the costs of temporary housing, storage costs, and other losses. In some states, an attempt in the lease to limit the new tenant's recovery to the return of prepaid sums alone would not hold up in court. To protect yourself, you will want to shift some of the financial liability to the holdover tenant. You'll have a stronger chance of doing this if the old tenant has given written notice of his intent to move out. (See Clause 4, above, which requires written notice.)

How to Fill In Clause 17:

You do not need to add anything to this clause.

Clause 18. Tenant Rules and Regulations

☐ Tenant acknowledges receipt of, and has read a copy of, tenant rules and regulations, which are labeled Attachment A and attached to and incorporated into this Agreement by this reference.

Many landlords don't worry about detailed rules and regulations, especially when they rent single-family homes or duplexes. However, in larger buildings with many tenants, rules are usually important to control the use of common areas and equipment—both for the convenience, safety, and welfare of the tenants and as a way to protect your property from damage. Rules and regulations also help avoid confusion and misunderstandings about day-to-day issues such as garbage disposal, lost key charges, and parking rules.

Not every minor rule needs to be incorporated in your lease or rental agreement. But it is a good idea to specifically incorporate important ones (especially those that are likely to be ignored by some tenants). Doing so gives you the authority to evict a tenant who persists in seriously violating your code of tenant rules and regulations. Also, to avoid charges of illegal discrimination, rules and regulations should apply equally to all tenants in your rental property.

Because tenant rules and regulations are often lengthy and may be revised occasionally, we suggest you prepare a separate attachment. (See "How to Prepare Attachment Pages" at the beginning of this section.) Be sure the rules and regulations (including any revisions) are dated on each page and signed by both you and the tenant.

What's Covered in Tenant Rules and Regulations

Tenant rules and regulations typically cover issues such as:

- elevator safety and use
- pool rules
- garbage disposal and recycling
- vehicles and parking regulations—for example, restrictions of repairs on the premises or types of vehicles (such as no RVs)
- lock-out and lost key charges
- pet rules
- no smoking in common areas
- security system use
- specific details on what's considered excessive noise
- dangerous materials—nothing explosive should be on the premises
- storage of bikes, baby strollers, and other equipment in halls, stairways, and other common areas
- specific landlord and tenant maintenance responsibilities (such as stopped-up toilets or garbage disposals, broken windows, rodent and pest control, and lawn and yard maintenance)
- use of the grounds and recreation areas
- maintenance of balconies and decks (for instance, no drying clothes on balconies)
- display of signs in windows
- laundry room rules, and
- waterbeds.

How to Fill In Clause 18:

If you have a set of tenant rules and regulations, check the box. If you do not, simply put a line through this clause or write the words "N/A" or "Not Applicable."

Clause 19. Payment of Court Costs and Attorney Fees in a Lawsuit

In any action or legal proceeding to enforce any part of this Agreement, the prevailing party ☐ shall not/ ☐ shall recover reasonable attorney fees and court costs.

Many landlords assume that if they sue a tenant and win (or prevail, in legalese), the court will order the losing tenant to pay the landlord's court costs (filing fees, service of process charges, deposition costs, and so on) and attorney fees. This is not generally true. In most states, a court will order the losing tenant to pay your attorney fees only if a written agreement specifically provides for it.

If, however, you have an "attorney fees" clause in your lease, all this changes. If you hire a lawyer to bring a lawsuit and win, the judge will order your tenant to pay your costs and attorney fees. (In rare instances, a court will order the loser to pay costs and fees on its own if it finds that the behavior of the losing party was particularly egregious.)

But there's another important issue you need to know about: By law in many states, an attorney fees clause in a lease or a rental agreement works both ways, even if you haven't written it that way. That is, even if the lease states only that you are entitled to attorney fees if you win a lawsuit, your tenants will be entitled to collect their attorney fees from you if they prevail. The amount you would be ordered to pay would be whatever the judge decides is reasonable.

So, especially if you live in a state that will read a "one-way" attorney fees clause as a two-way street, give some thought to whether you want to bind both of you to paying for the winner's costs and fees. Remember, if you can't actually collect a judgment containing attorney fees from an evicted tenant (which often happens), the clause will not help you. But if the tenant prevails, you will be stuck paying his costs and fees. In addition, the presence of a two-way clause will make it far easier for a tenant to secure a willing lawyer for even a doubtful claim, because the source of the lawyer's fee (you, if you lose) will probably appear more financially solid than if the client were paying the bill himself.

Especially if you intend to do all or most of your own legal work in any potential eviction or other lawsuit, you will almost surely be better off not to allow for attorney fees. Why? Because if the tenant wins, you will have to pay her fees; but if you win, she will owe you nothing, since you didn't hire an attorney. You can't even recover for the long hours you spent preparing for and handling the case.

Finally, be aware that attorney fees clauses only cover lawsuits concerning the meaning or implementation of the lease—such as a dispute about rent, security deposits, or your right to access. An attorney fees clause would not apply in a personal injury or discrimination lawsuit.

How to Fill In Clause 19:

If you don't want to allow for attorney fees, check the box before the words "shall not" and cross out the word "shall."

If you want to be entitled to attorney fees and costs if you win—and you're willing to pay them if you lose—check the box before the word "shall" and cross out the words "shall not."

Clause 20. Disclosures

Tenant acknowledges that Landlord has made the following disclosures regarding the premises:

☐ Disclosure of Information on Lead-Based Paint and/or Lead-Based Paint Hazards

☐ Other disclosures:

_____

_____

_____

Federal, state, or local laws may require you to make certain disclosures before a new tenant signs a lease or rental agreement or moves in.

Lead Disclosures

If your rental unit was built prior to 1978, before signing a lease or rental agreement you must tell new tenants about any known lead-based paint or lead-based paint hazards in the rental premises, including individual units and common areas, such as hallways, parking garages, or play areas. You must also give them an EPA pamphlet, *Protect Your Family From Lead in Your Home*. This is a requirement of the Residential Lead-Based Paint Hazard Reduction Act, commonly known as Title X (42 U.S.C. § 4852d), which is administered by the U.S. Environmental Protection Agency (EPA).

In addition, both you and the tenant must sign an EPA-approved form—*Disclosure of Information on Lead-Based Paint and/or Lead-Based Paint Hazards*—that will prove that you told your tenants what you know about these hazards on your premises. You must keep the disclosure form as part of your records for three years from the date of the start of the tenancy.

As discussed below, state laws on lead disclosure may also come into play.

CD-ROM

The Landlord Rental Forms CD includes copies of the *Disclosure of Information on Lead-Based Paint and/or Lead-Based Paint Hazards* form, and the EPA pamphlet *Protect Your Family From Lead in Your Home* (both in English and in Spanish). Appendix C includes blank tear-out copies of these forms.

CAUTION

Penalties are severe. Property owners who fail to comply with EPA regulations for disclosing lead-based paint hazards face penalties of up to $10,000 for each violation and treble (triple) damages if a tenant is injured by your willful noncompliance.

Rental Properties Exempt From Title X Regulations

Landlords who rent the following types of property are not required to comply with federal lead disclosure requirements:

- housing built after January 1978
- housing certified lead-free by an accredited lead inspector
- lofts, efficiencies, and studios
- short-term vacation rentals of 100 days or less
- a single room rented in a residential dwelling
- housing designed for persons with disabilities, unless children under age six are present, and
- retirement communities (housing designed for seniors, where one or more tenant is at least 62 years old), unless children under age six are present.

RESOURCE

Copies of Title X regulations and background information may be obtained by calling the National Lead Information Center at 800-424-LEAD, or checking its website, www.epa.gov/lead/pubs/nlic.htm. Information on the evaluation and control of lead may be obtained from the regional offices of the EPA or the EPA website, www.epa.gov.

Many states have also addressed the lead issue by prohibiting the use of lead-based paint in residences and requiring the careful maintenance of existing lead-based building materials. Some states require property owners to disclose lead hazards to prospective tenants. If you are subject to a state statute, you must comply with it as well as federal law. Check with your state housing department or local office of the U.S. Department of Housing and Urban Development (www.hud.gov) to find out if this applies to you.

Other Disclosures

State laws may impose disclosure requirements, too, such as the presence of mold on the property or shared utility arrangements. Local rent control ordinances often require disclosures, such as the name and address of the government agency or elected board that administers the ordinance. Some states require landlords to inform tenants of the name and address of the bank where their security deposit is being held. (Clause 8 covers security deposits.)

Here is a sampling of other state disclosure laws. This is not an exhaustive list. Check your state and local laws for details on these and other disclosure requirements:

- property located near former military ordnance (Cal. Civ. Code § 1940.7) or military noise or accident potential zone (Va. Code Ann. § 55-248. 12:1)

- tenant's gas or electric meter serves areas outside of the rental unit (Cal. Civ. Code § 1940.9; 765 Ill. Comp. Stat. §§ 735/1.2, 740/5)

- full explanation of utility rates, charges, and services (Iowa Code Ann. § 562A.13(4))

- existence of a state Department of Justice database that the tenant can access to learn if an individual is a registered sexual offender living within a community and zip code (Cal. Civ. Code § 2079.10a)

- fire safety and protection information (Fla. Stat. Ann. § 83.50; Wash. Rev. Code Ann. § 59.18.060)

- rental unit has been flooded within the past five years (Ga. Code Ann. § 44-7-20; Okla. Stat. Ann. tit. 41, § 113a)

- landlord's excise tax number, so that tenants may file for a low-income tax credit (Haw. Rev. Stat. § 521-43)

- outstanding inspection orders, condemnation orders, or declarations that the property is unfit. Citations for violations that do not involve threats to tenant health or safety must be summarized and posted in an obvious place, and the original must be available for review by the tenant. (Minn. Stat. Ann. § 504B.195), and

- presence of dangerous mold (Cal. Health & Safety Code § 26147) or of any "controlled substances" releases, such as waste from illegal drug labs, on or under the residential property (Cal. Civ. Code § 1940.7.5).

How to Fill In Clause 20:

If your rental property was built before 1978, you must meet federal lead disclosure requirements, so check the first box and follow the advice above.

If you are legally required to make other disclosures as described above, check the second box and provide details in the blank space, adding pages as necessary. (See "How to Prepare Attachment Pages" at the beginning of this section.)

Also, if there is a hidden (not obvious) problem with the property that could cause injury or substantially interfere with your tenant's safe enjoyment and use of the dwelling, and it is impossible to fix it, you are better off legally if you disclose the defective or dangerous condition before the tenant signs the lease. Examples include naturally occurring dangers, such as loose soil, and man-made dangers, such as steep stairs. See "Disclosures of Hidden Defects," below, for more on the subject.

Disclosures of Hidden Defects

Landlords have a duty to warn tenants and others about naturally occurring dangers (such as loose soil) and man-made dangers (like low doorways or steep stairs) that are hidden but which you know (or should know) about. Disclose hidden defects in Clause 20 of your lease or rental agreement, so that it can never be claimed that a tenant was not warned of a potentially dangerous condition. For example, if the building contains asbestos insulation that could be dangerous if anyone made a hole in the wall, disclose this to your tenants. If appropriate, also post warning signs near hazards, such as a ramp that's slippery when wet or a tree that drops entire strips of bark during windy weather.

While disclosure doesn't guarantee that you won't be legally liable (also make sure your insurance protects you), it will likely help. Putting the tenant on notice that a problem exists will help prevent injuries and limit your liability should an injury occur from a defective condition in the rental unit or on the premises.

> ⓘ **CAUTION**
>
> **Some problems need to be fixed, not merely disclosed.** Warning your tenants about a hidden defect does not absolve you of legal responsibility if the condition makes the dwelling uninhabitable or unreasonably dangerous. For example, you are courting liability if you rent an apartment with a gas heater that you know might blow up, even if you warn the tenant that the heater is faulty. Nor can you simply warn your tenants about prior crime on the premises and then fail to do anything (like installing deadbolts or hiring security) to promote safety.

Clause 21. Authority to Receive Legal Papers

The Landlord, any person managing the premises, and anyone designated by the Landlord are authorized to accept service of process and receive other notices and demands, which may be delivered to:

☐ The Landlord, at the following address:

_____

_____

☐ The manager, at the following address:

_____

_____

☐ The following person, at the following address:

_____

_____

It's the law in many states, and a good idea in all, to give your tenants information about everyone whom you have authorized to receive notices and legal papers, such as a tenant's notice that she is ending the tenancy or a tenant's court documents as part of an eviction defense. Of course, you may want to handle all of this yourself or delegate it to a manager or management company. Make sure the person you designate to receive legal papers is almost always available to receive tenant notices and legal papers. Also, be sure to keep your tenants up to date on any changes in this information.

How to Fill In Clause 21:

Provide your name and street address or the name and address of someone else you authorize to receive notices and legal papers on your behalf, such as a property manager.

Clause 22. Additional Provisions

Additional provisions are as follows: _____

_____

In this clause, you may list any additional provisions or agreements that are unique to you and the particular tenant signing the lease or rental agreement, such as a provision that allows limited business use of the premises—for example, for occasional weekday piano lessons.

If you don't have separate tenant rules and regulations (see Clause 18, above), you may spell out a few rules under this clause—for example, regarding lost key charges, use of a pool on the property, or no smoking rules.

How to Fill In Clause 22:

List additional provisions or rules here or in an attachment. If there are no additional provisions, write "N/A" or "Not Applicable."

TIP

There is no legal or practical imperative to put every small detail you want to communicate to the tenant into your lease or rental agreement. Instead, prepare a welcoming, but no-nonsense, "move-in letter" that dovetails with the lease or rental agreement and highlights important terms of the tenancy—for example, how and where to report maintenance problems. You may also use a move-in letter to cover issues not included in the lease or rental agreement—for example, rules for use of a laundry room. (Chapter 4 covers move-in letters.)

CAUTION

Do not include exculpatory ("If there's a problem, I'm not responsible") clauses or hold harmless ("If there's a problem, you are responsible") clauses. Many form leases include provisions that attempt to absolve you in advance from responsibility for your legal misdeeds. For example, one lease form generated by a popular software package contains a broad provision stating that you are not responsible for injuries to tenants and guests, even those you cause intentionally. Many exculpatory clauses are blatantly illegal: If a tenant is injured because of a dangerous condition you failed to fix for several months, no boilerplate lease provision will protect you from civil—and probably criminal—charges.

Clause 23. Validity of Each Part

If any portion of this Agreement is held to be invalid, its invalidity will not affect the validity or enforceability of any other provision of this Agreement.

This clause is known as a "savings" clause, and it is commonly used in contracts. It means that, in the unlikely event that one of the other clauses in the Agreement is found to be invalid by a court, the remainder of the Agreement will remain in force.

How to Fill In Clause 23:

You do not need to add anything to this clause.

Clause 24. Grounds for Termination of Tenancy

The failure of Tenant or Tenant's guests or invitees to comply with any term of this Agreement, or the misrepresentation of any material fact on Tenant's rental application, is grounds for termination of the tenancy, with appropriate notice to the Tenant and procedures as required by law.

This clause states that any violation of the Agreement by the tenant, or by the tenant's business or social guests, is grounds for terminating the tenancy, according to the procedures established by your state or local laws. Making the tenant responsible for the actions of his guests can be extremely important—for example, if you discover that the tenant's family or friends are dealing illegal drugs on the premises or have damaged the property.

How to Fill In Clause 24:

You do not need to add anything to this clause.

Clause 25. Entire Agreement

This document constitutes the entire Agreement between the parties, and no promises or representations, other than those contained here and those implied by law, have been made by Landlord or Tenant. Any modifications to this Agreement must be in writing, signed by Landlord and Tenant.

This clause establishes that the lease or rental agreement and any attachments (such as tenant rules and regulations) constitute the entire agreement between you and your tenant. It means that oral promises (by you or the tenant) to do something different with respect to any aspect of the rental are not binding. Any changes or additions must be in writing. For example, if your lease prohibits pets, and your tenant wants to get a dog and you agree, you should amend the Pets clause of the lease accordingly. This will help assure that a casual conversation about pets doesn't lead the tenant to bringing in a dog without your permission. (Chapter 5 discusses how to modify signed rental agreements and leases.)

How to Fill In Clause 25:

You do not need to add anything to this clause.

Signing the Lease or Rental Agreement

Make a copy of the lease or rental agreement, including all attachments. You and each tenant should sign both copies. At the end of the lease or rental agreement, there's space to include your signature, street address, and phone number, or that of the person you authorize as your agent, such as a property manager. There's also space for the tenants' signatures and phone numbers.

Again, as stressed in Clause 1, make sure all adults living in the rental unit, including both members of a married couple, sign the lease or rental agreement. And check that the tenant's name and signature match his or her driver's license or other legal document.

If the tenant has a cosigner (see "About Cosigners," below), you'll need to add a line for the cosigner's signature.

If you alter our form by writing or typing in changes, be sure that you and all tenants initial the changes when you sign the document, so as to forestall any possibility that a tenant will claim you unilaterally inserted changes after the tenant signed.

CAUTION

Don't sign a lease until all terms are final and the tenant understands all terms of the agreement and what's expected. All of your expectations should be written into the lease or rental agreement (or any attachments, such as tenant rules and regulations) before you and the tenant sign the document. Never sign an incomplete document assuming last-minute changes can be made later.

Give one copy of the signed lease or rental agreement to the tenant(s), and keep the other one for your files. (If you are renting to more than one tenant, you don't need to prepare a separate agreement for each cotenant. After the agreement is signed, cotenants may make their own copies of the signed document.)

TIP

Help tenants understand the lease or rental agreement before they sign it. Too many landlords thrust a lease or rental agreement at tenants and expect them to sign it unread. Far better to encourage tenants to ask questions about anything that's unclear, or to actually review each clause with new tenants. It will save you lots of hassles later on.

If English is not a tenant's first language—especially if you regularly rent to people in the tenant's ethnic group—prepare and give the tenant a written translation. Appendix C includes a Spanish version of our lease and rental agreement. Some states require this. California, for example, requires landlords to notify Spanish-speaking tenants, in Spanish, of the right to request a Spanish version. But even if it's not legally required, you want your tenants to know and follow the rules. Providing a written translation of your lease or rental agreement is a great way to establish rapport with tenants. Chapter 4 discusses how to get your new tenancy off to the right start.

About Cosigners

Some landlords require cosigners on rental agreements and leases, especially when renting to students who depend on parents for much of their income. The cosigner signs a separate agreement or the rental agreement or lease, under which she agrees to cover any rent or damage-repair costs the tenant fails to pay.

In practice, a cosigner's promise to guarantee the tenant's rent obligation may have less legal value than at first you might think. This is because the threat of eviction is the primary factor that motivates a tenant to pay the rent, and, obviously, you cannot evict a cosigner. Also, since the cosigner must be sued separately in either a regular civil lawsuit or in small claims court—for example, if a tenant stiffs you for a month's rent—actually doing so may be more trouble than it's worth. This is especially true if the cosigner lives in another state, since the amount of money you are out will rarely justify hiring a lawyer and collecting a judgment.

In sum, the benefits of having a lease or rental agreement cosigned by someone who won't be living on the property are largely psychological. But these benefits may still be worth something: A tenant who thinks you can (and will) notify and sue a cosigning relative or friend may be less likely to default on the rent. Similarly, a cosigner asked to pay the tenant's debts may persuade the tenant to pay.

Because of the practical difficulties associated with cosigners, many landlords refuse to consider them, which is legal in every situation but one: If a disabled tenant who has insufficient income (but is otherwise suitable) asks you to accept a cosigner who will cover the rent if needed, you must relax your blanket rule at least to the extent of investigating the suitability of the proposed cosigner. If that person is solvent and stable, federal law requires you to accommodate the applicant by accepting the cosigner, in spite of your general policy. (*Giebeler v. M & B Associates*, 343 F.3d 1143 (9th Cir. 2003).)

If you decide to accept a cosigner, you may want to have that person fill out a separate rental application and agree to a credit check—after all, a cosigner who has no resources or connection to the tenant will be completely useless. Should the tenant and her prospective cosigner object to these inquiries and the costs of a credit check, you may wonder how serious they are about the guarantor's willingness to stand behind the tenant. Once you are satisfied that the cosigner can genuinely back up the tenant, add a line at the end of the lease or rental agreement for the dated signature, phone, and address of the cosigner.

> **CAUTION**
>
> **If you later amend the rental agreement or change the lease, have the cosigner sign the new version.** Generally speaking, a cosigner is bound only to the terms of the exact lease or rental agreement he cosigns. If you later change a significant term, add a new tenant or otherwise create a new contract, the original cosigner will probably be off the hook, unless you again get him to sign.

Month-to-Month Residential Rental Agreement

Clause 1. Identification of Landlord and Tenant

This Agreement is entered into between _____Marty Nelson_____

_____ [Tenant] and

_____Alex Stevens_____ [Landlord].

Each Tenant is jointly and severally liable for the payment of rent and performance of all other terms of this Agreement.

Clause 2. Identification of Premises

Subject to the terms and conditions in this Agreement, Landlord rents to Tenant, and Tenant rents from

Landlord, for residential purposes only, the premises located at _____137 Howell St., Houston, Texas_____

_____ [the premises],

together with the following furnishings and appliances: _____

_____

Rental of the premises also includes _____

_____

Clause 3. Limits on Use and Occupancy

The premises are to be used only as a private residence for Tenant(s) listed in Clause 1 of this Agreement, and

their minor children. Occupancy by guests for more than _____ten days every six months_____

is prohibited without Landlord's written consent and will be considered a breach of this Agreement.

Clause 4. Term of the Tenancy

The rental will begin on _____September 15, 20xx_____, and continue on a month-to-month

basis. Landlord may terminate the tenancy or modify the terms of this Agreement by giving the Tenant

_____30_____ days' written notice. Tenant may terminate the tenancy by giving the Landlord

_____30_____ days' written notice.

Clause 5. Payment of Rent

Regular monthly rent

Tenant will pay to Landlord a monthly rent of $_____900_____ , payable in advance on the first day of

each month, except when that day falls on a weekend or legal holiday, in which case rent is due on the next

business day. Rent will be paid in the following manner unless Landlord designates otherwise:

Delivery of payment.

Rent will be paid:

☑ by mail, to __Alex Stevens, 28 Franklin St., Houston, Texas 77002__

☐ in person, at _____

Form of payment.

Landlord will accept payment in these forms:

☑ personal check made payable to __Alex Stevens__

☑ cashier's check made payable to __Alex Stevens__

☐ credit card

☑ money order

☐ cash

Prorated first month's rent.

For the period from Tenant's move-in date, __September 15, 20xx__, through the end of the

month, Tenant will pay to Landlord the prorated monthly rent of $__450__. This amount will

be paid on or before the date the Tenant moves in.

Clause 6. Late Charges

If Tenant fails to pay the rent in full before the end of the __third__ day after it's due, Tenant will pay

Landlord a late charge as follows: __$10 plus $5 for each additional day that the rent remains__

__unpaid. The total late charge for any one month will not exceed $45__.

Landlord does not waive the right to insist on payment of the rent in full on the date it is due.

Clause 7. Returned Check and Other Bank Charges

If any check offered by Tenant to Landlord in payment of rent or any other amount due under this Agreement

is returned for lack of sufficient funds, a "stop payment," or any other reason, Tenant will pay Landlord a

returned check charge of $__15__.

Clause 8. Security Deposit

On signing this Agreement, Tenant will pay to Landlord the sum of $__1,800__ as a security

deposit. Tenant may not, without Landlord's prior written consent, apply this security deposit to the last

month's rent or to any other sum due under this Agreement. Within __30 days__

after Tenant has vacated the premises, returned keys, and provided Landlord with a forwarding address,

Landlord will return the deposit in full or give Tenant an itemized written statement of the reasons for, and

the dollar amount of, any of the security deposit retained by Landlord, along with a check for any deposit

balance.

[optional clauses here, if any]

Clause 9. Utilities

Tenant will pay all utility charges, except for the following, which will be paid by Landlord:

garbage and water
_____.

Clause 10. Assignment and Subletting

Tenant will not sublet any part of the premises or assign this Agreement without the prior written consent of Landlord.

Clause 11. Tenant's Maintenance Responsibilities

Tenant will: (1) keep the premises clean, sanitary, and in good condition and, upon termination of the tenancy, return the premises to Landlord in a condition identical to that which existed when Tenant took occupancy, except for ordinary wear and tear; (2) immediately notify Landlord of any defects or dangerous conditions in and about the premises of which Tenant becomes aware; and (3) reimburse Landlord, on demand by Landlord, for the cost of any repairs to the premises damaged by Tenant or Tenant's guests or business invitees through misuse or neglect.

Tenant has examined the premises, including appliances, fixtures, carpets, drapes, and paint, and has found them to be in good, safe, and clean condition and repair, except as noted in the Landlord-Tenant Checklist.

Clause 12. Repairs and Alterations by Tenant

a. Except as provided by law, or as authorized by the prior written consent of Landlord, Tenant will not make any repairs or alterations to the premises, including nailing holes in the walls or painting the rental unit.

b. Tenant will not, without Landlord's prior written consent, alter, rekey, or install any locks to the premises or install or alter any burglar alarm system. Tenant will provide Landlord with a key or keys capable of unlocking all such rekeyed or new locks as well as instructions on how to disarm any altered or new burglar alarm system.

Clause 13. Violating Laws and Causing Disturbances

Tenant is entitled to quiet enjoyment of the premises. Tenant and guests or invitees will not use the premises or adjacent areas in such a way as to: (1) violate any law or ordinance, including laws prohibiting the use, possession, or sale of illegal drugs; (2) commit waste (severe property damage); or (3) create a nuisance by annoying, disturbing, inconveniencing, or interfering with the quiet enjoyment and peace and quiet of any other tenant or nearby resident.

Clause 14. Pets

No animal, bird, or other pet will be kept on the premises, even temporarily, except properly trained service animals needed by blind, deaf, or disabled persons and _____ under the following conditions: _____

_____

_____ .

Clause 15. Landlord's Right to Access

Landlord or Landlord's agents may enter the premises in the event of an emergency, to make repairs or improvements, or to show the premises to prospective buyers or tenants. Landlord may also enter the premises to conduct an annual inspection to check for safety or maintenance problems. Except in cases of emergency, Tenant's abandonment of the premises, court order, or where it is impractical to do so, Landlord shall give Tenant _____ 24 hours' _____ notice before entering.

Clause 16. Extended Absences by Tenant

Tenant will notify Landlord in advance if Tenant will be away from the premises for _____ seven _____ or more consecutive days. During such absence, Landlord may enter the premises at times reasonably necessary to maintain the property and inspect for needed repairs.

Clause 17. Possession of the Premises

a. *Tenant's failure to take possession.*

If, after signing this Agreement, Tenant fails to take possession of the premises, Tenant will still be responsible for paying rent and complying with all other terms of this Agreement.

b. *Landlord's failure to deliver possession.*

If Landlord is unable to deliver possession of the premises to Tenant for any reason not within Landlord's control, including, but not limited to, partial or complete destruction of the premises, Tenant will have the right to terminate this Agreement upon proper notice as required by law. In such event, Landlord's liability to Tenant will be limited to the return of all sums previously paid by Tenant to Landlord.

Clause 18. Tenant Rules and Regulations

☐ Tenant acknowledges receipt of, and has read a copy of, tenant rules and regulations, which are labelled Attachment A and attached to and incorporated into this Agreement by this reference.

Clause 19. Payment of Court Costs and Attorney Fees in a Lawsuit

In any action or legal proceeding to enforce any part of this Agreement, the prevailing party

☐ shall not / ☑ shall recover reasonable attorney fees and court costs.

Clause 20. Disclosures

Tenant acknowledges that Landlord has made the following disclosures regarding the premises:

☑ Disclosure of Information on Lead-Based Paint and/or Lead-Based Paint Hazards

☐ Other disclosures: _____

_____

_____

_____

Clause 21. Authority to Receive Legal Papers

The Landlord, any person managing the premises, and anyone designated by the Landlord are authorized to accept service of process and receive other notices and demands, which may be delivered to:

☑ The Landlord, at the following address: _28 Franklin St., Houston, Texas 77002_

☐ The manager, at the following address: _____

☐ The following person, at the following address: _____

Clause 22. Additional Provisions

Additional provisions are as follows: _____

_____

_____

_____

_____

_____

_____

_____

Clause 23. Validity of Each Part

If any portion of this Agreement is held to be invalid, its invalidity will not affect the validity or enforceability of any other provision of this Agreement.

Clause 24. Grounds for Termination of Tenancy

The failure of Tenant or Tenant's guests or invitees to comply with any term of this Agreement, or the misrepresentation of any material fact on Tenant's Rental Application, is grounds for termination of the tenancy, with appropriate notice to Tenant and procedures as required by law.

Clause 25. Entire Agreement

This document constitutes the entire Agreement between the parties, and no promises or representations, other than those contained here and those implied by law, have been made by Landlord or Tenant. Any modifications to this Agreement must be in writing signed by Landlord and Tenant.

Sept. 1, 20xx	*Alex Stevens*	Landlord
Date	Landlord or Landlord's Agent	Title
28 Franklin Street		
Street Address		
Houston	Texas	77002	713-555-1578
City	State	Zip Code	Phone
Sept. 1, 20xx	*Marty Nelson*		713-555-8751
Date	Tenant		Phone
Date	Tenant		Phone
Date	Tenant		Phone

Choosing Tenants: Your Most Important Decision

How to Advertise Rental Property 52

Renting Property That's Still Occupied 54

Accepting Rental Applications 54

Checking References, Credit History, and More 60

    Check With Previous Landlords and Other References 61

    Verify Income and Employment 61

    Obtain a Credit Report 64

    Verify Bank Account Information 65

    Review Court Records 66

    Use Megan's Law to Check State Databases 66

Avoiding Illegal Discrimination 67

Choosing—and Rejecting—an Applicant 68

    Information You Should Keep on Rejected Applicants 69

    Information You Must Provide Rejected Applicants 69

    Conditional Acceptances 73

Choosing a Tenant-Manager 73

Property Management Companies 74

Choosing tenants is the most important decision any landlord makes. To do it well and stay out of legal trouble, you need a good system. Follow the steps in this chapter to maximize your chances of selecting tenants who will pay their rent on time, keep their units in good condition, and not cause you any legal or practical problems later.

TIP

Before you advertise your property for rent, make a number of basic decisions—including how much rent to charge, whether to offer a fixed-term lease or a month-to-month tenancy, how many tenants can occupy each rental unit, how big a security deposit to require, and whether you'll allow pets. Making these important decisions should dovetail with writing your lease or rental agreement (see Chapter 2).

How to Advertise Rental Property

You can advertise rental property in many ways:

- putting an "Apartment for Rent" sign in front of the building or in one of the windows
- taking out classified newspaper ads
- posting flyers on neighborhood bulletin boards
- listing with a local homefinders' or apartment-finding service that provides a centralized listing of rental units for a particular geographic area
- listing with a local real estate broker that handles rentals
- buying ads in apartment rental guides or magazines
- hiring a property management company that will advertise your rentals as part of the management fee, or
- posting a notice online (see "Online Apartment Listing Services," below, for details).

Online Apartment Listing Services

Dozens of online services now make it easy to reach potential tenants, whether they already live in your community or are from out of state.

Community posting boards allow you to list your rentals at no or low charge and are a good place to start. *Craigslist,* one of the most established community boards, has local sites for many major metropolitan areas, including San Francisco, New York City, Atlanta, Miami, Phoenix, Chicago, Washington, DC, and Boston. Check out www.craigslist.org for details.

National apartment listing services are also available, with the largest ones representing millions of apartment units in the United States. Some of the most established are:

- www.move.com
- www.apartments.com
- www.rent.com, and
- www.apartmentguide.com.

These national sites offer a wide range of services, from simple text-only ads that provide basic information on your rental (such as the number of bedrooms) to full-scale virtual tours and floor plans of the rental property. Prices vary widely depending on the type of ad, how long you want it to run, and any services you purchase (some websites provide tenant-screening services).

What will work best depends on a number of factors, including the characteristics of the particular rental property (such as rent, size, and amenities), its location, your budget, and whether you are in a hurry to rent. Many smaller landlords find that instead of advertising widely and having to screen many potential tenants in an effort to sort the good from the bad, it makes better sense to market their rentals through word of mouth—telling friends, colleagues, neighbors, and current tenants. After all, people who already live in your property will want decent neighbors.

But no matter how you let people know about the availability of your rental units, you want to follow these simple rules and stay out of legal hot water:

Describe the rental unit accurately. Your ad should be easy to understand and scrupulously honest. Also, as a practical matter, you should avoid abbreviations and real estate jargon in your ad. Include basic details, such as:

- rent
- size—particularly number of bedrooms and baths
- location—either the general neighborhood or street address
- fixed-term lease or month-to-month rental agreement
- special features—such as fenced-in yard, view, washer/dryer, fireplace, remodeled kitchen, furnished, garage parking, doorman, hardwood floors, or wall-to-wall carpeting
- phone number or email for more details (unless you're going to show the unit only at an open house and don't want to take calls), and
- date and time of any open house.

If you have any important rules (legal and nondiscriminatory, of course), such as no pets, put them in your ad. Letting prospective tenants know about your important policies can save you from talking to a lot of unsuitable people.

Be sure your ad can't be construed as discriminatory. The best way to do this is to focus only on the rental property—not on any particular type of tenant. Specifically, ads should never mention sex, race, religion, disability, or age (unless yours is legally sanctioned senior citizens housing). And ads should never imply through words, photographs, or illustrations that you prefer to rent to people because of their age, sex, or race. (See "Avoiding

Illegal Discrimination," below, for more on the subject.)

Quote an honest price in your ad. Or, put another way, if a tenant who is otherwise acceptable (has a good credit history and impeccable references and meets all the criteria laid out below) shows up promptly, and agrees to all the terms set out in your ad, he or she should be able to rent your property for the price you have advertised. By contrast, if you suddenly find a reason why it will cost significantly more, you are likely to be in violation of your state's false advertising laws. This doesn't mean you are always legally required to rent at your advertised price, however. If a tenant asks for more services or significantly different lease terms that you feel require more rent, it's fine to bargain and raise your price, as long as your proposed increase doesn't violate any local rent control laws.

Don't advertise something you don't have. Some large landlords, management companies, and rental services have advertised units that weren't really available in order to produce a large number of prospective tenants who could then be directed to higher-priced or inferior units. Such bait-and-switch advertising is clearly illegal under consumer fraud laws, and many property owners have been prosecuted for such practices.

Don't overhype security measures. Don't exaggerate your written or oral description of security measures. Not only will you have begun the landlord-tenant relationship on a note of insincerity, but your descriptions of security may legally obligate you to actually provide what you have portrayed. Or, if you fail to do so, or fail to conscientiously maintain promised security measures in working order (such as outdoor lighting or an electronic gate on the parking garage), a court or jury may find your failure to be a material factor allowing a crime to occur on the premises. And, if this happens, chances are good you will be held liable for a tenant's losses or injuries.

Renting Property That's Still Occupied

Often, you can wait until the old tenant moves out to show a rental unit to prospective tenants. This gives you the chance to refurbish the unit and avoids problems such as promising the place to a new tenant, only to have the existing tenant not move out on time or leave the place a mess.

To eliminate any gap in rent, however, you may want to show a rental unit while its current tenants are still there. This can create a conflict; in most states, you have a right to show the still-occupied property to prospective tenants, but your current tenants are still entitled to a reasonable level of privacy. (For details, see Clause 15 of the lease and rental agreement in Chapter 2.)

To minimize disturbing your current tenant, follow these guidelines:

- Before implementing your plans to find a new tenant, discuss them with outgoing tenants so you can be as accommodating as possible.
- Give current tenants as much notice as possible before entering and showing a rental unit to prospective tenants.
- Try to limit the number of times you show the unit in a given week, and make sure your current tenants agree to any evening and weekend visits.
- Consider reducing the rent slightly for the existing tenant if showing the unit really will be an imposition.
- If possible, avoid putting a sign on the rental property itself, since this almost guarantees that your existing tenants will be bothered by strangers. Or, if you can't avoid putting up a sign, make sure any sign clearly warns against disturbing the occupant and includes a telephone number for information. Something on the order of "For Rent: Shown by Appointment Only. Call 555-1700. Do Not Disturb Occupants" should work fine.

If, despite your best efforts to protect their privacy, the current tenants are uncooperative or hostile, it really is best to avoid legal hassles and wait until they leave before showing the unit. Also, if the current tenant is a complete slob or has damaged the place, you'll be far better off to apply paint and elbow grease before trying to rerent it.

Accepting Rental Applications

It's good business, as well as a sound way to protect yourself from future legal problems, to carefully screen prospective tenants. To avoid legal problems and choose the best tenant, ask all prospective tenants to fill out a written rental application that includes information on the applicant's employment, income, credit, and rental housing history, including up-to-date references. It's legal and a good idea to ask for the applicant's Social Security and driver's license numbers or other identifying information. For example, instead of a Social Security number, you could accept an ITIN (Individual Taxpayer Identification Number), which is issued by the IRS to persons who are required to file income taxes but who can't obtain a Social Security number (SSN). ITINs are issued to nonimmigrants (people who are in the U.S. legally but don't have the right to live here permanently). Almost anyone planning on staying in the U.S. long enough to rent an apartment (like someone with a student visa) will have an ITIN. If you refuse to rent to someone who has an ITIN but not an SSN, you may be courting a fair housing claim. You can also ask if the applicant has declared bankruptcy, been evicted, or been convicted of a crime. (You'll also get much of this information from a credit report, as discussed below.)

CD-ROM

The Landlord Rental Forms CD includes a Rental Application and a sample is shown below. A blank tear-out version is in Appendix C at the back of this book.

Before giving prospective tenants a rental application, complete the box at the top, filling in the property address, the first month's rent, the rental term, and any deposit or credit check fee that tenants must pay before moving in. (Credit check fees are discussed later in this chapter.) If you're charging any other fee, such as a nonrefundable cleaning deposit, note this as well—if you are sure that the nonrefundable fee is legal in your state. (See "Don't Charge Nonrefundable Fees" in Chapter 2 for details.)

Here are some basic guidelines for accepting rental applications:

- Each prospective tenant—everyone age 18 or older who wants to live in your rental property—should completely fill out and sign a separate written application. This is true whether you're renting to a married couple or to unrelated roommates, a complete stranger, or the cousin of your current tenant.

- Always make sure that prospective tenants complete the entire rental application, including Social Security number, driver's license or other identifying information (such as a passport number), current employment, bank, and emergency contacts. You may need this information later to track down a tenant who skips town leaving unpaid rent or abandoned property. Also, you may need the Social Security number or other identifying information, such as a passport, to request an applicant's credit report.

- Request proof of identity and immigration status. In these security-sensitive times, many landlords ask prospective tenants to show their driver's license or other photo identification as a way to verify that the applicant is using his real name. You may also ask applicants for proof of identity and eligibility to work under U.S. immigration laws, such as a passport or naturalization certificate, using Form I-9 (*Employment Eligibility Verification*) of the U.S. Citizenship and Immigration Services or USCIS, a bureau of the U.S. Department of Homeland Security. This form (and instructions for completing it) are available from the USCIS website at www.uscis.gov, or by phone at 800-375-5283. Under federal fair housing laws, you may not selectively ask for such immigration information—that is, you must ask all prospective tenants, not just those you suspect may be in the country illegally. It is illegal to discriminate on the basis of national origin, although you may reject someone on the basis of immigration status.

Rental Application

Separate application required from each applicant age 18 or older.

Date and time received by landlord _____

Credit check fee _$35_____ Received _____

THIS SECTION TO BE COMPLETED BY LANDLORD

Address of Property to Be Rented: __178 West 81st St., Apt. 4F_____

Rental Term: ☐ month-to-month ☑ lease from _____March 1, 20xx____ to ____February 28, 20xx____

Amounts Due Prior to Occupancy

First month's rent .... $___1,500_____

Security deposit .... $___1,500_____

Other (specify): __Broker's fee_____ $___1,500_____

TOTAL .... $___4,530_____

Applicant

Full Name—include all names you use(d): ___Hannah Silver_____

Home Phone: (609) 555-3789_____ Work Phone: (609) 555-4567_____

Social Security Number: 123-000-4567_____ Driver's License Number/State: ___NJD123456_____

Other Identifying Information: _____

Vehicle Make: __Toyota_____ Model: __Tercel_____ Color: __White_____ Year: __1994____

License Plate Number/State: __NJ1234567_____

Additional Occupants

List everyone, including children, who will live with you:

Full Name	Relationship to Applicant
Dennis Olson	Husband

Rental History

FIRST-TIME RENTERS: ATTACH A DESCRIPTION OF YOUR HOUSING SITUATION FOR THE PAST FIVE YEARS.

Current Address: __39 Maple St., Princeton, NJ 08540_____

Dates Lived at Address: __May 1990– to date_____ Rent $ _2,000_____ Security Deposit $ _4,000____

Landlord/Manager: __Jane Tucker_____ Landlord/Manager's Phone: (609) ___555-7523____

Reason for Leaving: __New job in NYC_____

Previous Address: _1215 Middlebrook Lane, Princeton, NJ 08540_

Dates Lived at Address: _June 1987–May 1990_   Rent $_1,800_   Security Deposit $_1,000_

Landlord/Manager: _Ed Palermo_   Landlord/Manager's Phone: (609) _555-3711_

Reason for Leaving: _Better apartment_

Previous Address: _1527 Highland Dr., New Brunswick, NJ 08444_

Dates Lived at Address: _Jan. 1986–June 1987_   Rent $ _____   Security Deposit $ _____

Landlord/Manager: _Millie & Joe Lewis_   Landlord/Manager's Phone: (609) _555-9999_

Reason for Leaving: _Wanted to live closer to work_

Employment History

SELF-EMPLOYED APPLICANTS: ATTACH TAX RETURNS FOR THE PAST TWO YEARS

Name and Address of Current Employer: _Argonworks, 54 Nassau St., Princeton, NJ_

Phone: (609) _555-2333_

Name of Supervisor: _Tom Schmidt_   Supervisor's Phone: (609) _555-2333_

Dates Employed at This Job: _1983–date_   Position or Title: _Marketing Director_

Name and Address of Previous Employer: _Princeton Times_

13 Junction Rd., Princeton, NJ   Phone: (609) _555-1111_

Name of Supervisor: _Dory Krossber_   Supervisor's Phone: (609) _555-2366_

Dates Employed at This Job: _June 1982–Feb. 1983_   Position or Title: _Marketing Assistant_

ATTACH PAY STUBS FOR THE PAST TWO YEARS, FROM THIS EMPLOYER OR PRIOR EMPLOYERS.

Income

1. Your gross monthly employment income (before deductions): $_8,000_

2. Average monthly amounts of other income (specify sources): $_____

   Note: This does not include my husband's income. See his application. $_____

   $_____

   $_____

   TOTAL: $_8,000_

Bank/Financial Accounts

	Account Number	Bank/Institution	Branch
Savings Account:	1222345	N.J. Federal	Trenton, NJ
Checking Account:	789101	Princeton S&L	Princeton, NJ
Money Market or Similar Account:	234789	City Bank	Princeton, NJ

Credit Card Accounts

Major Credit Card: ☑VISA ☐MC ☐Discover Card ☐Am Ex ☐Other: _____

Issuer: _____City Bank_____   Account No. _1234 5555 6666 7777_

Balance $____1,000____   Average Monthly Payment: $ ___500___

Major Credit Card: ☐VISA ☐MC ☐Discover Card ☐Am Ex ☑Other: _____Dept. Store_____

Issuer: _____City Bank_____   Account No. _2345 0000 9999 8888_

Balance $____1,000____   Average Monthly Payment: $ ___500___

Loans

Type of Loan (mortgage, car, student loan, etc.)	Name of Creditor	Account Number	Amount Owed	Monthly Payment

Other Major Obligations

Type	Payee		Amount Owed	Monthly Payment

Miscellaneous

Describe the number and type of pets you want to have in the rental property: _____None now, but we might_ _want to get a cat some time_____

Describe water-filled furniture you want to have in the rental property: _____None_____

Do you smoke?   ☐ yes ☑ no

Have you ever:

Filed for bankruptcy?	☐ yes ☑ no	How many times _____
Been sued?	☐ yes ☑ no	How many times _____
Sued someone else?	☐ yes ☑ no	How many times _____
Been evicted?	☐ yes ☑ no	
Been convicted of a crime?	☐ yes ☑ no	How many times _____

Explain any "yes" listed above: _____

_____

_____

References and Emergency Contact

Personal Reference: _Joan Stanley_ Relationship: _Friend, coworker_

Address: _785 Spruce St., Princeton, NJ 08540_

_____ Phone: (609) _555-4578_

Personal Reference: _Marnie Swatt_ Relationship: _Friend_

Address: _82 East 59th St., #12B, NYC_

_____ Phone: (212) _555-8765_

Contact in Emergency: _Connie & Martin Silver_ Relationship: _Parents_

Address: _7852 Pierce St., Somerset, NJ 08321_

_____ Phone: (609) _555-7878_

Source

Where did you learn of this vacancy? _Ad in local paper._

_____

I certify that all the information given above is true and correct and understand that my lease or rental agreement may be terminated if I have made any material false or incomplete statements in this application. I authorize verification of the information provided in this application from my credit sources, credit bureaus, current and previous landlords and employers, and personal references. This permission will survive the expiration of my tenancy.

Hannah Silver _February 15, 20xx_
Applicant Date

Notes (Landlord/Manager): _____

Consent to Contact References and Perform Credit Check

I authorize _____ Jan Gold _____ to

obtain information about me from my credit sources, current and previous landlords, employers, and personal references, to enable

_____ Jan Gold _____ to evaluate my rental application.

I give permission for the landlord or its agent to obtain a consumer report about me for the purpose of this application, to ensure

that I continue to meet the terms of the tenancy, for the collection and recovery of any financial obligations relating to my tenancy,

or for any other permissible purpose.

_____ *Michael Clark* _____

Applicant signature

_____ Michael Clark _____

Printed name

_____ 123 State Street, Chicago, Illinois _____

Address

_____ 312-555-9876 _____

Phone Number

_____ February 2, 20xx _____

Date

- Be sure all potential tenants sign the rental application, authorizing you to verify the information and references and to run a credit report. (Some employers and banks require written authorization before they will talk to you.) You may also want to prepare a separate authorization, signed and dated by the applicant, so that you don't need to copy the entire application and send it off every time a bank or employer wants proof that the tenant authorized you to verify the information.

CD-ROM

The Landlord Rental Forms CD includes a copy of the Consent to Contact References and Perform Credit Check, and a sample is shown above. Appendix C includes a blank tear-out copy of this form.

Checking References, Credit History, and More

If an application looks good, your next step is to follow up thoroughly. The time and money you spend are some of the most cost-effective expenditures you'll ever make.

Be consistent in your screening. You risk a charge of illegal discrimination if you screen certain categories of applicants more stringently than others—for example, only requiring credit reports from racial minorities. See "Avoiding Illegal Discrimination," below, for more on the subject.

Here are six elements of a very thorough screening process. You should always go through at least the first three to check out the applicant's previous landlords and income and employment, and run a credit check.

Check With Previous Landlords and Other References

Always call current and previous landlords or managers for references—even if you have a written letter of reference from a previous landlord. It's worth the cost of a long-distance phone call to weed out a tenant who may cause problems down the road. Also call employers and personal references listed on the application.

To organize the information you gather from these calls, use the tenant references form, which lists key questions to ask previous landlords, employers, and other references.

TIP

Check out pets, too. If the prospective tenant has a dog or cat, be sure to ask previous landlords if the pet caused any damage or problems for other tenants or neighbors. It's also a good idea to meet the dog or cat, so you can make sure that it's well-groomed and well-behaved, before you make a final decision. You must, however, accommodate a mentally or physically disabled applicant whose pet serves as a support animal—no matter how mangy-looking the pet might be. (See the discussion of pet rules in Chapter 2, Clause 14.)

Be sure to take notes of all your conversations and keep them on file. You may indicate your reasons for refusing an individual on the tenant references form—for example, negative credit information, bad references from a previous landlord, or your inability to verify information. You'll want a record of this information so that you can survive a fair housing challenge if a disappointed applicant files a discrimination complaint against you.

CD-ROM

The Landlord Rental Forms CD includes a copy of the Tenant References screening form, and a sample is shown below. Appendix C includes a blank tear-out copy of the form.

Verify Income and Employment

Obviously, you want to make sure that all tenants have the income to pay the rent each month. Call the prospective tenant's employer to verify income and length of employment. Make notes on the tenant references form, discussed above.

Before providing this information, some employers require written authorization from the employee. You will need to mail or fax the employer a signed copy of the release included at the bottom of the rental application form or the separate "Consent to Contact References and Perform Credit Check" form. If for any reason you question the income information you get by telephone—for example, you suspect a buddy of the applicant is exaggerating on his behalf—you may also ask applicants for copies of recent paycheck stubs.

It's also reasonable to require documentation of other sources of income, such as Social Security, disability payments, workers' compensation, welfare, child support, or alimony.

Tenant References

Name of Applicant: _____Michael Clark_____

Address of Rental Unit: _____123 State Street, Chicago, Illinois_____

Previous Landlord or Manager

Contact (name, property owner or manager, address of rental unit): _____Kate Steiner, 345 Mercer St., Chicago, Illinois;_____

_____(312) 555-5432_____

Date: _____February 4, 20xx_____

Questions

When did tenant rent from you (move-in and move-out dates)? _____December 2003 to date_____

What was the monthly rent? __$1,250__   Did tenant pay rent on time?   ☐ Yes ☑ No

If rent was not paid on time, did you have to give tenant a legal notice demanding the rent?   ☐ Yes ☑ No

If rent was not paid on time, provide details _____He paid rent a week late a few times_____

Did you give tenant notice of any lease violation for other than nonpayment of rent?   ☐ Yes ☑ No

If you gave a lease violation notice, what was the outcome? _____

Was tenant considerate of neighbors—that is, no loud parties and fair, careful use of common areas?

_____Yes, considerate_____

Did tenant have any pets?   ☑ Yes ☐ No   If so, were there any problems? _____He had a cat, contrary to_____

_____rental agreement_____

Did tenant make any unreasonable demands or complaints?   ☐ Yes ☑ No   If so, explain: _____

Why did tenant leave? _____He wants to live someplace that allows pets_____

Did tenant give the proper amount of notice before leaving?   ☐ Yes ☑ No

Did tenant leave the place in good condition? Did you need to use the security deposit to cover damage?

_____No problems_____

Any particular problems you'd like to mention? _____No_____

Would you rent to this person again? _____Yes, but without pets_____

Other comments: _____

Employment Verification

Contact (name, company, position):   Brett Field, Manager, Chicago Car Company

Date: ____February 5, 20xx____   Salary: $ ____60,000 + bonus____

Dates of Employment: ____March 2004 to date____

Comments: ____No problems. Fine employee. Michael is responsible and hard-working.____

Personal Reference

Contact (name and relationship to applicant):   Sandy Cameron, friend

Date: ____February 5, 20xx____   How long have you known the applicant? ____Five years____

Would you recommend this person as a prospective tenant? ____Yes____

Comments: ____Michael is very neat and responsible. He's reliable and will be a great tenant.____

Credit and Financial Information

Mostly fine—see attached credit report

Notes, Including Reasons for Rejecting Applicant

Applicant had a history of late rent payments and kept a cat, contrary to the rental agreement.

How much income is enough? Think twice before renting to someone if the rent will take more than one-third of their income, especially if they have a lot of debts.

Obtain a Credit Report

Private credit reporting agencies collect and sell credit files and other information about consumers. Many landlords find it essential to check a prospective tenant's credit history with at least one credit reporting agency to see how responsible the person is about managing money. Jot your findings down on the Tenant References Form, discussed above.

How to Get a Credit Report

A credit report contains a gold mine of information on a prospective tenant. You can find out, for example, if a particular person has a history of paying rent or bills late or has gone through bankruptcy, been convicted of a crime, or ever been evicted. (Your legal right to get information on evictions, however, may vary from state to state.) Credit reports usually cover the past seven to ten years. To run a credit check, you'll normally need a prospective tenant's name, address, and Social Security number, or ITIN (Individual Taxpayer Identification Number).

Three credit bureaus have cornered the markett on credit reports:

- Equifax, www.equifax.com
- Experian (formerly TRW), www.experian.com, and
- TransUnion, www.transunion.com.

You cannot order a credit report directly from the big three bureaus. Instead, you'll need to work through a credit reporting agency or tenant screening service (type "tenant screening" into your browser's search box). Look for a company that operates in your area, has been in business for a while, and provides you with a sample report that's clear and informative. You can also find tenant screening companies in the Yellow Pages under "Credit Reporting Agencies." Your state or local apartment association may also offer credit reporting services. With credit reporting agencies, you can often obtain a credit report the same day it's requested. Fees depend on how many reports you order each month.

Tenants who are applying for more than one rental are understandably dismayed at the prospect of paying each landlord to pull the same credit report. They may obtain their own report, make copies, and ask you to accept their copy. Federal law does not require you to accept an applicant's copy—that is, you may require applicants to pay a credit check fee for you to run a new report. Wisconsin is an exception: State law in Wisconsin forbids landlords from charging for a credit report if, before the landlord asks for a report, the applicant offers one from a consumer reporting agency and the report is less than 30 days old. (Wis. Adm. Code ATCP 134.05(4)(b) (2004).)

Credit Check Fees

It's legal in most states to charge prospective tenants a fee for the cost of the credit report itself and your time and trouble. Any credit check fee should be reasonably related to the cost of the credit check—$20 to $30 is common. Check your state law for any limits. California, for example, sets a maximum screening fee per applicant and requires landlords to provide an itemized receipt when accepting a credit check fee. (Cal. Civ. Code § 1950.6.)

Some landlords don't charge credit check fees, preferring to absorb the cost as they would any other cost of business. For low-end units, charging an extra fee can be a barrier to getting tenants in the first place, and a tenant who pays a fee, but is later rejected, is likely to be annoyed and possibly more apt to claim that you have rejected her for a discriminatory reason.

The rental application form in this book informs prospective tenants if you charge a credit check fee. Be sure prospective tenants understand that paying a credit check fee does not guarantee the tenant will get the rental unit.

> **TIP**
>
> **It's a mistake to collect a credit check fee from lots of people.** If you expect a large number of applicants, you'd be wise not to accept fees from everyone. Instead, read over the applications first and do a credit check only on applicants you're seriously considering. That way, you won't waste your time (and prospective tenants' money) collecting fees from unqualified applicants.

> **CAUTION**
>
> **It is generally illegal to charge a credit check fee if you do not use it for the stated purpose and pocket it instead.** Return any credit check fees you don't use for that purpose.

What You're Looking For in a Credit Report

It makes sense to be leery of applicants with lots of debts—this clearly includes people whose monthly payments plus the rent obligation exceed 40% of their after-tax income. Also, look at the person's bill-paying habits, and, of course, pay attention to lawsuits and evictions.

Sometimes, your only choice is to rent to someone with poor or fair credit—or even no credit (for example, a student or recent graduate). If that's your situation, you should still adopt sensible screening requirements such as these:

- positive references from previous landlords and employers
- a creditworthy cosigner of the lease (see the discussion on cosigners at the end of Chapter 2)

- a good-sized deposit—as much as you can collect under state law and the market will bear (see Clause 8 of the form agreements in Chapter 2), and
- proof of specific steps taken to improve bad credit—for example, enrollment in a debt counseling group.

> **CAUTION**
>
> **Take special care to store credit reports in a safe place, where only you and those who "need to know" have access to them.** In fact, under the "Disposal Rule" of the Fair and Accurate Credit Transactions Act of 2003, you must destroy the report when you have reviewed it and no longer need it. Use a shredder or burn the credit report.

Verify Bank Account Information

If an individual's credit history raises questions about financial stability, you may want to double-check the bank accounts listed on the rental application. If so, you'll probably need an authorization form such as the one included at the bottom of the rental application, or the separate "Consent to Check References and Perform Credit Check" form (discussed above). Banks differ as to the type of information they will provide over the phone. Generally, without a written authorization, banks will only confirm that an individual has an account there and that it is in good standing.

> **CAUTION**
>
> **Be wary of an applicant who has no checking or savings account.** Tenants who offer to pay cash or with a money order should be viewed with extreme caution. Perhaps the individual bounced so many checks that the bank dropped the account or the income comes from a shady or illegitimate source—for example, from drug dealing.

Review Court Records

If your prospective tenant has previously lived in your area, you may want to review local court records to see if collection or eviction lawsuits have ever been filed against him. Checking court records may seem like overkill, since some of this information may be available on credit reports, but now and then it's an invaluable tool if you are able to weed out a prospective tenant who is almost sure to be a troublemaker. Especially if you fear that the person who rubs you the wrong way might accuse you of illegal discrimination if you turn down her application, you'll want to have good documentation of your decision. Because court records are kept for many years, this kind of information can supplement references from recent landlords. Talk to the court clerk at the local court that handles eviction cases for information on how to check court records.

Use Megan's Law to Check State Databases

Not surprisingly, most landlords do not want tenants with criminal records, particularly convictions for violent crimes or crimes against children. Checking a prospective tenant's credit report, as recommended above, is one way to find out about a person's criminal history. Self-reporting is another: Rental applications, such as the one in this book, typically ask whether the prospective tenant has ever been convicted of a crime. "Megan's Law" may also be a useful source of information. Named after a young girl who was killed by a convicted child molester who lived in her neighborhood, this federal crime prevention law charges the FBI with keeping a nationwide database of persons convicted of sexual offenses against minors and violent sexual offenses against anyone. (42 U.S.C. §§ 14071 and following.) Every state has its own version of Megan's Law that requires certain convicted sexual offenders to register with local law enforcement officials who keep a database on their whereabouts. For information on your access to this type of database, and restrictions on your use of information derived from a Megan's Law database, contact your local law enforcement agency. To find out how to access your state's sex offender registry, you can also contact the Parents for Megan's Law (PFML) hotline at 888-ASK-PFML, or check this organization's website at www.parentsformeganslaw.com.

The Rights of Disabled Tenants

The Fair Housing Act requires that landlords *accommodate* the needs of disabled tenants, at the landlord's own expense. (42 U.S.C. § 3604(f)(3)(B).) You are expected to adjust your rules, procedures, or services in order to give a person with a disability an equal opportunity to use and enjoy a dwelling unit or a common space. Accommodations include such things as providing a close-in, spacious parking space for a wheelchair-bound tenant (assuming you provide parking). Your duty to accommodate disabled tenants does not mean that you must bend every rule and change every procedure at the tenant's request. You are expected to accommodate "reasonable" requests, but need not undertake changes that would seriously impair your ability to run your business.

The Fair Housing Act also requires landlords to allow disabled tenants to make reasonable *modifications* of their living unit at their expense if that is what is needed for the person to comfortably and safely live in the unit. (42 U.S.C. § 3604(f)(3)(A).)

For example, a disabled person has the right to modify his living space to the extent necessary to make the space safe and comfortable, as long as the modifications will not make the unit unacceptable to the next tenant or the disabled tenant agrees to undo the modification when he leaves. An example of a modification undertaken by a disabled tenant is lowering countertops for a wheelchair-bound tenant.

You are not obliged to allow a disabled tenant to modify his unit at will, without your prior approval. You are entitled to ask for a reasonable description of the proposed modifications, proof that they will be done in a workmanlike manner, and evidence that the tenant is obtaining any necessary building permits. Moreover, if a tenant proposes to modify the unit in such a manner that will require restoration when the tenant leaves (such as the repositioning of lowered kitchen counters), you may require that the tenant pay into an interest-bearing escrow account the amount estimated for the restoration. (The interest belongs to the tenant.)

Avoiding Illegal Discrimination

Federal and state antidiscrimination laws limit what you can say and do in the tenant selection process. Basically, you need to keep in mind three important points:

1. You are legally free to choose among prospective tenants as long as your decisions are based on legitimate business criteria. You are entitled to reject people for the following reasons:

- poor credit history

- income that you reasonably regard as insufficient to pay the rent

- negative references from previous landlords indicating problems—such as property damage or consistently late rent payments—that make someone a bad risk

- convictions for criminal offenses

- inability to meet the legal terms of a lease or rental agreement, such as someone who can't come up with the security deposit or who wants to keep a pet and your policy is no pets, or

- more people than you want to live in the unit—assuming that your limit on the number of tenants is clearly tied to health and safety or legitimate business needs. (See Clause 3 discussion of occupancy limits in Chapter 2.)

2. Antidiscrimination laws specify clearly illegal reasons to refuse to rent to a tenant. The federal Fair Housing Act and Fair Housing Amendments Act (42 U.S.C. §§ 3601-3619, 3631) prohibit discrimination on the basis of race or color, religion, national origin, gender, age, familial status (pregnancy or children), and physical or mental disability (including recovering alcoholics and people with a past drug addiction). Many states and cities also prohibit discrimination based on marital status, military status, or sexual orientation.

RESOURCE

For more information on the rules and regulations of the Fair Housing Act, contact HUD's Housing Discrimination Hotline at 800-669-9777 or check the HUD website at www.hud.gov. You can also contact a local HUD office.

For information on state and local housing discrimination laws, contact your state fair housing agency. For a list of state agencies and contact information, see www.fairhousing.com, a website maintained by the National Fair Housing Advocate Online.

3. Consistency is crucial when dealing with prospective tenants. If you don't treat all tenants more or less equally—for example, if you arbitrarily set tougher standards (such as a higher income level or proof of legal status, such as legal papers) for renting to a member of an ethnic minority—you are violating federal laws and opening yourself up to expensive lawsuits and the possibility of being hit with large judgments. On the other hand, if you require all prospective tenants to meet the same income standard and to supply satisfactory proof of their legal eligibility to work (as well as meet your other criteria), you will get the needed information, but in a nondiscriminatory way.

CAUTION

Show the property to and accept applications from everyone who's interested. Even if, after talking to someone on the phone, you doubt that a particular tenant can qualify, it's best to politely take all applications. Unless you can point to something in writing that clearly disqualifies a tenant, you are always on shaky legal ground. Refusing to take an application may unnecessarily anger a prospective tenant, and may make him or her more likely to look into the possibility of filing a discrimination complaint. Make decisions later about who will rent the property. Be sure to keep copies of all applications. (See discussion of recordkeeping in Chapter 4, Section D.)

 CD-ROM

The Landlord Law Forms CD includes a special *Legal Guide to Complying With Discrimination Laws.* Check it out for details on legal reasons for rejecting applications and specifics on avoiding illegal discrimination under federal law (race, disability, and the like) as well as state laws that prohibit discrimination on the basis of marital status, sexual orientation, and source of income.

Choosing—and Rejecting— an Applicant

After you've collected applications and done some screening, you can start sifting through the applicants, using the basic criteria discussed above for evaluating and choosing tenants. Start by eliminating the worst risks: people with negative references from previous landlords, a history of nonpayment of rent, or poor credit or previous evictions. Then make your selection.

Assuming you choose the best-qualified candidate (based on income, credit history, and references), you have no legal problem. But what if you have a number of more or less equally qualified applicants? Can you safely choose an older white man over a young black woman? The answer is a qualified "yes." If two people rate equally, you can legally choose either one without legal risk in any particular situation. But be extra careful not to take the further step of always selecting a person of the same sex, age, or ethnicity. For example, if you are a larger landlord who is frequently faced with tough choices and who always avoids an equally qualified minority or disabled applicant, you are exposing yourself to charges of discrimination.

Information You Should Keep on Rejected Applicants

A crucial use of any tenant-screening system is to document how and why you chose a particular tenant.

Be sure to note your reasons for rejection—such as poor credit history, pets (if you don't accept pets), or a negative reference from a previous landlord—on the tenant references form or other document so that you have a paper trail if a tenant ever accuses you of illegal discrimination. You want to be able to back up your reason for rejecting the person. Keep organized files of applications and other materials and notes on prospective tenants for at least three years after you rent a particular unit. (See "Organize Your Tenant Records" in Chapter 4.) Keep in mind that if a rejected applicant files a complaint with a fair housing agency or files a lawsuit, your file will be made available to the applicant's lawyers. Knowing that, choose your words carefully, avoiding the obvious (slurs and exaggerations) and being scrupulously truthful.

Information You Must Provide Rejected Applicants

If you do not rent to someone because of an insufficient credit report or negative information in the report, you must give the applicant the name and address of the agency that reported the negative information or furnished the insufficient report. This is a requirement of the federal Fair Credit Reporting Act (FCRA). (15 U.S.C. §§ 1681 and following.) The notices are known as "adverse action reports."

In these cases, you must tell the applicant that he or she has a right to obtain a copy of the file from the agency that reported the negative information, by requesting it within the next 60 days, or by asking within one year of having asked for their last free report. You must also tell the rejected applicant that the credit reporting agency did not make the decision to reject them and cannot explain the reason for the rejection. Finally, you must tell applicants that they can dispute the accuracy of their credit report and add their own consumer statement to their report. The law doesn't require you to communicate an applicant's right to disclosure in writing, but it's a good idea to do so (and to keep a copy of the rejection letter in your files). That way, you'll have irrefutable proof that you complied with the law if you're ever challenged in court. Use the "Notice of Denial Based on Credit Report or Other Information" form, shown below, to comply with the federal Fair Credit Reporting Act when you reject an applicant because of an insufficient credit report or negative information in the report.

CD-ROM

The Landlord Rental Forms CD includes a copy of the "Notice of Denial Based on Credit Report or Other Information" form, and a sample is shown below. Appendix C includes a blank tear-out copy of the form.

Exceptions: The federal requirements do not apply if you reject someone based on information that the applicant furnished.

Notice of Denial Based on Credit Report or Other Information

To: _Ryan Paige_
Applicant

1 Mariner Square
Street Address

Seattle, Washington 98101
City, State, and Zip Code

Your rights under the Fair Credit Reporting Act and Fair and Accurate Credit Transactions (FACT) Act of 2003.

(15 U.S.C. §§ 1681 and following.)

THIS NOTICE is to inform you that your application to rent the property at _75 Starbucks Lane, Seattle, WA 98108_

[rental property address] has been denied because of [*check all that apply*]:

☑ Insufficient information in the credit report provided by:

Credit reporting agency: _ABC Credit Bureau_

Address, phone number, URL: _310 Griffey Way, Seattle, WA 98140; Phone: 206-555-1212;_
www.abccredit.com

☐ Negative information in the credit report provided by:

Credit reporting agency: _____

Address, phone number, URL: _____

☑ The consumer credit reporting agency noted above did not make the decision not to offer you this rental. It only provided information about your credit history. You have the right to obtain a free copy of your credit report from the consumer credit reporting agency named above, if your request is made within 60 days of this notice or if you have not requested a free copy within the past year. You also have the right to dispute the accuracy or completeness of your credit report. The agency must reinvestigate within a reasonable time, free of charge, and remove or modify inaccurate information. If the reinvestigation does not resolve the dispute to your satisfaction, you may add your own "consumer statement" (up to 100 words) to the report, which must be included (or a clear summary) in future reports.

☐ Information supplied by a third party other than a credit reporting agency or you and gathered by someone other than myself or any employee. You have the right to learn of the nature of the information if you ask me in writing within 60 days of the date of this notice.

Jason McGuire
Landlord/Manager

_10-01-xx_
Date

Notice of Conditional Acceptance Based on Credit Report or Other Information

To: <u>William McGee</u>
Applicant

<u>1257 Bay Avenue</u>
Street Address

<u>Anytown, FL 12345</u>
City, State, and Zip Code

Your application to rent the property at <u>37 Ocean View Drive, #10-H, Anytown, FL 12345</u>

_____ [rental property address] has been accepted, conditioned on your

willingness and ability to: <u>Supply a cosigner that is acceptable to the landlord</u>

Your rights under the Fair Credit Reporting Act and Fair and Accurate Credit Transactions (FACT) Act of 2003. (15 U.S.C. §§ 1681 and following.)

Source of information prompting conditional acceptance

My decision to conditionally accept your application was prompted in whole or in part by:

☑ Insufficient information in the credit report provided by

Credit reporting agency: <u>Mountain Credit Bureau</u>

Address, phone number, URL: <u>75 Baywood Drive, Anytown FL 12345. 800-123-4567.</u>
<u>www.mountaincredit.com</u>

☐ Negative information in the credit report provided by :

Credit reporting agency:_____

Address, phone number, URL: _____

☑ The consumer credit reporting agency noted above did not make the decision to offer you this conditional acceptance. It only provided information about your credit history. You have the right to obtain a free copy of your credit report from the consumer credit reporting agency named above, if your request is made within 60 days of this notice or if you have not requested a free copy within the past year. You also have the right to dispute the accuracy or completeness of your credit report. The agency must reinvestigate within a reasonable time, free of charge, and remove or modify inaccurate information. If the reinvestigation does not resolve the dispute to your satisfaction, you may add your own "consumer statement" (up to 100 words) to the report, which must be included (or a clear summary) in future reports.

☐ Information supplied by a third party other than a credit reporting agency or you and gathered by someone other than myself or any employee. You have the right to learn of the nature of the information if you ask me in writing within 60 days of the date of this notice.

Jane Thomas
_____
Landlord/Manager

May 15, 20xx
_____
Date

Conditional Acceptances

You may want to make an offer to an applicant but condition that offer on the applicant paying more rent or a higher security deposit (one that's within any legal limits, of course), supplying a cosigner, or agreeing to a different rental term than you originally advertised. If your decision to impose the condition resulted from information you gained from a credit report or a report from a tenant screening service, you have to accompany the offer with an adverse action report (described in the section immediately above). Use the Notice of Conditional Acceptance Based on Credit Report or Other Information, shown above.

CD-ROM

The Landlord Rental Forms CD includes a copy of the Notice of Conditional Acceptance Based on Credit Report or Other Information, and a sample is shown above. Appendix C includes a blank tear-out copy of the form.

Choosing a Tenant-Manager

Many landlords hire a manager to handle all the day-to-day details of running a rental property, including fielding tenants' routine repair requests and collecting the rent. If you hire a resident manager, make sure he or she (like all other tenants) completes a rental application and that you check references and other information carefully. If you use a property management company, it will do this work for you. (See below.)

The person you hire as a manager will occupy a critical position in your business. Your manager will interact with every tenant and will often have access to her personal files and her home. Legally,

you have a duty to protect your tenants from injuries caused by employees you know (or should know) pose a risk of harm to others. If someone gets hurt or has property stolen or damaged by a manager whose background you didn't check carefully, you could be sued, so it's crucial that you be especially vigilant when hiring a manager.

When you hire a manager, you should sign two separate agreements:

- an employment agreement that covers manager responsibilities, hours, and pay, and that can be terminated at any time for any reason by either party

- a month-to-month rental agreement that can be terminated by either of you with the amount of written notice, typically 30 days, required under state law.

Whether or not you compensate a manager with reduced rent or regular salary, be sure you comply with your legal obligations as an employer, such as following laws governing minimum wage and overtime.

RESOURCE

Every Landlord's Legal Guide by Marcia Stewart, Ralph Warner, & Janet Portman (Nolo), provides detailed advice on hiring a manager, including how to prepare a property manager agreement, and your legal obligations as an employer, such as following laws governing minimum wage and overtime.

The Employer's Legal Handbook, by Fred S. Steingold (Nolo), is a complete guide to the latest workplace laws and regulations. It covers everything you need to know about hiring and firing employees, personnel policies, employee benefits, discrimination, and other laws affecting small business practices.

Property Management Companies

Property management companies are often used by owners of large apartment complexes and by absentee owners too far away from the property to be directly involved in everyday details. Property management companies generally take care of renting units, collecting rent, taking tenant complaints, arranging repairs and maintenance, and evicting troublesome tenants. Of course, some of these responsibilities may be shared with or delegated to resident managers who, in some instances, may work for the management company.

A variety of relationships between owners and management companies is possible, depending on your wishes and how the particular management company chooses to do business. For example, if you own one or more big buildings, the management company will probably recommend hiring a resident manager. But if your rental property has only a few units, or you own a number of small buildings spread over a good-sized geographical area, the management company will probably suggest simply responding to tenant requests and complaints from its central office.

One advantage of working with a management company is that you avoid all the legal hassles of being an employer: paying payroll taxes, buying workers' compensation insurance, and withholding income tax. The management company is an independent contractor, not an employee. It hires and pays the people who do the work. Typically, you sign a contract spelling out the management company's duties and fees. Most companies charge a fixed percentage—about 5% to 10%—of the total rent collected. (The salary of any resident manager is additional.) This gives the company a good incentive to keep the building filled with rent-paying tenants.

Another advantage is that management companies are usually well informed about the law, keep good records, and are adept at staying out of legal hot water in such areas as discrimination, invasion of privacy, and returning deposits.

The primary disadvantage of hiring a management company is the expense. For example, if you pay a management company 10% of the $14,000 you collect in rent each month from tenants in a 20-unit building, this amounts to $1,400 a month and $16,800 per year. While many companies charge less than 10%, it's still quite an expense. Also, if the management company works from a central office with no one on-site, tenants may feel that management is too distant and unconcerned with their day-to-day needs.

Management companies have their own contracts, which you should read thoroughly and understand before signing. Be sure you understand how the company is paid and its exact responsibilities. ●

Getting the Tenant Moved In

Inspect and Photograph the Unit..76

    Use a Landlord-Tenant Checklist..76

    How to Fill Out the Checklist..81

    Photograph the Rental Unit..82

Send New Tenants a Move-In Letter..82

Cash Rent and Security Deposit Checks..85

Organize Your Tenant Records..85

Organize Income and Expenses for Schedule E...86

Legal disputes between landlords and tenants can be almost as emotional as divorce court battles. While some may be inevitable, many disputes could be defused at the start if tenants were better educated as to their legal rights and responsibilities. A clearly written and easy-to-understand lease or rental agreement that details a tenant's obligations and is signed by all adult occupants of your rental unit is the key to starting a tenancy. (See Chapter 2.) But there's more that can be done to help establish a positive relationship when new tenants move in. Most important, you should:

- inspect the property, fill out a landlord-tenant checklist with the tenant, and photograph the rental unit, and

- prepare a move-in letter highlighting important terms of the tenancy and your expectations, such as how to report repair problems.

Inspect and Photograph the Unit

To eliminate the possibility of all sorts of future arguments, it is absolutely essential that you (or your representative) and prospective tenants (together, if possible) check the place over for damage and obvious wear and tear before the tenant moves in. The best way to document what you find is to jointly fill out a landlord-tenant checklist form and take photographs of the rental unit.

Use a Landlord-Tenant Checklist

A landlord-tenant checklist, inventorying the condition of the rental property at the beginning and end of the tenancy, is an excellent device to protect both you and your tenant when the tenant moves out and wants the security deposit returned. Without some record as to the condition of the unit, the tenant is all too likely to make unreasonable demands. For example, is there a landlord alive who has not been falsely told that a stained rug or a cracked mirror or broken stove was already damaged when the tenant moved in?

The checklist provides good evidence as to why you withheld all or part of a security deposit. Coupled with a system to regularly keep track of the rental property's condition, the checklist will also be extremely useful to you if a tenant withholds rent, breaks the lease and moves out, or sues you outright, claiming the unit needs substantial repairs.

CD-ROM

The Landlord Rental Forms CD includes a copy of the Landlord-Tenant Checklist and a sample is shown below. Appendix C includes a blank tear-out copy of the form.

States That Require A Landlord-Tenant Checklist

A number of states require landlords to give new tenants a written statement on the condition of the rental premises at move-in time, including a comprehensive list of existing damages: Arizona, Georgia, Hawaii, Kansas, Kentucky, Maryland, Massachusetts, Michigan, Montana, Nevada, North Dakota, Virginia, and Washington. Tenants in these states often have the right to inspect the premises to verify the accuracy of the landlord's list and note any problems. Check your state's statutes for the exact requirements in your state, including the type of inspection required at the end of the tenancy.

Landlord-Tenant Checklist

GENERAL CONDITION OF RENTAL UNIT AND PREMISES

572 Fourth St.		Apt. 11	Washington, D.C.
Street Address		Unit No.	City

	Condition on Arrival	Condition on Departure	Estimated Cost of Repair/ Replacement
Living Room			
Floors & Floor Coverings	OK		
Drapes & Window Coverings	Miniblinds discolored		
Walls & Ceilings	OK		
Light Fixtures	OK		
Windows, Screens, & Doors	Window rattles		
Front Door & Locks	OK		
Fireplace	N/A		
Other			
Other			
Kitchen			
Floors & Floor Coverings	Cigarette burn hole		
Walls & Ceilings	OK		
Light Fixtures	OK		
Cabinets	OK		
Counters	Stained		
Stove/Oven	Burners filthy (grease)		
Refrigerator	OK		
Dishwasher	OK		
Garbage Disposal	N/A		
Sink & Plumbing	OK		
Windows, Screens, & Doors	OK		
Other			
Other			
Dining Room			
Floors & Floor Covering			
Walls & Ceilings	Crack in ceiling		
Light Fixtures	OK		
Windows, Screens, & Doors	OK		
Other			

	Condition on Arrival			Condition on Departure			Estimated Cost of Repair/ Replacement
Bathroom(s)	Bath #1	Bath #2		Bath #1	Bath #2		
Floors & Floor Coverings	OK						
Walls & Ceilings	Mold on the ceiling						
Windows, Screens, & Doors	OK						
Light Fixtures	OK						
Bathtub/Shower	Tub chipped						
Sink & Counters	OK						
Toilet	Base of toilet very dirty						
Other							
Other							
Bedroom(s)	Bdrm #1	Bdrm #2	Bdrm #3	Bdrm #1	Bdrm #2	Bdrm #3	
Floors & Floor Coverings	OK	OK					
Windows, Screens, & Doors	OK	OK					
Walls & Ceilings	OK	OK					
Light Fixtures	Dented	OK					
Other	Mildew in closet						
Other							
Other							
Other							
Other Areas							
Heating System	OK						
Air Conditioning	OK						
Lawn/Garden	OK						
Stairs and Hallway	OK						
Patio, Terrace, Deck, etc.	N/A						
Basement	OK						
Parking Area	OK						
Other							
Other							
Other							
Other							
Other							

✓ Tenants acknowledge that all smoke detectors and fire extinguishers were tested in their presence and found to be in working order, and that the testing procedure was explained to them. Tenants agree to test all detectors at least once a month and to report any problems to Landlord/Manager in writing. Tenants agree to replace all smoke detector batteries as necessary.

	Condition on Arrival			Condition on Departure			Estimated Cost of Repair/ Replacement
Living Room							
Coffee Table	Two scratches on top						
End Tables	OK						
Lamps	OK						
Chairs	OK						
Sofa	OK						
Other							
Other							
Kitchen							
Broiler Pan	N/A						
Ice Trays	N/A						
Other							
Other							
Dining Room							
Chairs	OK						
Stools	N/A						
Table	Leg bent slightly						
Other							
Other							
Bathroom(s)	**Bath #1**		**Bath #2**	**Bath #1**		**Bath #2**	
Mirrors	OK						
Shower Curtain	Torn						
Hamper	N/A						
Other							
Bedroom(s)	**Bdrm #1**	**Bdrm #2**	**Bdrm #3**	**Bdrm #1**	**Bdrm #2**	**Bdrm #3**	
Beds (single)	OK	N/A					
Beds (double)	N/A	OK					
Chairs	OK	OK					
Chests	N/A	N/A					
Dressing Tables	OK	N/A					
Lamps	OK	OK					
Mirrors	OK	OK					
Night Tables	OK	N/A					

	Condition on Arrival	Condition on Departure	Estimated Cost of Repair/ Replacement
Other	N/A		
Other	N/A		
Other Areas			
Bookcases			
Desks			
Pictures	Hallway picture frame chipped		
Other			
Other			

Use this space to provide any additional explanation:

_____

_____

_____

_____

_____

_____

_____

_____

_____

_____

_____

_____

Landlord-Tenant Checklist completed on moving in on _____May 1, 20xx_____ and approved by:

_Bernard Cohen_____   and   _Maria Crouse_____
Landlord/Manager   Tenant

                                                                      _Sandra Martino_____
                                                                      Tenant

                                                                      _____
                                                                      Tenant

Landlord-Tenant Checklist completed on moving out on _____ and approved by:

_____   and   _____
Landlord/Manager   Tenant

                                                                      _____
                                                                      Tenant

                                                                      _____
                                                                      Tenant

How to Fill Out the Checklist

You and the tenant should fill out the checklist together. If that's impossible, complete the form and then make a copy and give it to the tenant to review. You should ask the tenant to note any disagreement promptly and return the checklist to you.

The checklist is in two parts. The first side covers the general condition of each room, such as the kitchen floor. The second side covers furnishings, such as a living room lamp or bathroom shower curtain. You should simply mark "Not Applicable" or "N/A" in most of these boxes if your unit is not furnished or does not have a particular item listed, such as a fireplace.

If your rental property has rooms or furnishings not listed on the form, note them in the rows labelled "Other," or cross out something that you don't have and write in the changes. If you are renting out a large house or apartment or providing many furnishings, you should attach a separate sheet of furnishings. Use the same headings (Condition on Arrival and so on).

In the Condition on Arrival column, mark "OK" in the space next to items that are in satisfactory condition. Make a note—as specific as possible—on items that are not working or are dirty, worn, scratched, or simply not in the best condition. For example, don't simply note that the refrigerator "needs fixing" if an ice maker doesn't work—it's just as easy to write "ice maker broken, should not be used." This way, if the tenant uses the ice maker anyway and causes water damage in the unit below, he cannot claim that you failed to tell him.

The last two columns—Condition on Departure and Estimated Cost of Repair/Replacement—are for use when the tenant moves out and, ideally, the two of you inspect the unit again. At that time,

the checklist will document your need to make deductions from the security deposit for repairs or cleaning or to replace missing items. (Chapter 5 discusses returning security deposits and using the checklist as part of your final inspection.) If you don't know what it will cost to fix or replace something, simply write in "Cost will be documented by Landlord."

> **CAUTION**
>
> **As part of your move-in procedures, make sure you test all smoke detectors and fire extinguishers in the tenant's presence and show them to be in good working order.** Clearly explain to the tenant how to test the smoke detectors and point out the signs—for example, a beeping noise—of a failing detector. Alert tenants to their responsibility to regularly test smoke detectors, and explain how to replace the battery when necessary. Be sure the tenant checks the box on the bottom of the second page of the checklist acknowledging that the smoke detector was tested in his presence and shown to be in working order. By doing this, you'll limit your liability if the smoke detector fails and results in fire damage or injury.

After you and the tenant agree on all of the particulars on the rental unit, you each should sign and date the checklist, as well as any attachments (such as a separate list of furnishings), on both sides. Keep the original checklist for yourself and attach a copy to the tenant's lease or rental agreement. (This checklist is referred to in Clause 11 of the form agreements in Chapter 2.)

Be sure to keep the checklist up to date if you repair, replace, add, or remove items or furnishings after the tenant moves in. Both you and the tenant should initial and date any changes on the original, signed checklist.

Photograph the Rental Unit

Taking photos or videotapes of the unit before the tenant moves in is another excellent way to avoid disputes over a tenant's responsibility for damage and dirt. In addition to the checklist, you'll be able to compare "before" and "after" pictures when a tenant leaves. This should help refresh your tenant's memory and may result in her being more reasonable. Certainly, if you end up in mediation or court for not returning the full security deposit, being able to document your point of view with photos will be invaluable. In addition, photos or a video can also help if you have to sue a former tenant for cleaning and repair costs above the deposit amount.

Both you and the tenant should date and sign the pictures, each keeping a set.

If you make a video, get the tenant on tape saying the date and time so that you can prove when the video was made, and, later, provide him with a copy.

If possible, you should repeat this process after the tenant leaves, as part of your standard move-out procedure. (Chapter 5 discusses how to prepare a move-out letter.)

Send New Tenants a Move-In Letter

A move-in letter should dovetail with the lease or rental agreement and provide basic information, such as the manager's phone number and office hours.

You can also use a move-in letter to explain any procedures and rules that are too detailed or numerous to include in your lease or rental agreement. (Alternatively, large landlords may use a set of tenant rules and regulations to cover some of these issues. See Clause 18 of the form agreements in Chapter 2.)

Here are some items you may want to cover in a move-in letter:

- how and where to report maintenance and repair problems
- any lock-out or re-key fees
- use of grounds and garage
- your policy regarding rent increases for additional roommates
- location of garbage cans, available recycling programs, and trash pickup days
- maintenance dos and don'ts, such as how to avoid overloading circuits and use the garbage disposal properly
- renter's insurance, and
- other issues, such as pool hours, elevator operation, building access during evening hours, and use of a laundry room and storage space, should be covered as needed.

Because every rental situation is at least a little different, we cannot supply you with a generic move-in letter that will work for everyone. We can, however, give you a template for a move-in letter that you can easily fill in with your own details. You can use the sample shown here as a model in preparing your own move-in letter.

We recommend that you make a copy of each tenant's move-in letter for yourself and ask him to sign the last page, indicating that he has read it.

Be sure to update the move-in letter from time to time as necessary.

Move-In Letter

September 1, 20xx
_____
Date
Frank O'Hara
_____
Tenant
139 Porter Street
_____
Street Address
Madison, Wisconsin 53704
_____
City and State

Dear Frank
_____,
                Tenant

Welcome to Apartment 45 B at Happy Hill Apartments
_____

_____ (address of rental unit). We hope you will enjoy living here.

This letter is to explain what you can expect from the management and what we'll be looking for from you.

1. **Rent:** Rent is due on the first day of the month. There is no grace period for the payment of rent. (See Clauses 5 and 6 of your rental agreement for details, including late charges.) Also, we don't accept postdated checks.

2. **New Roommates:** If you want someone to move in as a roommate, please contact us first. If your rental unit is big enough to accommodate another person, we will arrange for the new person to fill out a rental application. If it's approved, all of you will need to sign a new rental agreement. Depending on the situation, there may be a rent increase to add a roommate.

3. **Notice to End Tenancy:** To terminate your month-to-month tenancy, you must give at least 30 days' written notice. We have a written form available for this purpose. We may also terminate the tenancy, or change its terms, on 30 days' written notice. If you give less than 30 days' notice, you will still be financially responsible for rent for the balance of the 30-day period.

4. **Deposits:** Your security deposit will be applied to costs of cleaning, damages, or unpaid rent after you move out. You may not apply any part of the deposit toward any part of your rent in the last month of your tenancy. (See Clause 8 of your rental agreement.)

5. **Manager:** Sophie Beauchamp (Apartment #15, phone 555-1234) is your resident manager. You should pay your rent to her and promptly let her know of any maintenance or repair problems (see #7, below) and any other questions or problems. She's in her office every day from 8 a.m. to 10 a.m. and from 4 p.m. to 6 p.m. and can be reached by phone at other times.

6. **Landlord-Tenant Checklist:** By now, Sophie Beauchamp should have taken you on a walk-through of your apartment to check the condition of all walls, drapes, carpets, and appliances and to test the smoke alarms and fire extinguisher. These are all listed on the Landlord-Tenant Checklist, which you should have reviewed carefully and signed. When you move out, we will ask you to check each item against its original condition as described on the Checklist.

7. **Maintenance/Repair Problems:** We are determined to maintain a clean, safe building in which all systems are in good repair. To help us make repairs promptly, we will give you Maintenance/Repair Request forms to report to the manager any problems in your apartment, such as a broken garbage disposal, or on the building or grounds, such a burned-out light in the garage. (Extra copies are available from the manager.) In an emergency, or when it's not convenient to use this form, please call the manager at 555-1234.

8. **Semiannual Safety and Maintenance Update:** To help us keep your unit and the common areas in excellent condition, we'll ask you to fill out a form every six months updating any problems on the premises or in your rental unit. This will allow you to report any potential safety hazards or other problems that otherwise might be overlooked.

9. **Annual Safety Inspection:** Once a year, we will ask to inspect the condition and furnishings of your rental unit and update the Landlord-Tenant Checklist. In keeping with state law, we will give you reasonable notice before the inspection, and you are encouraged to be present for it.

10. **Insurance:** We highly recommend that you purchase renters' insurance. The building property insurance policy will not cover the replacement of your personal belongings if they are lost due to fire, theft, or accident. In addition, you could be found liable if someone is injured on the premises you rent as a result of your negligence. If you damage the building itself—for example, if you start a fire in the kitchen and it spreads—you could be responsible for large repair bills.

11. **Moving Out:** It's a little early to bring up moving out, but please be aware that we have a list of items that should be cleaned before we conduct a move-out inspection. If you decide to move, please ask the manager for a copy of our Move-Out Letter, explaining our procedures for inspection and returning your deposit.

12. **Telephone Number Changes:** Please notify us if your home or work phone number changes, so we can reach you promptly in an emergency.

Please let us know if you have any questions.

Sincerely,

Tom Quiliano
_____
Landlord/Manager

September 1, 20xx
_____
Date

I have read and received a copy of this statement.

Frank O'Hara
_____
Tenant

September 1, 20xx
_____
Date

Cash Rent and Security Deposit Checks

Every landlord's nightmare is a new tenant whose first rent or deposit check bounces and who must be dislodged with time-consuming and expensive legal proceedings.

To avoid this, never sign a rental agreement, or let a tenant move furniture into your property or take a key, until you have the tenant's cash, certified check, or money order for the first month's rent and security deposit. An alternative is to cash the tenant's check at the bank before the move-in date. (While you have the tenant's first check, photocopy it for your records. The information on it can be helpful if you ever need to sue to collect a judgment from the tenant.) Be sure to give the tenant a signed receipt for the deposit.

Clause 5 of the form lease and rental agreements in Chapter 2 requires tenants to pay rent on the first day of each month. If the move-in date is other than the first day of the month, rent is prorated between that day and the end of that month.

Organize Your Tenant Records

A good system to record all significant tenant complaints and repair requests will provide a valuable paper trail should disputes develop later—for example, regarding your right to enter a tenant's unit to make repairs, or the time it took for you to fix a problem. Without good records, the outcome of a dispute may come down to your word against your tenant's—always a precarious situation.

Set up a file folder on each property with individual files for each tenant. Include the following documents:

- rental application and references, including information about any cosigners
- a signed lease or rental agreement, plus any changes made along the way
- landlord-tenant checklist and photos or video made at move-in, and
- signed move-in letter.

CAUTION

Don't keep copies of tenant credit reports. Under the "Disposal Rule" of the Fair and Accurate Credit Transactions Act of 2003, you must destroy the report when you have reviewed it and no longer need it. Use a shredder or burn the credit report.

After a tenant moves in, add these documents to the individual's file:

- your written requests for entry
- rent increase notices
- records of repair requests and details of how and when they were handled. If you keep repair records on the computer, you should regularly print out and save files from past months; if you have a master system to record all requests and complaints in one log, you would save that log separately, not necessarily put it in every tenant's file.
- safety and maintenance updates and inspection reports, and
- correspondence and other relevant information.

Your computer can also be a valuable tool to keep track of tenants. Set up a simple database for each tenant with spaces for the following information:

- address or unit number
- move-in date
- home phone number
- name, address, and phone number of employer
- credit information, including up-to-date information as to where tenant banks
- monthly rent amount and rent due date
- amount and purpose of deposits plus any information your state requires on location of deposit and interest payments

- vehicle make, model, color, year, and license plate number, and

- emergency contacts, and whatever else is important to you.

Once you enter the information into your database, you can sort the list by address or other variables and easily print labels for rent increases or other notices.

If you own many rental properties, you should check into commercial computer programs that allow you to keep track of every aspect of your business, from the tracking of rents to the follow-up on repair requests.

Organize Income and Expenses for Schedule E

If you file IRS Form 1040 to pay your taxes, you'll report your rental property income and expenses on Schedule E. The schedule is relatively simple: For each address (which may include multiple rental units), you report the year's rent and list enumerated expenses (Schedule E is reproduced below). You can download a fillable version of Schedule E by going to the IRS website (www.irs. gov) and typing "Schedule E" in the Forms and Publications search box.

A quick glance at the schedule suggests how you might keep track of rental income and expenses so that you can complete it easily at tax time. If you're partial to paper and file folders, gather one folder for every rental property address. If you have many properties, identify each as Property A, Property B, and so on, to correspond to the columns on Schedule E. Inside, place a ledger, with column headers corresponding to the lines on Schedule E. For example, the first column will be "3: Rent," the second, "5: Advertising," and so on. Use the rows to place your dated entries. When you prepare your taxes, you can sum up the entries in your columns and easily transfer the information. A portion of a sample ledger is shown below.

You can accomplish the same end by using your computer. Design a master spreadsheet with interior sheets for each rental property address. Again, label the columns according to the lines on Schedule E, and add the information as it comes along.

RESOURCE

For detailed information on completing Schedule E, and valuable tax advice in general for landlords, see *Every Landlord's Tax Deduction Guide*, by Stephen Fishman (Nolo).

Sample Schedule E Ledger

Rental Property: 1256 Fourteenth Street, San Ardo, Arizona (Units 1 and 2)
Schedule E Property: A

Date	3: Rent	5: Advertising	6: Auto & Travel	7: Cleaning & Maintenance
May 5, 20xx		$45.50		
June 1, 20xx	$1,200			
December 2, 20xx				$500

SCHEDULE E
(Form 1040)

Department of the Treasury
Internal Revenue Service (99)

Supplemental Income and Loss

(From rental real estate, royalties, partnerships,
S corporations, estates, trusts, REMICs, etc.)

▶ Attach to Form 1040, 1040NR, or Form 1041.   ▶ See Instructions for Schedule E (Form 1040).

OMB No. 1545-0074

2006

Attachment
Sequence No. **13**

Name(s) shown on return

Your social security number

Part I | **Income or Loss From Rental Real Estate and Royalties** Note. If you are in the business of renting personal property, use **Schedule C** or **C-EZ** (see page E-3). Report farm rental income or loss from **Form 4835** on page 2, line 40.

1	List the type and location of each **rental real estate property:**	**2** For each rental real estate property listed on line 1, did you or your family use it during the tax year for personal purposes for more than the greater of:		**Yes** / **No**
A	....		A	
B	....	● 14 days **or**		
C	....	● 10% of the total days rented at fair rental value? (See page E-3.)	B / C	

Income:			Properties			Totals (Add columns A, B, and C.)
			A	B	C	
3	Rents received	**3**				**3**
4	Royalties received	**4**				**4**
Expenses:						
5	Advertising	**5**				
6	Auto and travel (see page E-4).	**6**				
7	Cleaning and maintenance	**7**				
8	Commissions	**8**				
9	Insurance	**9**				
10	Legal and other professional fees	**10**				
11	Management fees	**11**				
12	Mortgage interest paid to banks, etc. (see page E-4)	**12**				**12**
13	Other interest	**13**				
14	Repairs	**14**				
15	Supplies	**15**				
16	Taxes	**16**				
17	Utilities	**17**				
18	Other (list) ▶	**18**				
19	Add lines 5 through 18	**19**				**19**
20	Depreciation expense or depletion (see page E-4)	**20**				**20**
21	Total expenses. Add lines 19 and 20	**21**				
22	Income or (loss) from rental real estate or royalty properties. Subtract line 21 from line 3 (rents) or line 4 (royalties). If the result is a (loss), see page E-5 to find out if you must file **Form 6198**	**22**				
23	Deductible rental real estate loss. **Caution.** Your rental real estate loss on line 22 may be limited. See page E-5 to find out if you must file **Form 8582**. Real estate professionals must complete line 43 on page 2	**23**	( )	( )	( )	
24	**Income.** Add positive amounts shown on line 22. **Do not** include any losses				**24**	
25	**Losses.** Add royalty losses from line 22 and rental real estate losses from line 23. Enter total losses here				**25**	( )
26	**Total rental real estate and royalty income or (loss).** Combine lines 24 and 25. Enter the result here. If Parts II, III, IV, and line 40 on page 2 do not apply to you, also enter this amount on Form 1040, line 17, or Form 1040NR, line 18. Otherwise, include this amount in the total on line 41 on page 2				**26**	

For Paperwork Reduction Act Notice, see page E-7 of the instructions.   Cat. No. 11344L   **Schedule E (Form 1040) 2006**

Changing or Ending a Tenancy

How to Modify Signed Rental Agreements and Leases.. 90

    Amending a Fixed-Term Lease.. 90

    Amending a Month-to-Month Rental Agreement.. 90

    Preparing a New Lease or Rental Agreement 91

Ending a Month-to-Month Tenancy.. 91

    Giving Notice to the Tenant.. 91

    How Much Notice the Tenant Must Give... 92

    You Should Insist on a Tenant's Written Notice of Intent to Move 93

    Accepting Rent After a 30-Day Notice Is Given 95

    When the Tenant Doesn't Give the Required Notice 95

    When You or Your Tenant Violates the Rental Agreement... 98

How Fixed-Term Leases End... 98

    Giving Notice to the Tenant.. 98

    If the Tenant Remains After the Lease Expires... 100

    If the Tenant Leaves Early 100

    Your Duty to Mitigate Your Loss If the Tenant Leaves Early................................... 102

    How to Mitigate Your Damages... 102

    The Tenant's Right to Find a Replacement Tenant 102

    When You Can Sue 103

Returning Security Deposits When a Tenancy Ends 103

    Inspecting the Unit When a Tenant Leaves.. 103

    Basic Rules for Returning Deposits... 104

    Penalties for Violating Security Deposit Laws.. 105

    If the Deposit Doesn't Cover Damage and Unpaid Rent 105

Sometime after you've signed a lease or rental agreement, you may want to make changes—perhaps you need to increase the rent, or you agree to let the tenant bring in a roommate or keep a small pet. This chapter shows how to modify a signed lease or rental agreement. It also discusses how you—or your tenant—may end a tenancy, and offers tips on how to take steps to try and avoid problems, such as a tenant giving inadequate notice and breaking the lease. This chapter also summarizes basic rules for returning security deposits when a tenant leaves.

 CROSS REFERENCE

If you haven't done so already, see the following chapters for related discussions:

- Writing clear lease and rental agreement provisions on notice required to end a tenancy: Chapter 2
- How to advertise and rent property before a current tenant leaves: Chapter 3
- Highlighting notice requirements in a move-in letter to the tenant: Chapter 4.

How to Modify Signed Rental Agreements and Leases

All amendments to your lease or rental agreement should be in writing and signed by both you and the tenant.

Amending a Fixed-Term Lease

If you use a fixed-term lease, you cannot unilaterally alter the terms of the tenancy. For the most part, the lease fixes the terms of the tenancy for the length of the lease. You can't raise the rent or change the terms of the lease until the end of the lease period unless the lease allows it or the tenant agrees. If the tenant agrees to changes, however, simply follow the directions below for amending the rental agreement.

Amending a Month-to-Month Rental Agreement

If you want to change one or more clauses in a month-to-month rental agreement, there is no legal requirement that you get the tenant's consent. Legally, you need simply to send the tenant a notice of the change.

Most states require 30 days' advance notice (subject to any rent control ordinances) to change a month-to-month tenancy—for example, to increase the rent. See the "Notice Required to Change or Terminate a Month-to-Month Tenancy" table in Appendix A for a list of each state's notice requirements, and Clause 4 of the rental agreement in Chapter 2. You'll need to consult your state statutes for the specific information on how you must deliver a 30-day notice to the tenant. (Most allow you to use first-class mail.)

TIP

Contact the tenant and explain the changes. It makes good personal and business sense for you or your manager to contact the tenant personally and tell him about a rent increase or other changes before you follow up with a written notice. If the tenant is opposed to your proposal, your personal efforts will allow you to explain your reasons.

You don't generally need to redo the rental agreement in order to make a change or two. Just keep a copy of the change with the rental agreement. In some cases, however, you may want the tenant to sign a new rental agreement—for example, if the tenant initiates a change. If the change is small and simply alters part of an existing clause—such as increasing the rent or making the rent payable every 14 days instead of every 30 days—you can cross out the old language, write in the new and sign in the margin next to the new words. Make sure the tenant also signs next to the change. Be sure to add the date, in case there is a dispute later as to when the change became effective.

Preparing a New Lease or Rental Agreement

If you're adding a clause or making several changes to your lease or rental agreement, you will probably find it easiest to substitute a whole new agreement for the old one. If you prepare an entire new agreement, be sure that you and the tenant write "Canceled by mutual consent, effective (date)" on the old one, and sign it. In order to avoid the possibility of two inconsistent agreements operating at the same time, be sure that there is no time overlap between the old and new agreements. Similarly, so that the tenant is always subject to a written agreement, do not allow any gap between the cancellation date of the old agreement and the effective date of the new one.

TIP

A new tenant should mean a new agreement. Even if a new tenant is filling out the rest of a former tenant's lease term under the same conditions, it is never wise to allow her to operate under the same lease or rental agreement. Start over and prepare a new agreement in the new tenant's name. (See Clause 10 of the form agreements in Chapter 2.)

Ending a Month-to-Month Tenancy

This section discusses a landlord's and a tenant's responsibilities to end a month-to-month tenancy.

Giving Notice to the Tenant

If you want a tenant to leave, you can end a month-to-month tenancy simply by giving the proper amount of notice. You don't usually have to state a reason, unless state or local law requires it. In most places, all you need to do is give the tenant a simple written notice that complies with your state's minimum notice requirement and states the date on which the tenancy will end. After that date, the tenant no longer has the legal right to occupy the premises.

In most states, and for most rentals, a landlord who wants to terminate a month-to-month tenancy must provide the same amount of notice as a tenant—typically 30 days (discussed below). But this is not true everywhere. For example, in Georgia, landlords must give 60 days' notice to terminate a month-to-month tenancy, while tenants need only give 30 days' notice. (See the "Notice Required to Change or Terminate a Month-to-Month Tenancy" table in Appendix A.) State and local rent control laws can also impose notice requirements on landlords. Things are different if you want a tenant to move because he or she has violated a material term of the rental agreement—for example, by failing to pay rent. If so, notice requirements are commonly greatly shortened, sometimes to as little as three days.

Each state (and even some cities) has its own very detailed rules and procedures for preparing and serving termination notices, and it is impossible for this book to provide all specific forms and instructions. Consult a landlords' association or local rent control board and your state statutes for information and sample forms. Once you understand how much notice you must give, how the notice must be delivered, and any other requirements, you'll be in good shape to handle this work yourself—usually with no lawyer needed.

How Much Notice the Tenant Must Give

In most states, the tenant who decides to move out must give you at least 30 days' notice. Some states allow less than 30 days' notice in certain situations—for example, because a tenant must leave early due to military orders or health problems. And, in some states, tenants who pay rent more frequently than once a month can give notice to terminate that matches their rent payment interval—for example, tenants who pay rent every two weeks would have to give 14 days' notice. If your tenant joins the military and wants to terminate a rental agreement, federal law specifies the maximum amount of notice you may require. But if state law requires less notice, you must follow state rules. See "Special Rules for Tenants Who Enter Military Service," below.

To educate your tenants as to what they can expect, make sure your rental agreement includes your state's notice requirements for ending a tenancy. (See Clause 4 of the form agreements in Chapter 2.) It is also wise to list termination notice requirements in the move-in letter (discussed in Chapter 4) you send to new tenants.

For details on your state's rules, see the "Notice Required to Change or Terminate a Month-to-Month Tenancy" table in Appendix A.

Restrictions to Ending a Tenancy

The general rules for terminating a tenancy described in this chapter often don't apply in the following situations:

- **Rent control ordinances.** Many rent control cities require "just cause" (a good reason) to end a tenancy, which typically includes moving in a close relative and refurbishing the unit. You will likely have to state your legal reason in the termination notice you give the tenant.

- **Discrimination.** It is illegal to end a tenancy because of a tenant's race, religion, or sex; because they have children; or for any other reason constituting illegal discrimination. (Chapter 3 discusses antidiscrimination laws.)

- **Retaliation.** You can not legally terminate a tenancy to retaliate against a tenant for exercising any right under the law, such as the tenant's right to complain to governmental authorities about defective housing conditions or, in many states, to withhold rent because of a health or safety problem the landlord has failed to correct. Chapter 16 of *Every Landlord's Legal Guide*, by Marcia Stewart, Ralph Warner, & Janet Portman (Nolo), covers how to avoid tenant retaliation claims.

Special Rules for Tenants Who Enter Military Service

Tenants who enter military service after signing a lease or rental agreement have a federally legislated right to get out of their rental obligations. (War and National Defense Servicemembers Civil Relief Act, 50 App. U.S.C.A. §§ 501 and following.) Tenants must mail written notice of their intent to terminate their tenancy for military reasons to the landlord or manager.

Rental agreements. Once the notice is mailed or delivered, the tenancy will terminate 30 days after the day that rent is next due. For example, if rent is due on the first of June and the tenant mails a notice on May 28, the tenancy will terminate on July 1. This rule takes precedence over any longer notice periods that might be specified in your rental agreement or by state law. If state law or your agreement provides for shorter notice periods, however, the shorter notice will control. Recently, many states have passed laws that offer the same or greater protections to members of the state militia or national guard.

Leases. A tenant who enters military service after signing a lease may terminate the lease by following the procedure for rental agreements, above. For example, suppose a tenant signs a one-year lease in April, agreeing to pay rent on the first of the month. The tenant enlists October 10 and mails you a termination notice on October 11. In this case, you must terminate the tenancy on December 1, 30 days after the first time that rent is due (November 1) following the mailing of the notice. This tenant will have no continuing obligation for rent past December 1, even though this is several months before the lease expires.

You Should Insist on a Tenant's Written Notice of Intent to Move

In many states, a tenant's notice must be in writing and give the exact date the tenant plans to move out. Even if it is not required by law, it's a good idea to insist that the tenant give you notice in writing (as does Clause 4 of the form agreements in Chapter 2). Why bother, especially if the tenant politely calls you to say she will be out on a particular date?

Insisting on written notice will prove essential should the tenant not move as planned after you have signed a lease or rental agreement with a new tenant. Not only will this be true if, at the last minute, the tenant tries to claim that he didn't really set a firm move-out date, but it will also be invaluable if a new tenant sues you to recover the costs of temporary housing or storage fees for her belongings because you could not deliver possession of the unit. In turn, you will want to sue the old (holdover) tenant for causing the problem by failing to move out. Should this be necessary, you will have a much stronger case against the holdover tenant if you can produce a written promise to move on a specific date instead of your version of a conversation (which will undoubtedly be disputed by the tenant).

A sample tenant's notice of intent to move out form is shown below. Give a copy of this form to any tenant who tells you he or she plans to move.

CD-ROM

The Landlord Rental Forms CD includes a copy of the Tenant's Notice of Intent to Move Out form. Appendix C includes a blank tear-out copy of the form.

Tenant's Notice of Intent to Move Out

April 3, 20xx
Date

Anne Sakamoto
Landlord

888 Mill Avenue
Street Address

Nashville, Tennessee 37126
City and State

Dear _____ Ms. Sakamoto _____ ,
Landlord

This is to notify you that the undersigned tenants, Patti and Joe Ellis

_____ , will be moving from

999 Brook Lane, Apartment Number 11

on _____ May 3, 20xx _____ , _____ 30 days _____ from today. This

provides at least _____ 30 days' _____ written notice as required in our rental

agreement.

Sincerely,

Patti Ellis
Tenant

Joe Ellis
Tenant

_____
Tenant

Preparing a Move-Out Letter

Chapter 4 explains how a move-in letter can help get a tenancy off to a good start. Similarly, a move-out letter can also help reduce the possibility of disputes, especially over the return of security deposits. Send the letter as soon as you receive notice of the tenant's intent to leave. Your move-out letter should explain the following to the tenant:

- how you expect the rental unit to be left, including specific cleaning requirements

- details on your final inspection procedures and how you will determine what cleaning and damage repair is necessary, requiring a deduction from the tenant's security deposit

- what kinds of deposit deductions you may legally make, and

- when and how you will send any refund that is due.

See below for more detail on returning security deposits and final inspection procedures.

CD-ROM

The Landlord Rental Forms CD includes a copy of the Move-Out Letter, and a sample is shown below. Appendix C includes a blank tear-out copy of the form.

Accepting Rent After a 30-Day Notice Is Given

If you accept rent for any period beyond the date the tenant told you he is moving out, this likely cancels the termination notice and creates a new tenancy. An exception would be where a tenant pays you past-due rent and you document this in writing.

Suppose, after giving notice, the tenant asks for a little more time in which to move out. Assuming no new tenant is moving in and you are willing to accommodate this request, prepare a written agreement setting out what you have agreed to in detail, and have the tenant sign it. See the sample letter, below, extending the tenant's move-out date.

! CAUTION

If you collected the "last month's rent" when the tenant moved in, do not accept rent for the last month of the tenancy. You are legally obligated to use this money for the last month's rent. Accepting an additional month's rent may extend the tenant's tenancy.

When the Tenant Doesn't Give the Required Notice

All too often, a tenant will send or give you a "too short" notice of intent to move. And it's not unheard of for a tenant to move out with no notice or with a wave as he tosses the keys on your doorstep.

A tenant who leaves without giving enough notice has lost the right to occupy the premises but is still obligated to pay rent through the end of the required notice period. For example, if the notice period is 30 days, but the tenant moves out after telling you 20 days ago that he intended to move, he still owes you rent for the remaining ten days.

In most states, you have a legal duty to try to re-rent the property before you can charge the tenant for giving you too little notice, but few courts expect a landlord to accomplish this in less than a month. (This rule, called the landlord's duty to mitigate damages, is discussed below.) You can also use the security deposit to cover unpaid rent, (also discussed below).

Move-Out Letter

July 5, 20xx
Date

Jane Wasserman
Tenant

123 North Street, Apartment #23
Street Address

Atlanta, Georgia 30360
City and State

Dear _____ Jane _____,
Tenant

We hope you have enjoyed living here. In order that we may mutually end our relationship on a positive note, this move-out letter describes how we expect your unit to be left and what our procedures are for returning your security deposit.

Basically, we expect you to leave your rental unit in the same condition it was when you moved in, except for normal wear and tear. To refresh your memory on the condition of the unit when you moved in, I've attached a copy of the Landlord-Tenant Checklist you signed at the beginning of your tenancy. I'll be using this same form to inspect your unit when you leave.

Specifically, here's a list of items you should thoroughly clean before vacating:

- ☑ Floors
    - ☑ sweep wood floors
    - ☑ vacuum carpets and rugs (shampoo if necessary)
    - ☑ mop kitchen and bathroom floors
- ☑ Walls, baseboards, ceilings, and built-in shelves
- ☑ Kitchen cabinets, countertops and sink, stove and oven—inside and out
- ☑ Refrigerator—clean inside and out, empty it of food, and turn it off, with the door left open
- ☑ Bathtubs, showers, toilets, and plumbing fixtures
- ☑ Doors, windows, and window coverings
- ☑ Other

Microwave oven—clean inside and out

_____

_____

_____

_____

_____

_____

_____

If you have any questions as to the type of cleaning we expect, please let me know.

Please don't leave anything behind—that includes bags of garbage, clothes, food, newspapers, furniture, appliances, dishes, plants, cleaning supplies, or other items that belong to you.

Please be sure you have disconnected phone and utility services, canceled all newspaper subscriptions, and sent the post office a change of address form.

Once you have cleaned your unit and removed all your belongings, please call me at _____555-1234_____ to arrange for a walk-through inspection and to return all keys. Please be prepared to give me your forwarding address where we may mail your security deposit.

It's our policy to return all deposits either in person or at an address you provide within _____one month_____ _____ after you move out. If any deductions are made—for past due rent or because the unit is damaged or not sufficiently clean—they will be explained in writing.

If you have any questions, please contact me at _____555-1234_____.

Sincerely,

Denise Parsons
Landlord/Manager

When You or Your Tenant Violates the Rental Agreement

If you seriously violate the rental agreement and fail to fulfill your legal responsibilities—for example, by not correcting serious health or safety problems—a tenant may be able to legally move out with no written notice or by giving less notice than is otherwise required. Called a "constructive eviction," this doctrine typically applies only when living conditions are intolerable—for example, if the tenant has had no heat for an extended period in the winter, or if a tenant's use and enjoyment of the property has been substantially impaired because of drug dealing in the building.

What exactly constitutes a constructive eviction varies slightly under the laws of different states. Generally, if you are on notice that a rental unit has serious habitability problems for an extended time, the tenant is entitled to move out on short notice or, in extreme cases, without giving notice.

Along the same lines, a landlord may evict a tenant who violates a lease or rental agreement. For example, you may give a "notice to quit" to a tenant who fails to pay rent or damages the premises, with less notice than is normally required to end a tenancy (typically three to five days, rather than 30 days). And, in the case of drug dealing, many states provide for expedited eviction procedures. Because of the wide state-by-state variations on eviction rules and procedures, the details of how to evict a tenant are beyond the scope of this book.

How Fixed-Term Leases End

A lease lasts for a fixed term, typically one year. As a general rule, neither you nor the tenant may unilaterally terminate the tenancy or change a material condition during the period of the lease, unless the other party has violated the terms of the lease. (There's an exception for tenants who join the military and want to terminate a lease, as explained in "Special Rules for Tenants Who Enter Military Service," above.)

If you and the tenant both live up to your promises, the lease simply ends of its own accord at the end of the lease term, and the tenant moves out. Alternatively, you may sign a new lease, with the same or different terms. As every landlord knows, however, life is not always so simple. Sooner or later, a tenant will stay beyond the end of the term without signing a new lease, or leave before the lease term ends without any legal right to do so.

Giving Notice to the Tenant

Because a lease clearly states when it will expire, you may not think it's necessary to remind the tenants of the expiration date. But doing so is a very good practice, and some states or cities (especially those with rent control) actually require it.

We suggest giving the tenant at least 60 days' written notice that the lease is going to expire. This reminder has several advantages:

- **Getting the tenant out on time.** Two months' notice allows plenty of time for the tenant to look for another place if he doesn't—or you don't—want to renew the lease.

- **Giving you time to renegotiate the lease.** If you would like to continue renting to your present tenant but also want to change some lease terms or increase the rent, your notice serves to remind the tenant that the terms of the old lease will not automatically continue. Encourage the tenant to stay, but mention that you need to make some changes to the lease.

- **Getting a new tenant in quickly.** If you know a tenant is going to move, you can show the unit to prospective tenants ahead of time and minimize the time the space is vacant. You must still respect the current tenant's privacy. (Chapter 3 discusses showing the unit to prospective tenants.)

Sample Letter Extending Tenant's Move-Out Date

June 20, 20xx

Hannah Lewis
777 Broadway Terrace, Apartment #3
Richmond, Virginia 23233

Dear Hannah:

On June 1, you gave me a 30-day notice of your intent to move out on July 1. You have since requested to extend your move-out to July 18 because of last-minute problems with closing escrow on your new house. This letter is to verify our understanding that you will move out on July 18, instead of July 1, and that you will pay prorated rent for 18 days (July 1 through July 18). Prorated rent for 18 days, based on your monthly rent of $900 or $30 per day, is $540.

Please sign below to indicate your agreement to these terms.

Sincerely,

Fran Moore, Landlord

Agreed to by Hannah Lewis, Tenant:

Signature *Hannah Lewis*

Date *June 20, 20xx*

RENT CONTROL

Your options may be limited in a rent control area. If your property is subject to rent control, you may be limited in your ability to end your relationship with a current tenant. Many ordinances require "just cause" for refusing to renew a lease, which generally means that only certain reasons (such as the tenant's failure to pay rent, or your desire to move in a close relative) justify nonrenewal. If your city requires "just cause," and if your decision not to renew does not meet the city's test, you may end up with a perpetual month-to-month tenant. Check your city's rent control ordinance carefully.

If the Tenant Remains After the Lease Expires

It's fairly common for a tenant to remain in a unit even though the lease has run out. If this happens, you have a choice: You can continue renting to the tenant, or you can take legal steps to get the tenant out.

If a tenant stays beyond the end of the lease, and you accept rent money without signing a new lease, in most states you will have created a new, month-to-month tenancy on the same terms as applied for the old lease. In a few states, you may create a new lease for the same term—such as one year. In other words, you'll be stuck with the terms and rent in the old lease, at least for the first 30 days and possibly longer. If you want to change the terms in a new lease, you must abide by the law regarding giving notice for a month-to-month tenancy (discussed above). It will usually take you at least a month while you go about giving notice to your now month-to-month tenant.

To avoid problems of tenants staying longer than you want, be sure to notify the tenant that you expect him to leave at the lease expiration date, and don't accept rent after this date. If a tenant just wants to stay an extra few days after a lease expires and you agree, it is wise to put your understanding on this arrangement in a letter. (See the sample letter extending the tenant's move-out date, above.)

If the Tenant Leaves Early

A tenant who leaves (with or without notifying you beforehand) before a fixed-term lease expires and refuses to pay the remainder of the rent due under the lease is said to have "broken the lease." Once the tenant leaves for good, you have the legal right to take possession of the premises and rerent to another tenant.

A key question that arises is, how much does a tenant with a lease owe if she walks out early? Let's start with the general legal rule. A tenant who signs a lease agrees at the outset to pay a fixed amount of rent: the monthly rent multiplied by the number of months of the lease. The tenant is obligated to pay this amount in monthly installments over the term of the lease. The fact that payments are made monthly doesn't change the tenant's responsibility to pay rent for the entire lease term. And the fact that a tenant who breaks a lease gives you notice of her intention to leave early changes nothing—you are still owed the money for the rest of the term. As discussed below, depending on the situation, you may use the tenant's security deposit to cover part of the shortfall, or sue the tenant for rent owed.

TIP

Require tenants to notify you of extended absences. Clause 16 of the form lease and rental agreements (Chapter 2) requires tenants to inform you when they will be gone for an extended time, such as two or more weeks.

By requiring tenants to notify you of long absences, you'll know whether property has been abandoned or the tenant is simply on vacation. In addition, if you have such a clause and, under its authority, enter an apparently abandoned unit only to be confronted later by an indignant tenant, you can defend yourself by pointing out that the tenant violated the lease.

When Leaving Early Is Justified

There are some important exceptions to the blanket rule that a tenant who breaks a lease owes you the rent for the entire lease term. A tenant who leaves early may *not* owe if:

- **Your rental unit is unsafe or otherwise uninhabitable.** If you don't live up to your obligations to provide habitable housing— for example, if you fail to maintain the unit in accordance with health and safety codes—a court will conclude that you have "constructively evicted" the tenant. That releases the tenant from further obligations under the lease.

- **You have rented—or could rent—the unit to someone else.** Most courts require landlords to try to soften ("mitigate") the ex-tenant's liability for the remaining rent by attempting to find a new rent-paying tenant as soon as possible. The new tenant's rent is credited against what the former tenant owed. (This "mitigation of damages" rule is discussed below.)

- **State law allows the tenant to leave early.** A few states have laws that list allowable reasons to break a lease. For example, in Delaware, a tenant need only give 30 days' notice to end a long-term lease if he needs to move because his present employer relocated or because health problems (of the tenant or a family member) require a permanent move. In Oregon, a victim of domestic violence, sexual assault, or stalking may terminate a lease with 14 days' notice. In all states, tenants who enter active military duty after signing a lease must be released after delivering proper notice. (See "Special Rules for Tenants Who Enter Military Service," above.) If your tenant has a good reason for a sudden move, you may want to research your state's law to see whether or not he's still on the hook for rent.

- **The rental unit is damaged or destroyed.** If a tenant's home is significantly damaged—either by natural disaster or any other reason beyond his control—he has the right to consider the lease at an end and to move out. State laws vary on the extent of the landlord's responsibility, depending on the cause of the damage. If a fire, flood, tornado, earthquake, or other natural disaster makes the dwelling unlivable, or if a third party is the cause of the destruction (for instance, a fire due to an arsonist), your best bet is to look to your insurance policy for help in repairing or rebuilding the unit and to assist your tenants in resettlement.

Your Duty to Mitigate Your Loss If the Tenant Leaves Early

If a tenant breaks the lease and moves out without legal justification, you can't just sit back and wait until the end of the term of the lease, and then sue the departed tenant for the total amount of your lost rent. In most states, you must try to rerent the property reasonably quickly and subtract the rent you receive from the amount the original tenant owed you.

Even if this isn't the legal rule in your state, trying to rerent is obviously a sound business strategy. It's much better to have rent coming in every month than to wait, leaving a rental unit vacant for months, and then try to sue (and collect from) a tenant who may be long gone, broke, or otherwise difficult to collect from.

If you don't make an attempt (or make an inadequate one) to rerent, and instead sue the former tenant for the whole rent, you will collect only what the judge thinks is the difference between the fair rental value of the property had you rerented it and the original tenant's promised rent. This can depend on how easy it is to rerent in your area. Also, a judge is sure to give you some time (probably at least 30 days) to find a new tenant.

How to Mitigate Your Damages

When you're sure that a tenant has left permanently, then you can turn your attention to rerenting the unit.

You do not need to relax your standards for acceptable tenants—for example, you are entitled to reject applicants with poor credit or rental histories. Also, you need not give the suddenly available property priority over other rental units that you would normally attend to first.

You are not required to rent the premises at a rate substantially below its fair market value. Keep in mind, however, that refusing to rent at less than the original rate may be foolish. If you are unable to ultimately collect from the former tenant, you will get *no* income from the property instead of less. You will have ended up hurting no one but yourself.

> ### Keep Good Records
>
> If you end up suing a former tenant, you will want to be able to show the judge that you acted reasonably in your attempts to rerent the property. Don't rely on your memory and powers of persuasion to convince the judge. Keep detailed records, including:
> - the original lease
> - receipts for cleaning and painting, with photos of the unit showing the need for repairs, if any
> - your expenses for storing or properly disposing of any belongings the tenant left
> - receipts for advertising the property and bills from credit reporting agencies investigating potential renters
> - a log of the time you spent showing the property, and the value of that time
> - a log of any people who offered to rent and, if you rejected them, documentation as to why, and
> - if the current rent is less than what the original tenant paid, a copy of the new lease.

The Tenant's Right to Find a Replacement Tenant

A tenant who wishes to leave before the lease expires may offer to find a suitable new tenant, so that the flow of rent will remain uninterrupted, and he will be off the hook for future rent payments. Unless you have a new tenant waiting, you have nothing to lose by cooperating. And refusing to cooperate could hurt you: If you refuse to accept an excellent new tenant and then withhold the lease-breaking tenant's deposit or sue for unpaid rent, you may wind up losing in court since, after all, you turned down the chance to reduce your losses (mitigate your damages).

Of course, if the rental market is really tight in your area, you may be able to lease the unit easily at a higher rent, or you may already have an even better prospective tenant on your waiting list. In that case, you won't care if a tenant breaks the lease, and you may not be interested in any new tenant he provides.

If you and the outgoing tenant agree on a replacement tenant, you and the new tenant should sign a new lease.

When You Can Sue

If a tenant leaves prematurely, you may need to go to court and sue for your rerental costs and the difference between the original and the replacement rent. (Obviously, you should first use the tenant's deposit, if possible, to cover these costs, as discussed below.)

Deciding *where* to sue is usually easy: Small claims court is usually the court of choice, because it's fast and affordable and doesn't require a lawyer. The only exception is in states where small claims courts have very low dollar limits and you are owed lots more.

Knowing *when* to sue is trickier. You may be eager to start legal proceedings as soon as the original tenant leaves, but, if you do, you won't know the extent of your losses, because you might find another tenant who will make up part of the lost rent. Must you wait until the end of the original tenant's lease? Or can you bring suit when you rerent the property?

The standard approach, and one that all states allow, is to go to court after you rerent the property. At this point, your losses—your expenses and the rent differential, if any—are known and final. The disadvantage is that you have had no income from that property since the original tenant left, and the original tenant may be long gone and not, practically speaking, worth chasing down.

 RESOURCE

Nolo's Book on Small Claims Court. *Everybody's Guide to Small Claims Court* (National Edition), by Ralph Warner (Nolo), provides detailed advice on bringing or defending a small claims court case, preparing evidence and witnesses for court, and collecting your court judgment when you win. *Everybody's Guide to Small Claims Court* will also be useful in defending yourself against a tenant who sues you in small claims court—for example, claiming that you failed to return a cleaning or security deposit.

Returning Security Deposits When a Tenancy Ends

Most states set very specific rules for the return of security deposits when a tenant leaves—whether voluntarily or by your ending the tenancy. A landlord's failure to return security deposits as legally required can result in substantial financial penalties if a tenant files suit.

Inspecting the Unit When a Tenant Leaves

After the tenant leaves, you will need to inspect the unit to assess what cleaning and damage repair is necessary. At the final inspection, check the condition of each item—for example, bathroom walls—on the landlord-tenant checklist (described in Chapter 4) or a similar document that you and the tenant signed when the tenant moved in. If you did not use a landlord-tenant checklist or a similar form to inventory the condition of the rental property at move-in, you should still do a walk-through inspection when the tenant moves out. You won't have the benefit of the "before" documentation, but you can still review the condition of the unit together and identify items that need cleaning, repair, or replacement. It's a good idea (and the law in some states) to involve the tenants in the final inspection. (See "Alerting Tenants to Final Inspection Procedures," below.)

Alerting Tenants to Final Inspection Procedures

Many landlords do a final inspection of the rental unit on their own and simply send the tenant an itemized statement with any remaining balance of the deposit. If at all possible, you should make the inspection with the tenant who's moving out, rather than by yourself. A few states actually require this. Laws in Arizona, Maryland, and Virginia, for example, specifically give tenants the right to be present when you conduct the final inspection. Other states (including Florida, Georgia, Kentucky, Michigan, and Tennessee) give tenants the opportunity to inspect the rental unit to determine the accuracy of the landlord's list of damages before the final itemization is done. A tenant who disagrees with any proposed deduction has a specified amount of time to send the landlord a written explanation as to this disagreement. Only then can the tenant sue over deductions that he or she considers improper. Because state laws can be quite detailed as to rules and procedures for itemizing and returning security deposits, be sure to check your state statutes. (See "State Security Deposit Rules" in Appendix A.)

! **CAUTION**

California has special rules and procedures for move-out inspections. California tenants are entitled to a pre-move-out inspection, when you tell the tenant what defects, if any, need to be corrected in order for the tenant to optimize the security deposit refund. California landlords must notify the tenant in writing of the right to request an initial inspection, at which the tenant has a right to be present. (Cal. Civ. Code §1950.5 (f).) For details, see *The California Landlord's Law Book*, by David Brown, Ralph Warner, & Janet Portman (Nolo).

Basic Rules for Returning Deposits

You are generally entitled to deduct from a tenant's security deposit whatever amount you need to fix damaged or dirty property (outside of "ordinary wear and tear") or to make up unpaid rent. But you must make your deductions and return deposits correctly. While the specific rules vary from state to state, you usually have between 14 and 30 days after the tenant leaves to return the deposit. (See "State Security Deposit Rules" in Appendix A.)

State security deposit statutes typically require you to mail the following within the time limit to the tenant's last known address (or forwarding address if you have one):

- the tenant's entire deposit with interest if required (see "States That Require Landlords to Pay Interest on Deposits" in Appendix A)

- a written itemized accounting of deductions, including back rent and costs of cleaning and damage repair, together with payment for any deposit balance, including any interest that is required. The statement should list each deduction and briefly explain what it's for.

Even if there is no specific time limit in your state or law requiring itemization, promptly presenting the tenant with a written itemization of all deductions and a clear reason why each was made is an essential part of a savvy landlord's overall plan to avoid disputes with tenants. In general, we recommend three to four weeks as a reasonable time to return deposits.

Penalties for Violating Security Deposit Laws

If you don't follow state security deposit laws to the letter, you may pay a heavy price if a tenant sues you and wins. In addition to whatever amount you wrongfully withheld, you may have to pay the tenant extra or punitive damages (penalties imposed when the judge feels that the defendant has acted especially outrageously) and court costs. In many states, if you "willfully" (deliberately and not through inadvertence) violate the security deposit statute, you may forfeit your right to retain any part of the deposit and may be liable for two or three times the amount wrongfully withheld, plus attorney fees and costs.

If the Deposit Doesn't Cover Damage and Unpaid Rent

If the security deposit doesn't cover what a tenant owes you for back rent, cleaning, or repairs, you may wish to file a small claims lawsuit against the former tenant.

RESOURCE

Every Landlord's Legal Guide, by Marcia Stewart, Ralph Warner, & Janet Portman (Nolo), provides complete details on state laws and sample forms for returning and itemizing security deposits.

State Landlord-Tenant Law Charts

State Landlord-Tenant Statutes 108

Notice Required to Change or Terminate a Month-to-Month Tenancy 109

State Rent Rules...112

State Security Deposit Rules...114

Required Security Deposit Disclosures..120

States That Require Landlords to Pay Interest on Deposits 123

Attachment to Florida Leases and Rental Agreements (Security Deposits)...........124

State Laws on Landlord's Access to Rental Property...125

Where to Find Landlord-Tenant Laws

Every landlord is governed by state, local, and federal law. If you're a typical landlord, you'll primarily be concerned with state law. Citations for state laws on important subjects such as security deposit rules are provided in this Appendix. Most states have made their statutes available online. You can find these by going to Nolo's website at www.nolo.com. See the legal research area of Nolo's website at www. nolo.com/statute/state.cfm. If you are looking for a local ordinance, for example, rent control rules or health and safety standards that affect landlords, check out State and Local Government on the Net at www.statelocalgov. net. This is an excellent source for finding local governments online. First click your state, then scroll down the page to find your local government's site.

State Landlord-Tenant Statutes

Here are some of the key statutes pertaining to landlord-tenant law in each state. In some states, important legal principles are contained in court opinions, not codes or statutes. Court-made law and rent stabilization—rent control—laws and regulations are not reflected in this chart.

State	Statute	State	Statute
Alabama	Ala. Code §§ 35-9-1 to 35-9-100; 35-9A-101 et seq.	Montana	Mont. Code Ann. §§ 70-24-101 to 70-26-110
Alaska	Alaska Stat. §§ 34.03.010 to 34.03.380	Nebraska	Neb. Rev. Stat. §§ 76-1401 to 76-1449
Arizona	Ariz. Rev. Stat. Ann. §§ 12-1171 to 12-1183; §§ 33-1301 to 33-1381; 33-301 to 33-381	Nevada	Nev. Rev. Stat. Ann. §§ 118A.010 to 118A.520; 40.215 to 40.280
Arkansas	Ark. Code Ann. §§ 18-16-101 to 18-16-306; 18-17-101 to 18-7-913	New Hampshire	N.H. Rev. Stat. Ann. §§ 540:1 to 540:29, 540-A:1 to 540-A:8
California	Cal. Civ. Code §§ 1925 to 1954, 1961 to 1962.7	New Jersey	N.J. Stat. Ann. §§ 46:8-1 to 46:8-50; 2A:42-1 to 42-96
Colorado	Colo. Rev. Stat. §§ 38-12-101 to 38-12-104, 38-12-301 to 38-12-302, 13-40-101 to 13-40-123	New Mexico	N.M. Stat. Ann. §§ 47-8-1 to 47-8-51
Connecticut	Conn. Gen. Stat. Ann. §§ 47a-1 to 47a-74	New York	N.Y. Real Prop. Law §§ 220 to 238; Real Prop. Acts. §§ 701 to 853; Mult. Dwell. Law (all); Mult. Res. Law (all); Gen. Oblig. Law §§ 7-103 to 7-109
Delaware	Del. Code Ann. tit. 25, §§ 5101 to 5907	North Carolina	N.C. Gen. Stat. §§ 42-1 to 42-14.2, 42-25.6 to 42-76
Dist. of Columbia	D.C. Code Ann. §§ 42-3201 to 42-3610; D.C. Mun. Regs., tit. 14, §§ 300 to 311	North Dakota	N.D. Cent. Code §§ 47-16-01 to 47-16-41
Florida	Fla. Stat. Ann. §§ 83.40 to 83.682	Ohio	Ohio Rev. Code Ann. §§ 5321.01 to 5321.19
Georgia	Ga. Code Ann. §§ 44-7-1 to 44-7-81	Oklahoma	Okla. Stat. Ann. tit. 41, §§ 101 to 136
Hawaii	Haw. Rev. Stat. §§ 521-1 to 521-78	Oregon	Or. Rev. Stat. §§ 90.100 to 91.225
Idaho	Idaho Code §§ 6-201 to 6-324, §§ 55-208 to 55-308	Pennsylvania	68 Pa. Cons. Stat. Ann. §§ 250.101; 399.18
Illinois	735 Ill. Com § 5/9-201 to 321 & 765 Ill. Comp. Stat. §§ 705/0.01 to 742/30	Rhode Island	R.I. Gen. Laws §§ 34-18-1 to 34-18-57
Indiana	Ind. Code Ann. §§ 32-31-1-1 to 32-31-9-15; 32-31-2.9-d to 2.9-5	South Carolina	S.C. Code Ann. §§ 27-40-10 to 27-40-940
Iowa	Iowa Code Ann. §§ 562A.1 to 562A.37	South Dakota	S.D. Codified Laws Ann. §§ 43-32-1 to 43-32-30
Kansas	Kan. Stat. Ann. §§ 58-2501 to 58-2573	Tennessee	Tenn. Code Ann. §§ 66-28-101 to 66-28-521
Kentucky	Ky. Rev. Stat. Ann. §§ 383.010 to 383.715	Texas	Tex. Prop. Code Ann. §§ 91.001 to 92.354
Louisiana	La. Rev. Stat. Ann. §§ 9:3251 to 9:3261; La. Civ. Code Ann. art. 2668 to 2729	Utah	Utah Code Ann. §§ 57-17-1 to 57-17-5, 57-22-1 to 57-22-6
Maine	Me. Rev. Stat. Ann. tit. 14, §§ 6001 to 6046	Vermont	Vt. Stat. Ann. tit. 9, §§ 4451 to 4468
Maryland	Md. Code Ann. [Real Prop.] §§ 8-101 to 8-604	Virginia	Va. Code Ann. §§ 55-218.1 to 55-248.40
Massachusetts	Mass. Gen. Laws Ann. ch. 186, §§ 1 to 22	Washington	Wash. Rev. Code Ann. §§ 59.04.010 to 59.04.900, 59.18.010 to 59.18.911
Michigan	Mich. Comp. Laws §§ 554.131 to .201 & 554.601 to 554.641	West Virginia	W. Va. Code §§ 37-6-1 to 37-6-30
Minnesota	Minn. Stat. Ann. §§ 504B.001 to 504B.471	Wisconsin	Wis. Stat. Ann. §§ 704.01 to 704.50; Wis. Admin. Code 134.01 to 134.10
Mississippi	Miss. Code Ann. §§ 89-7-1 to 89-8-27	Wyoming	Wyo. Stat. §§ 1-21-1201 to 1-21-1211, §§ 34-2-128 to 34-2-129
Missouri	Mo. Rev. Stat. §§ 441.005 to 441.880, §§ 535.150 to 535.300		

Notice Required to Change or Terminate a Month-to-Month Tenancy

Except where noted, the amount of notice a landlord must give to increase rent or change another term of the rental agreement in month-to-month tenancy is the same as that required to end a month-to-month tenancy. Be sure to check state and local rent control laws, which may have different notice requirements.

State	Tenant	Landlord	Statute	Comments
Alabama	30 days	30 days	Ala. Code §§ 35-9-5, 35-9A-441	No state statute on the amount of notice required to change rent or other terms
Alaska	30 days	30 days	Alaska Stat. § 34.03.290(b)	
Arizona	30 days	30 days	Ariz. Rev. Stat. Ann. § 33-1375	
Arkansas		10 days	Ark. Code Ann. § 18-16-101; 18-17-704	No state statute on the amount of notice required to change rent or other terms
California	30 days	30 or 60 days	Cal. Civ. Code § 1946; Cal. Civ. Code § 827a	30 days to change rental terms, but if landlord is raising the rent, tenant gets 60 days' notice if the sum of this and all prior rent increases during the previous 12 months is more than 10% of the lowest rent charged during that time. 60 days to terminate (landlord), 30 days (tenant).
Colorado	10 days	10 days	Colo. Rev. Stat. § 13-40-107	
Connecticut		3 days	Conn. Gen. Stat. Ann. § 47a-23	Landlord must provide 3 days' notice to terminate tenancy. Landlord is not required to give a particular amount of notice of a proposed rent increase unless prior notice was previously agreed upon.
Delaware	60 days	60 days	Del. Code Ann. tit. 25, §§ 5106, 5107	After receiving notice of landlord's proposed change terms, tenant has 15 days to terminate tenancy. Otherwise, changes will take effect as announced.
District of Columbia	30 days	30 days	D.C. Code Ann. § 42-3202	No state statute on the amount of notice required to change rent or other terms
Florida	15 days	15 days	Fla. Stat. Ann. § 83.57	No state statute on the amount of notice required to change rent or other terms
Georgia	30 days	60 days	Ga. Code Ann. § 44-7-6 & -7	No state statute on the amount of notice required to change rent or other terms
Hawaii	28 days	45 days	Haw. Rev. Stat. §§ 521-71, 521-21(d)	
Idaho	One month	One month	Idaho Code §§ 55-208, 55-307	Landlords must provide 15 days' notice to increase rent or change tenancy.
Illinois	30 days	30 days	735 Ill. Comp. Stat. § 5/9-207	
Indiana	One month	One month	Ind. Code Ann. § 32-31-1-1, 32-31-5-4	Unless agreement states otherwise, landlord must give 30 days' written notice to modify written rental agreement.
Iowa	30 days	30 days	Iowa Code Ann. §§ 562A.34, 562A.13(5)	
Kansas	30 days	30 days	Kan. Stat. Ann. § 58-2570	No state statute on the amount of notice required to change rent or other terms
Kentucky	30 days	30 days	Ky. Rev. Stat. Ann. § 383.695	
Louisiana	10 days	10 days	La. Civ. Code Art. 2728	No state statute on the amount of notice required to change rent or other terms
Maine	30 days	30 days	Me. Rev. Stat. Ann. tit. 14 §§ 6002, 6015	Landlord must provide 45 days' notice to increase rent.
Maryland	One month	One month	Md. Code Ann. [Real Prop.] § 8-402(b)(3), (b)(4)	Two months notice required in Montgomery County. Does not apply in Baltimore.

Notice Required to Change or Terminate a Month-to-Month Tenancy (continued)

State	Tenant	Landlord	Statute	Comments
Massachusetts	See 1 below	See 1 below	Mass. Gen. Laws Ann. ch. 186, § 12	
Michigan	See 2	See 2	Mich. Comp. Laws § 554.134	No state statute on the amount of notice required to
Minnesota	See 3 below	See 3 below	Minn. Stat. Ann. § 504B.135	No state statute on the amount of notice required to change rent or other terms
Mississippi	30 days	30 days	Miss. Code Ann. § 89-8-19	No state statute on the amount of notice required to change rent or other terms
Missouri	One month	One month	Mo. Rev. Stat. § 441.060	No state statute on the amount of notice required to change rent or other terms
Montana	30 days	30 days	Mont. Code Ann. § 70-24-441, 70-26-109	Landlord may change terms of tenancy with 15 days' notice.
Nebraska	30 days	30 days	Neb. Rev. Stat. § 76-1437	No state statute on the amount of notice required to
Nevada	30 days	30 days	Nev. Rev. Stat. Ann. §§ 40.251, 118A.300	Landlords must provide 45 days' notice to increase rent.
New Hampshire	30 days	30 days	N.H. Rev. Stat. Ann. §§ 540:2, 540:3	Landlord may terminate only for just cause.
New Jersey			No statute	
New Mexico	30 days	30 days	N.M. Stat. Ann. §§ 47-8-37, 47-8-15(F)	Landlord must deliver rent increase notice at least 30
New York	One	One	N.Y. Real Prop. Law § 232-b	No state statute on the amount of notice required to
North Carolina	7 days	7 days	N.C. Gen. Stat. § 42-14	No state statute on the amount of notice required to
North Dakota	30 days	30 days	N.D. Cent. Code § 47-16-15, 47-16-07	Tenant may terminate with 25 days' notice if landlord has changed the terms of the lease.
Ohio	30 days	30 days	Ohio Rev. Code Ann. § 5321.17	No state statute on the amount of notice required to change rent or other terms
Oklahoma	30 days	30 days	Okla. Stat. Ann. tit. 41, § 111	No state statute on the amount of notice required to change rent or other terms
Oregon	30 days	30 days	Or. Rev. Stat. § 91.070 , 90.427	No state statute on the amount of notice required to change rent or other terms
Pennsylvania			No statute	
Rhode Island	30 days	30 days	R.I. Gen. Laws §§ 34-18-16.1, 34-18-37	Landlord must provide 30 days' notice to increase rent.
South Carolina	30 days	30 days	S.C. Code Ann. § 27-40-770	No state statute on the amount of notice required to change rent or other terms
South Dakota	One month	One month	S.D. Codified Laws Ann. §§ 43-32-13, 43-8-8	Tenant may terminate within 15 days of receiving landlord's modification notice.
Tennessee	30 days	30 days	Tenn. Code Ann. § 66-28-512	No state statute on the amount of notice required to change rent or other terms

1 Interval between days of payment or 30 days, whichever is longer.
2 Interval between times of payment.
3 Interval between time rent is due or three months, whichever is less.

			Notice Required to Change or Terminate a Month-to-Month Tenancy (continued)	
State	**Tenant**	**Landlord**	**Statute**	**Comments**
Texas	One month	One month	Tex. Prop. Code Ann. § 91.001	No state statute on the amount of notice required to change rent or other terms
Utah		15 days	Ut. Code Ann. § 78-36-3	No state statute on the amount of notice required to change rent or other terms
Vermont	One rental period	30 days	Vt. Code Ann. tit. 9, §§ 4467, 4456(d)	If there is no written rental agreement, for tenants who have continuously resided in the unit for two years or less, 60 days' notice to terminate; for those who have resided longer than two years, 90 days. If there is a written rental agreement, for tenants who have lived continuously in the unit for two years or less, 30 days; for those who have lived there longer than two years, 60 days.
Virginia	30 days	30 days	Va. Code Ann. §§ 55-248.37, 55-248.7	No state statute on the amount of notice required to change rent or other terms, but landlord must abide by notice provisions in the rental agreement, if any, and tenant must consent in writing to any change.
Washington	20 days	20 days	Wash. Rev. Code Ann. §§ 59.18.200, 59.18.140	Landlord must give 30 days to change rent or other lease terms.
West Virginia	One month	One month	W. Va. Code § 37-6-5	No state statute on the amount of notice required to change rent or other terms
Wisconsin	28 days	28 days	Wis. Stat. Ann. § 704.19	No state statute on the amount of notice required to change rent or other terms
Wyoming			No statute	

Current as of July 2007

State Rent Rules

Here are citations for statues that set out rent rules in each state. When a state has no statute, the space is left blank. See the "Notice Required to Change or Terminate a Month-to-Month Tenancy" chart in this Appendix for citations to raising rent.

State	When Rent Is Due	Grace Period	Where Rent Is Due	Late Fees
Alabama	Ala. Code § 35-9A-161 (c)		Ala. Code § 35-9A-161 (c)	
Alaska	Alaska Stat. § 34.03.020(c)		Alaska Stat. § 34.03.020(c)	
Arizona	Ariz. Rev. Stat. Ann. §§ 33-1314(C), 33-1368(B)		Ariz. Rev. Stat. Ann. § 33-1314(C)	Ariz. Rev. Stat. Ann. § 33-1368(B)
Arkansas	Ark. Code Ann. § 18-17-401	Ark. Code Ann. §§ 18-17-401, 18-17-701, 18-17-901	Ark Code Ann. 18-17-401	
California	Cal. Civil Code § 1947		Cal. Civil Code § 1962	*Orozco V. Casimiro*, 121 Cal.App.4th Supp. 7 (2004)
Colorado				
Connecticut	Conn. Gen. Stat. Ann. § 47a-3a	Conn. Gen. Stat. Ann. § 47a-15a	Conn. Gen. Stat. Ann. § 47a-3a	Conn. Gen. Stat. Ann. §§ 47a-4(a)(8), 47a-15a [1]
Delaware	Del. Code Ann. tit. 25, § 5501(b)	Del. Code Ann. tit. 25, § 5501(d)	Del. Code Ann. title 25, § 5501(b)	Del. Code Ann. tit. 25, § 5501(d) [2]
D.C.				
Florida	Fla. Stat. Ann. § 83.46(1)			
Georgia				
Hawaii	Haw. Rev. Stat. § 521-21(b)		Haw. Rev. Stat. § 521-21(b)	
Idaho				
Illinois	765 Ill. Comp. Stat. Ann. 705/3			
Indiana	*Watson v. Penn*, 108 Ind. 21 (1886), 8 N.E. 636 (1886)			
Iowa	Iowa Code Ann. § 562A.9(3)		Iowa Code Ann. § 562A.9(3)	Iowa Code Ann. § 535.2(7) [3]
Kansas	Kan. Stat. Ann. § 58-2545(c)		Kan. Stat. Ann. § 58-2545(c)	
Kentucky	Ky. Rev. Stat. Ann. § 383.565(2)		Ky. Rev. Stat. Ann. § 383.565(2)	
Louisiana	La. Civ. Code Ann. art. 2703(1)		La. Civ. Code Ann. art. 2703(2)	
Maine		Me. Rev. Stat. Ann. tit. 14, § 6028		Me. Rev. Stat. Ann. tit. 14, § 6028 [4]
Maryland				Md. Code Ann. [Real Prop.] § 8-208(d)(3) [5]
Massachusetts		Mass. Gen. Laws Ann. ch. 186, § 15B(1)(c); ch. 239, § 8A		Mass. Gen. Laws Ann. ch. 186, § 15B(1)(c) [6]

1 Landlords may not charge a late fee until 9 days after rent is due. (Connecticut)
2 To charge a late fee, landlord must maintain an office in the county where the rental unit is located at which tenants can pay rent. If a landlord doesn't have a local office for this purpose, tenant has 3 extra days (beyond the due date) to pay rent before the landlord can charge a late fee. Late fee cannot exceed 5% of rent and cannot be imposed until the rent is more than 5 days late. (Delaware)
3 Late fees cannot exceed $10 per day or $40 per month. (Iowa)
4 Late fees cannot exceed 4% of the amount due for 30 days. Landlord must notify tenants, in writing, of any late fee at the start of the tenancy, and cannot impose it until rent is 15 days late. (Maine)
5 Late fees cannot exceed 5% of the rent due. (Maryland)
6 Late fees, including interest on late rent, may not be imposed until the rent is 30 days late. (Massachusetts)

		State Rent Rules (continued)		
State	**When Rent Is Due**	**Grace Period**	**Where Rent Is Due**	**Late Fees**
Michigan	*Hilsendegen v. Scheich*, 21 N.W. 2d 894 (1885)			
Minnesota				
Mississippi				
Missouri	Mo. Rev. Stat. § 535.060			
Montana	Mont. Code Ann. § 70-24-201(2)(c)		Mont. Code Ann. § 70-24-201(2)(b)	
Nebraska	Neb. Rev. Stat. § 76-1414(3)		Neb. Rev. Stat. § 76-1414(3)	
Nevada	Nev. Rev. Stat. Ann. § 118A.210		Nev. Rev. Stat. Ann. § 118A.210	Nev. Rev. Stat. Ann. § 118A.200(3)(g), (4)(c)
New Hampshire				
New Jersey	N.J. Stat. Ann. § 2A:42-6.1	N.J. Stat. Ann. § 2A:42-6.1		N.J. Stat. Ann. § 2A:42-6.1 [7]
New Mexico	N.M. Stat. Ann. § 47-8-15(B)		N.M. Stat. Ann. § 47-8-15(B)	N.M. Stat. Ann § 47-8-15(D) [8]
New York				
North Carolina		N.C. Gen Stat. § 42-46		N.C. Gen. Stat. § 42-46 [9]
North Dakota	N.D. Cent. Code § 47-16-07			
Ohio				
Oklahoma	Okla. Stat. Ann. tit. 41, § 109	Okla. Stat. Ann. tit. 41, § 132(B)	Okla. Stat. Ann. tit. 41, § 109	*Sun Ridge Investors, Ltd. v. Parker*, 956 P.2d 876 (1998) [10]
Oregon	Or. Rev. Stat. § 90.220	Or. Rev. Stat. § 90.260	Or. Rev. Stat. § 90.220	Or. Rev. Stat. § 90.260 [11]
Pennsylvania				
Rhode Island	R.I. Gen. Laws § 34-18-15(c)	R.I. Gen. Laws § 34-18-35	R.I. Gen. Laws § 34-18-15(c)	
South Carolina	S.C. Code Ann. § 27-40-310(c)		S.C. Code Ann. § 27-40-310(c)	
South Dakota	S.D. Codified Laws Ann. § 43-32-12			
Tennessee	Tenn. Code Ann. § 66-28-201(c)	Tenn. Code Ann. § 66-28-201(d)	Tenn. Code Ann. § 66-28-201(c)	Tenn. Code Ann. § 66-28-201(d) [12]
Texas				
Utah				
Vermont	Vt. Stat. Ann. tit. 9, § 4455			
Virginia	Va. Code Ann. § 55-248.7(C)		Va. Code Ann. § 55-248.7(C)	
Washington				
West Virginia				
Wisconsin				
Wyoming				

7 Landlord must wait until 5 days before charging a late fee. (New Jersey)

8 Late fee may not exceed 10% of the rent specified per rental period. (New Mexico)

9 Late fee cannot be higher than $15 or 5% of the rental payment, whichever is greater, and may not be imposed until the tenant is 5 days late paying rent. (North Carolina)

10 Preset late fees are invalid. (Oklahoma)

11 Landlord must wait 4 days after the rent due date to assess a late fee, and must disclose the late fee policy in the rental agreement. A flat fee must be "reasonable." A daily late fee may not be more than 6% of a reasonable flat fee, and cannot add up to more than 5% of the monthly fee. (Oregon)

12 Landlord can't charge late fee until 5 days have passed. If day five is a Saturday, Sunday or legal holiday, landlord cannot impose a fee if the rent is paid on the next business day. Fee can't exceed 10% of the amount past due. (Tennessee)

State Security Deposit Rules

Here are citations for statutes pertaining to security deposits in each state. Details on various aspects of security deposits are provided in the chapters. You should read your state's statute carefully for more detail.

This table is limited to security deposit statutes. West Virginia does not have statutes on security deposits. That doesn't mean that there is no law on the subject. Court decisions (what lawyers call "case law") in your state may set out quite specific requirements for refunding of deposits, whether they should be held in interest-bearing accounts, and the like. This book does not cover all case or local law. To find out whether courts or local governments in your state have made decisions or ordinances you need to be aware of, you may need to do some legal research on your own.

State	Statute	Limit	Separate Account	Interest	Deadline for Landlord to Itemize and Return Deposit	Exemptions
Alabama	Ala. Code § 35-9A-201	One month's rent, except for pet deposits, deposits to cover undoing tenant's alterations, deposits to cover tenant activities that pose increased liability risks			5 days after termination of tenancy and delivery of possession	
Alaska	Alaska Stat. § 34.03.070	Two months' rent, unless rent exceeds $2,000 per month	✔		14 days if the tenant gives proper notice to terminate tenancy; 30 days if the tenant does not give proper notice	Any rental unit where the rent exceeds $2,000 per month
Arizona	Ariz. Rev. Stat. Ann. § 33-1321	One and one-half months' rent (unless tenant voluntarily agrees to pay more)			14 days	
Arkansas	Ark. Code Ann. §§ 18-16-303 to 18-16-305, 18-17-501	Two months' rent			30 days	Landlord who owns five or fewer rental units, unless these units are managed by a third party for a fee
California	Cal. Civ. Code §§ 1950.5, 1940.5(g)	Two months' rent (unfurnished); 3 months' rent (furnished). Add extra one-half month's rent for waterbed			21 days	
Colorado	Colo. Rev. Stat. §§ 38-12-102 to 38-12-104	No statutory limit			One month, unless lease agreement specifies longer period of time (which may be no more than 60 days); 72 hours (not counting weekends or holidays) if a hazardous condition involving gas equipment requires tenant to vacate	

State	Statute	Limit	Separate Account	Interest	Deadline for Landlord to Itemize and Return Deposit	Exemptions
					State Security Deposit Rules (continued)	
Connecticut	Conn. Gen. Stat. Ann. § 47a-21 to 47a-22a	Two months' rent (tenant under 62 years of age); one month's rent (tenant 62 years of age or older)	✔	✔	30 days, or within 15 days of receiving tenant's forwarding address, whichever is later	
Delaware	Del. Code Ann. tit. 25, § 5514	One month's rent on leases for one year or more; no limit for month-to-month rental agreements (may require additional pet deposit of up to one month's rent)	✔		20 days	
District of Columbia	D.C. Code Ann § 42-3502.17; D.C. Mun. Regs. tit. 14, §§ 308 to 311	One month's rent	✔	✔	45 days	
Florida	Fla. Stat. Ann. §§ 83.49, 83.43 (12)	No statutory limit	✔	[1]	15 to 60 days depending on whether tenant disputes deductions	
Georgia	Ga. Code Ann. §§ 44-7-30 to 44-7-37	No statutory limit	✔		One month	Landlord who owns ten or fewer rental units, unless these units are managed by an outside party
Hawaii	Haw. Rev. Stat. §§ 521-44, 521-42	One month's rent			14 days	
Idaho	Idaho Code § 6-321	No statutory limit			21 days or up to 30 days if landlord and tenant agree	
Illinois	765 Ill. Comp. Stat. 710/0.01 to 715/3	No statutory limit		✔ [2]	30 to 45 days depending on whether tenant disputes deductions or if statement and receipts are furnished	Landlord who owns four or fewer dwelling units
Indiana	Ind. Code Ann. §§ 32-31-3-9 to 32-31-3-19	No statutory limit			45 days	
Iowa	Iowa Code Ann. § 562A.12	Two months' rent	✔	[1]	30 days	
Kansas	Kan. Stat. Ann. §§ 58-2550, 58-2548	One month's rent (unfurnished); one and one-half months' rent (furnished); for pets, add extra one-half month's rent			30 days	

1 Interest payments are not required, but when they are made, certain rules apply.
2 Applies only to landlords with 25 or more rental units.

State Security Deposit Rules (continued)						
State	Statute	Limit	Separate Account	Interest	Deadline for Landlord to Itemize and Return Deposit	Exemptions
Kentucky	Ky. Rev. Stat. Ann. § 383.580	No statutory limit	✔		30 to 60 days depending on whether tenant disputes deductions	
Louisiana	La. Rev. Stat. Ann. §§ 9:3251 to 9:3254	No statutory limit			One month	
Maine	Me. Rev. Stat. Ann. tit. 14, §§ 6031 to 6038	Two months' rent	✔		30 days (if written rental agreement) or 21 days (if tenancy at will)	Entire security deposit law does not apply to rental unit that is part of structure with five or fewer units, one of which is occupied by landlord
Maryland	Md. Code Ann. [Real Prop.] § 8-203, § 8-203.1	Two months' rent	✔	✔	45 days	
Massachusetts	Mass. Gen. Laws Ann. ch. 186, § 15B	One month's rent	✔	✔	30 days	
Michigan	Mich. Comp. Laws §§ 554.602 to 554.616	One and one-half months' rent	✔		30 days	
Minnesota	Minn. Stat. Ann. §§ 504B.175 to 504B.178	No statutory limit		✔	Three weeks after tenant leaves and landlord receives forwarding address; five days if tenant must leave due to building condemnation	
Mississippi	Miss. Code Ann. § 89-8-21	No statutory limit			45 days	
Missouri	Mo. Ann. Stat. § 535.300	Two months' rent			30 days	
Montana	Mont. Code Ann. §§ 70-25-101 to 70-25-206	No statutory limit			30 days 10 days if no deductions	
Nebraska	Neb. Rev. Stat. § 76-1416	One month's rent (no pets); one and one-quarter months' rent (pets)			14 days	
Nevada	Nev. Rev. Stat. Ann. §§ 118A.240 to 118A.250	Three months' rent			30 days	

	State Security Deposit Rules (continued)					
State	**Statute**	**Limit**	**Separate Account**	**Interest**	**Deadline for Landlord to Itemize and Return Deposit**	**Exemptions**
New Hampshire	N.H. Rev. Stat. Ann. §§ 540-A:5 to 540-A:8; 540-B:10	One month's rent or $100, whichever is greater; when landlord and tenant share facilities, no statutory limit	✔	✔[3]	30 days For shared facilities, if the deposit is more than 30 days' rent, landlord must provide written agreement acknowledging receipt and specifying when deposit will be returned—if no written agreement, 20 days after tenant vacates.	Entire security deposit law does not apply to landlord who leases a single-family residence and owns no other rental property, or landlord who leases rental units in an owner-occupied building of five units or fewer (exemption does not apply to any individual unit in owner-occupied building that is occupied by a person 60 years of age or older)
New Jersey	N.J. Stat. Ann. §§ 46:8-19 to 46:8-26	One and one-half months' rent; an additional amount of security deposit, collected annually, no greater than 10% of current security deposit	✔	✔[4]	30 days; five days in case of fire, flood, condemnation, or evacuation	Owner-occupied building with two or fewer units where tenant fails to provide 30 days' written notice to landlord invoking provisions of act
New Mexico	N.M. Stat. Ann. §§ 47-8-18	One month's rent (for rental agreement of less than one year); no limit for leases of one year or more		✔	30 days	
New York	N.Y. Gen. Oblig. Law §§ 7-103 to 7-108	No statutory limit for nonregulated units	✔	✔	Reasonable time	Landlord who rents out non-regulated units in buildings with five or fewer units need not pay interest.
North Carolina	N.C. Gen. Stat. §§ 42-50 to 42-56	One and one-half months' rent for month-to-month rental agreements; two months' rent if term is longer than two months; reasonable, non-refundable pet deposit	✔		30 days	Not applicable to single rooms rented on a weekly, monthly, or annual basis

3   When landlord holds deposit for one year or longer
4   Does not apply when landlord owns fewer than ten rental units, unless required by the Commissioner of Banking and Insurance

State Security Deposit Rules (continued)

State	Statute	Limit	Separate Account	Interest	Deadline for Landlord to Itemize and Return Deposit	Exemptions
North Dakota	N.D. Cent. Code §§ 47-16-07.1, 47-16-07.2	One month's rent (or if tenant has a pet not to exceed the greater of $2,500 or amount equal to two months' rent)	✔	✔	30 days	
Ohio	Ohio Rev. Code Ann. § 5321.16	No statutory limit		✔	30 days	
Oklahoma	Okla. Stat. Ann. tit. 41, § 115	No statutory limit	✔		30 days	
Oregon	Or. Rev. Stat. § 90.300	No statutory limit			31 days	
Pennsylvania	68 Pa. Cons. Stat. Ann. §§ 250.511a to 250.512	Two months' rent for first year of renting; one month's rent during second and subsequent years of renting	✔	✔	30 days	
Rhode Island	R.I. Gen. Laws § 34-18-19	One month's rent			20 days	
South Carolina	S.C. Code Ann. § 27-40-410	No statutory limit			30 days	
South Dakota	S.D. Codified Laws Ann. § 43-32-6.1, § 43-32-24	One month's rent (Higher deposit may be charged if special conditions pose a danger to maintenance of the premises.)			Two weeks to return entire deposit or a portion, and supply reasons for withholding; 45 days for a written, itemized accounting, if tenant requests it	
Tennessee	Tenn. Code Ann. § 66-28-301	No statutory limit	✔		No statutory deadline to return; 10 days to itemize	
Texas	Tex. Prop. Code Ann. §§ 92.101 to 92.109	No statutory limit			30 days	
Utah	Utah Code Ann. §§ 57-17-1 to 57-17-5	No statutory limit			30 days, or within 15 days of receiving tenant's forwarding address, whichever is later	
Vermont	Vt. Stat. Ann. tit. 9, § 4461	No statutory limit			14 days	
Virginia	Va. Code Ann. §§ 55-248.15:1	Two months' rent		✔	45 days	

			State Security Deposit Rules (continued)			
State	**Statute**	**Limit**	**Separate Account**	**Interest**	**Deadline for Landlord to Itemize and Return Deposit**	**Exemptions**
Washington	Wash. Rev. Code Ann. §§ 59.18.260 to 59.18.285	No statutory limit	✔		14 days	
W. Virginia	No statute					
Wisconsin	Wis. Admin. Code ATCP 134.06	No statutory limit			21 days	
Wyoming	Wyo. Stat. §§ 1-21-1207 to 1-21-1208	No statutory limit			30 days, or within 15 days of receiving tenant's forwarding address, whichever is later; 60 days if there is damage	

Current as of July 2007

Required Security Deposit Disclosures

State	Statute	In writing	In the lease	Orally or in writing	Disclosure
Alabama	No statute				
Alaska	Alaska Stat. § 34.03.070(c)			x	Landlord must disclose the conditions under which landlord may withhold all or part of the deposit.
Arizona	No statute				
Arkansas	No statute				
California	Ca. Civil Code §1950.5(f)	x			No earlier than two weeks before tenancy ends, landlord must advise tenant of the right to a pre-move-out inspection and tenant's right to be present.
Colorado	No statute				
Connecticut	No statute				
District of Columbia	D.C. Mun. Regs., tit. 14, § 308.6	x	x		In the lease, rental agreement, or receipt, landlord must state the purpose of the security deposit.
Delaware	Del. Code Ann. Tit. 25, § 5514				The landlord must disclose to the tenant the location of the security deposit account.
Florida	Fla. Stat. Ann. § 83.49(2)	x			Within 30 days of receiving the security deposit, the landlord must disclose whether it will be held in an interest- or non-interest-bearing account; the name of the account depository; and the rate and time of interest payments. Landlord must include a copy of Florida Statutes § 89.49(3).
Georgia	Ga. Code Ann. §§ 44-7-32	x			Landlord must place the deposit in an escrow account in a state or federally regulated depository, and must inform the tenant of the location of this account.
Hawaii	No statute				
Idaho	No statute				
Illinois	No statute				
Indiana	No statute				
Iowa	No statute				
Kansas	No statute				
Kentucky	Ky. Rev. Stat. § 383.580			x	Landlord must disclose where the security deposit is being held and the account number.
Louisiana	No statute				
Maine	Me .Rev. Stat. Ann. tit.14, § 6038			x	Upon request by the tenant, landlord must disclose the name of the institution and the account number where the security deposit is being held.
Maryland	Md. Code Ann. [Real Prop.] § 8-203.1	x			Landlord must provide a receipt that describes tenant's right to move-in and move-out inspections.
Massachusetts	Mass. Gen. Laws Ann. Ch. 186 §15B(3)(a)	x			Within 30 days of receiving security deposit, landlord must disclose the name and location of the bank in which the security deposit has been deposited, and the amount and account number of the deposit
Michigan	No statute				

Required Security Deposit Disclosures (continued)

State	Statute	In writing	In the lease	Orally or in writing	Disclosure
Minnesota	No statute				
Mississippi	No statute				
Missouri	No statute				
Montana	No statute				
Nebraska	No statute				
Nevada	Nev. Rev. Stat. §118A.200(2)(f)		x		Lease or rental agreement must explain the conditions under which the landlord will refund the deposit.
New Hampshire	N.H. Rev. Stat. Ann § 540-A:6I(b) and N.H. Rev. Stat. Ann. § 540-A:6IV(b)	x			Landlord must provide a receipt stating the amount of the deposit and the institution where it will be held, and stating that if tenant finds any conditions in the rental in need of repair, tenant may note them and return the receipt within five days. Upon request, landlord must disclose the account number, the amount on deposit, and the interest rate.
New Jersey	N.J. Stat. Ann. § 46:8-19c			x	Within 30 days of receiving the deposit and specified times thereafter, landlord must disclose the name and address of the banking organization where the deposit is being held, the type of account, current rate of interest, and the amount of the deposit.
New Mexico	No statute				
New York	N.Y. Gen. Oblig. Law § 7-103(3)	x			Landlord must disclose the name and address of the banking organization where the deposit is being held, and the amount of such deposit.
North Carolina	N.C. Gen. Stat. § 42-50			x	Within 30 days of the beginning of the lease term, landlord must disclose the name and address of the banking institution where the deposit is located.
North Dakota	No statute				
Ohio	No statute				
Oklahoma	No statute				
Oregon	No statute				
Pennsylvania	68 Pa. Cons. Stat. Ann. § 250.511b	x			For deposits over $100, landlord must deposit them in a federally or state regulated institution, and give tenant the name and address of the banking institution and the amount of the deposit.
Rhode Island	No statute				
South Carolina	No statute				
South Dakota	No statute				
Tennessee	Tenn. Code Ann. § 66-28-301			x	Landlord must disclose the location of the separate account used by landlord for the deposit.
Texas	No statute				
Utah	Utah Code Ann. § 57-17-2	x			For written leases or rental agreements only, if part of the deposit is nonrefundable, landlord must disclose this feature.

Required Security Deposit Disclosures (continued)					
State	Statute	In writing	In the lease	Orally or in writing	Disclosure
Vermont	No statute				
Virginia	No statute				
Washington	Wash. Rev. Code Ann. § 59.18.260 and Wash. Rev. Code Ann. § 59.81.270		x		Landlord must disclose the circumstances under which all or part of the deposit may be withheld, and must provide a receipt with the name and location of the banking institution where the deposit is being held.
West Virginia	No statute				
Wisconsin	Wis. Admin. Code § 134.06	x			Before accepting the deposit, landlord must inform tenant of tenant's inspection rights.
Wyoming	Wyo. Stat. Ann. § 1-21-1207	x	x		Lease or rental agreement must state whether any portion of a deposit is nonrefundable, and landlord must give tenant written notice of this fact when collecting the deposit.

States That Require Landlords to Pay Interest on Deposits	
Connecticut	Interest payments must be made annually and at termination of tenancy. The interest rate must be equal to the average rate paid on savings deposits by insured commercial banks, as published by the Federal Reserve Board Bulletin, but not less than 1.5%.
Dist. of Columbia	Interest payments at the prevailing statement savings rate must be made at termination of tenancy.
Florida	Interest payments (if any—account need not be interest-bearing) must be made annually and at termination of tenancy. However, no interest is due a tenant who wrongfully terminates the tenancy before the end of the rental term. If landlord is paying interest, details on interest rate and time of payment must be provided in lease or rental agreement.
Illinois	Landlords who rent 25 or more units in either a single building or a complex of buildings located on contiguous properties must pay interest on deposits held for more than six months.
Iowa	Interest payment (if any—account need not be interest-bearing) must be made at termination of tenancy. Interest earned during first five years of tenancy belongs to landlord.
Maryland	Within 45 days of termination of tenancy, interest must be paid (at an annual rate of 3%, not compounded) only on security deposits of $50 or more.
Massachusetts	Landlord must pay tenant 5% interest per year or the amount received from the bank where the deposit has been held. Interest should be paid to the tenant yearly, and within 30 days of termination date. Interest will not accrue for the last month for which rent was paid in advance.
Minnesota	Landlord must pay 1% (simple, noncompounded) annual interest per year. (Rate prior to 8/1/2003 was 3%.) Any interest amount less than $1 is excluded.
New Hampshire	Landlord who holds a security deposit for a year or longer must pay interest at a rate equal to the interest rate paid on regular savings accounts in the New Hampshire bank, savings and loan association or credit union where it is deposited. If a landlord mingles security deposits in a single account, the landlord must pay the actual interest earned proportionately to each tenant. A tenant may request the interest accrued every three years, 30 days before that year's tenancy expires. The landlord must comply with the request within 15 days of the expiration of that year's tenancy.
New Jersey	Landlord with 10 or more units must place security deposit in an insured money market fund account where the investments mature in one year or less, or in another account that pays quarterly interest at a rate comparable to the money market fund. Landlords with fewer than 10 units may place deposit in an interest-bearing account in any New Jersey financial institution insured by the FDIC. All landlords must pay tenant interest earned on account annually or credit it toward payment of rent due.
New Mexico	Landlord who receives more than one month's rent deposit on a year lease must pay the tenant, annually, interest equal to the passbook interest.

States That Require Landlords to Pay Interest on Deposits (continued)	
New York	Interest must be paid at the "prevailing rate" on deposits received from tenants who rent units in buildings containing six or more units. The landlord may retain an administrative fee of 1% per year on the sum deposited. Interest can be subtracted from the rent, paid at the end of the year, or paid at the end of the tenancy according to the tenant's choice.
North Dakota	Landlord must pay interest if the period of occupancy is at least nine months. Money must be held in a federally insured interest-bearing savings or checking account for benefit of the tenant. Interest must be paid upon termination of the lease.
Ohio	Any security deposit in excess of $50 or one month's rent, whichever is greater, must bear interest on the excess at the rate of 5% per annum if the tenant stays for six months or more. Interest must be paid annually and upon termination of tenancy.
Pennsylvania	Tenant who occupies rental unit for two or more years is entitled to interest beginning with the 25th month of occupancy. Landlord must pay tenant interest (minus fee of 1%) at the end of the third and subsequent years of the tenancy.
Virginia	Landlord must accrue interest on all money held as security at an annual rate equal to 4% below the Federal Reserve Board discount rate as of January 1 of each year. No interest is payable unless the landlord holds the deposit for over 13 months after the date of the rental agreement for continuous occupancy of the same unit. Interest begins accruing from the effective date of the rental agreement and must be paid only upon termination of tenancy.

Attachment to Florida Leases and
Rental Agreements (Security Deposits)

Fla. Stat. Ann. § 83.49(3)(a). Upon the vacating of the premises for termination of the lease, if the landlord does not intend to impose a claim on the security deposit, the landlord shall have 15 days to return the security deposit together with interest if otherwise required, or the landlord shall have 30 days to give the tenant written notice by certified mail to the tenant's last known mailing address of his or her intention to impose a claim on the deposit and the reason for imposing the claim. The notice shall contain a statement in substantially the following form:

This is a notice of my intention to impose a claim for damages in the amount of $ _____ upon your security deposit, due to _____.

It is sent to you as required by § 83.49(3), Florida Statutes. You are hereby notified that you must object in writing to this deduction from your security deposit within 15 days from the time you receive this notice or I will be authorized to deduct my claim from your security deposit. Your objection must be sent to _____

_____ (landlord's address).

If the landlord fails to give the required notice within the 30-day period, he forfeits his right to impose a claim upon the security deposit.

(b) Unless the tenant objects to the imposition of the landlord's claim of the amount thereof within 15 days after receipt of the landlord's notice of intention to impose a claim, the landlord may then deduct the amount of his claim and shall remit the balance of the deposit to the tenant within 30 days after the date of the notice of intention to impose a claim for damages.

(c) If either party institutes an action in a court of competent jurisdiction to adjudicate the party's right to the security deposit, the prevailing party is entitled to receive his or her court costs plus a reasonable fee for his or her attorney. The court shall advance the cause on the calendar.

(d) Compliance with this section by an individual or business entity authorized to conduct business in this state, including Florida-licensed real estate brokers and salespersons, shall constitute compliance with all other relevant Florida Statutes pertaining to security deposits held pursuant to a rental agreement or other landlord-tenant relationship. Enforcement personnel shall look solely to this section to determine compliance. This section prevails over any conflicting provisions in chapter 475 and in other sections of the Florida Statutes, and shall operate to permit licensed real estate brokers to disburse security deposits and deposit money without having to comply with the notice and settlement procedures contained in § 475.25(1)(d).

State Laws on Landlord's Access to Rental Property

This is a synopsis of state laws that specify circumstances when a landlord may enter rental premises and the amount of notice required for such entry.

State	State Law Citation	Amount of Notice Required in Nonemergency Situations	Reasons Landlord May Enter				
			To Deal With an Emergency	To Inspect the Premises	To Make Repairs, Alterations, or Improvements	To Show Property to Prospective Tenants or Purchasers	During Tenant's Extended Absence
Alabama	Ala. Code § 35-9A-303 to 304	Two days	✔	✔	✔	✔	✔
Alaska	Alaska Stat. § 34.03.140	24 hours	✔	✔	✔	✔	✔
Arizona	Ariz. Rev. Stat. Ann. § 33-1343	Two days	✔	✔	✔	✔	
Arkansas	Ark. Code Ann. § 18-17-602	No notice specified		✔	✔	✔	
California	Cal. Civ. Code § 1954	24 hours (48 hours for initial move-out inspection)	✔	✔	✔	✔	
Colorado	No statute						
Connecticut	Conn. Gen. Stat. Ann. §§ 47a-16 to 47a-16a	Reasonable notice	✔	✔	✔	✔	✔
Delaware	Del. Code Ann. tit. 25, §§ 5509, 5510	Two days	✔	✔	✔	✔	
District of Columbia	No statute						
Florida	Fla. Stat. Ann. § 83.53	12 hours	✔	✔	✔	✔	✔
Georgia	No statute						
Hawaii	Haw. Rev. Stat. §§ 521-53, 521-70(b)	Two days	✔	✔	✔	✔	✔

			To Deal With an Emergency	To Inspect the Premises	To Make Repairs, Alterations, or Improvements	To Show Property to Prospective Tenants or Purchasers	During Tenant's Extended Absence
State	**State Law Citation**	**Amount of Notice Required in Nonemergency Situations**					
Idaho	No statute						
Illinois	No statute						
Indiana	Ind. Code Ann. § 32-31-5-6(e)	Reasonable notice	✔	✔	✔	✔	
Iowa	Iowa Code Ann. §§ 562A.19, 562A.28, 562A.29	24 hours	✔	✔	✔	✔	✔
Kansas	Kan. Stat. Ann. §§ 58-2557, 58-2565	Reasonable notice	✔	✔	✔	✔	✔
Kentucky	Ky. Rev. Stat. Ann. §§ 383.615, 383.670	Two days	✔	✔	✔	✔	✔
Louisiana	La. Civ. Code art. 2693				✔		
Maine	Me. Rev. Stat. Ann. tit. 14, § 6025	24 hours	✔	✔	✔	✔	
Maryland	No statute						
Massachusetts	Mass. Gen. Laws Ann. ch. 186, § 15B(1)(a)	No notice specified	✔	✔	✔	✔	
Michigan	No statute						
Minnesota	Minn. Stat. Ann. § 504B.211	Reasonable notice	✔	✔	✔	✔	
Mississippi	No statute						

Table title: **State Laws on Landlord's Access to Rental Property (continued)** — with spanning header **Reasons Landlord May Enter**.

State Laws on Landlord's Access to Rental Property (continued)							
			Reasons Landlord May Enter				
State	State Law Citation	Amount of Notice Required in Nonemergency Situations	To Deal With an Emergency	To Inspect the Premises	To Make Repairs, Alterations, or Improvements	To Show Property to Prospective Tenants or Purchasers	During Tenant's Extended Absence
Missouri	No statute						
Montana	Mont. Code Ann. § 70-24-312	24 hours	✔	✔	✔	✔	✔
Nebraska	Neb. Rev. Stat. §§ 76-1423, 76-1432	One day	✔	✔	✔	✔	✔
Nevada	Nev. Rev. Stat. Ann. § 118A.330	24 hours	✔	✔	✔	✔	
New Hampshire	N.H. Rev. Stat. Ann. § 540-A:3	Notice that is adequate under the circumstances	✔	✔	✔	✔	
New Jersey	No statute						
New Mexico	N.M. Stat. Ann. §§ 47-8-24, 47-8-34	24 hours	✔	✔	✔	✔	✔
New York	No statute						
North Carolina	No statute						
North Dakota	N.D. Cent. Code § 47-16-07.3	Reasonable notice	✔	✔	✔	✔	
Ohio	Ohio Rev. Code Ann. §§ 5321.04(A)(8), 5321.05(B)	24 hours	✔	✔	✔	✔	
Oklahoma	Okla. Stat. Ann. tit. 41, § 128	One day	✔	✔	✔	✔	
Oregon	Or. Rev. Stat. § 90.322	24 hours	✔	✔	✔	✔	✔

			Reasons Landlord May Enter				
State	**State Law Citation**	**Amount of Notice Required in Nonemergency Situations**	**To Deal With an Emergency**	**To Inspect the Premises**	**To Make Repairs, Alterations, or Improvements**	**To Show Property to Prospective Tenants or Purchasers**	**During Tenant's Extended Absence**
Pennsylvania	No statute						
Rhode Island	R.I. Gen. Laws § 34-18-26	Two days	✔	✔	✔	✔	✔
South Carolina	S.C. Code Ann. § 27-40-530	24 hours	✔	✔	✔	✔	✔
South Dakota	No statute						
Tennessee	Tenn. Code Ann. § 66-28-403, 66-28-507	No notice specified	✔	✔	✔	✔	✔
Texas	No statute						
Utah	Utah Code Ann. § 57-22-5(2)(c)	No notice specified	✔		✔		
Vermont	Vt. Stat. Ann. tit. 9, § 4460	48 hours	✔	✔	✔	✔	
Virginia	Va. Code Ann. § 55-248.18	24 hours	✔	✔	✔	✔	✔
Washington	Wash. Rev. Code Ann. § 59.18.150	Two days	✔	✔	✔	✔	
West Virginia	No statute						
Wisconsin	Wis. Stat. Ann. § 704.05(2)	Advance notice	✔	✔	✔	✔	
Wyoming	No statute						

State Laws on Landlord's Access to Rental Property (continued)

How to Use the Landlord Rental Forms CD-ROM

Installing the Form Files Onto Your Computer...132
    Windows 2000, XP, and Vista Users 132
    Macintosh Users...132

Using the Word Processing Files to Create Documents..133
    Step 1: Opening a File..133
    Step 2: Editing Your Document..133
    Step 3: Printing Out the Document..134
    Step 4: Saving Your Document..134

Using Print-Only Files...134
    Step 1: Opening PDF Files..135
    Step 2: Printing PDF files...135
    Step 3: Filling in PDF files..135

Files Included on the CD-ROM..136

The tear-out forms in Appendix C are included on a CD-ROM in the back of the book. This CD-ROM, which can be used with Windows computers, installs files that you use with software programs that are already installed on your computer. It is not a standalone software program. Please read this appendix and the README.TXT file included on the CD-ROM for instructions on using the Forms CD.

Note to Mac users: This CD-ROM and its files should also work on Macintosh computers. Please note, however, that Nolo cannot provide technical support for non-Windows users.

How to View the README File

If you do not know how to view the file README. TXT, insert the Forms CD-ROM into your computer's CD-ROM drive and follow these instructions.

- Windows 2000, XP, and Vista: (1) On your PC's desktop, double click the My Computer icon; (2) double click the icon for the CD-ROM drive into which the Forms CD-ROM was inserted; (3) double click the file README.TXT.

- Macintosh: (1) On your Mac desktop, double click the icon for the CD-ROM that you inserted and (2) double click the file README.TXT.

While the README file is open, print it out by using the Print command in the File menu.

Two different kinds of forms are on the CD-ROM:

- Word processing (RTF) forms that you can open, complete, print, and save with your word processing program (see "Using the Word Processing Files to Create Documents," below), and

- Forms (PDF) that can be viewed only with Adobe Acrobat Reader 4.0 or higher (see "Using Print-Only Files," below). These forms are designed to be printed out and filled in by hand or with a typewriter.

See the end of this appendix for a list of forms, their file names, and their file formats.

Installing the Form Files Onto Your Computer

Before you can do anything with the files on the CD-ROM, you need to install them onto your hard disk. In accordance with U.S. copyright laws, remember that copies of the CD-ROM and its files are for your personal use only.

Insert the Forms CD and do the following:

Windows 2000, XP, and Vista Users

Follow the instructions that appear on the screen. (If nothing happens when you insert the Forms CD-ROM, then (1) double click the My Computer icon; (2) double click the icon for the CD-ROM drive into which the Forms CD-ROM was inserted; (3) double click the file WELCOME. EXE.)

By default, all the files are installed to the \Rental Forms folder in the \Program Files folder of your computer. A folder called "Rental Forms" is added to the "Programs" folder of the Start menu.

Macintosh Users

Step 1: If the "Rental Forms" window is not open, open it by double clicking the "Rental Forms" icon.

Step 2: Select the "Rental Forms" folder icon.

Step 3: Drag and drop the folder icon onto the icon of your hard disk.

Using the Word Processing Files to Create Documents

This section concerns the files for forms that can be opened and edited with your word processing program.

All word processing forms come in rich text format. These files have the extension ".RTF." For example, the tenant references form discussed in Chapter 3 is on the file References.rtf. All forms, their file names, and their file formats are listed at the end of this appendix.

RTF files can be read by most recent word processing programs including all versions of MS Word for Windows and Macintosh, WordPad for Windows, and recent versions of WordPerfect for Windows and Macintosh.

To use a form from the CD to create your documents you must: (1) open a file in your word processor or text editor; (2) edit the form by filling in the required information; (3) print it out; (4) rename and save your revised file.

The following are general instructions. However, each word processor uses different commands to open, format, save, and print documents. Please read your word processor's manual for specific instructions on performing these tasks.

Do not call Nolo's technical support if you have questions on how to use your word processor or computer.

Step 1: Opening a File

There are three ways to open the word processing files included on the CD-ROM after you have installed them onto your computer.

Windows users can open a file by selecting its "shortcut" as follows: (1) Click the Windows "Start" button; (2) open the "Programs" folder; (3) open the "Rental Forms" subfolder; (4) open the "RTF" subfolder; (5) click the shortcut to the form you want to work with.

Both Windows and Macintosh users can open a file directly by double clicking on it. Use My Computer or Windows Explorer (Windows 2000, XP, or Vista) or the Finder (Macintosh) to go to the folder you installed or copied the CD-ROM's files to. Then, double click the specific file you want to open.

You can also open a file from within your word processor. To do this, you must first start your word processor. Then, go to the File menu and choose the Open command. This opens a dialog box where you will tell the program (1) the type of file you want to open (*.RTF) and (2) the location and name of the file (you will need to navigate through the directory tree to get to the folder on your hard disk where the CD's files have been installed).

Where Are the Files Installed?

Windows Users: RTF files are installed by default to a folder named \Rental Forms\RTF in the \Program Files folder of your computer.

Macintosh Users: RTF files are located in the "RTF" folder within the "Rental Forms" folder.

Step 2: Editing Your Document

Fill in the appropriate information according to the instructions and sample agreements in the book. Underlines are used to indicate where you need to enter your information, frequently followed by instructions in brackets. Be sure to delete the underlines and instructions from your edited document. You will also want to make sure that any signature lines in your completed documents appear on a page with at least some text from the document itself.

Editing Forms That Have Optional or Alternative Text

Some of the forms have check boxes before text. The check boxes indicate:

- Optional text, where you choose whether to include or exclude the given text.
- Alternative text, where you select one alternative to include and exclude the other alternatives.

If you are using the tear-out forms in Appendix C, you simply mark the appropriate box to make your choice.

If you are using the Forms CD, however, we recommend that instead of marking the check boxes, you do the following:

Optional text

If you *don't want* to include optional text, just delete it from your document.

If you *do want* to include optional text, just leave it in your document.

In either case, delete the check box itself as well as the italicized instructions that the text is optional.

Alternative text

First delete all the alternatives that you do not want to include.

Then delete the remaining check boxes, as well as the italicized instructions that you need to select one of the alternatives provided.

Step 3: Printing Out the Document

Use your word processor's or text editor's "Print" command to print out your document.

Step 4: Saving Your Document

After filling in the form, use the "Save As" command to save and rename the file. Because all the files are "read-only," you will not be able to use the "Save" command. This is for your protection. If you save the file without renaming it, the underlines that indicate where you need to enter your information will be lost and you will not be able to create a new document with this file without recopying the original file from the CD-ROM.

Using Print-Only Files

Electronic copies of useful forms are included on the CD-ROM in Adobe Acrobat PDF format. You must have the Adobe Reader installed on your computer to use these forms. Adobe Reader is available for all types of Windows and Macintosh systems. If you don't already have this software, you can download it for free at www.adobe.com.

All forms, their file names, and their file formats are listed at the end of this appendix.

These forms cannot be filled out using your computer. To create your document using these files, you must: (1) open the file; (2) print it out; (3) complete it by hand or typewriter.

Step 1: Opening PDF Files

PDF files, like the word processing files, can be opened one of three ways.

Windows users can open a file by selecting its "shortcut" as follows: (1) Click the Windows "Start" button; (2) open the "Programs" folder; (3) open the "Rental Forms" subfolder; (4) open the "PDF" folder; (5) click the shortcut to the form you want to work with.

Both Windows and Macintosh users can open a file directly by double clicking on it. Use My Computer or Windows Explorer (Windows 2000, XP, or Vista) or the Finder (Macintosh) to go to the folder you created and copied the CD-ROM's files to. Then, double click the specific file you want to open.

You can also open a PDF file from within Adobe Reader. To do this, you must first start Reader. Then, go to the File menu and choose the Open command. This opens a dialog box where you will tell the program the location and name of the file (you will need to navigate through the directory tree to get to the folder on your hard disk where the CD's files have been installed).

Where Are the PDF Files Installed?

- **Windows Users:** PDF files are installed by default to a folder named \Rental Forms\ PDF in the \Program Files folder of your computer.
- **Macintosh Users:** PDF files are located in the "PDF" folder within the "Rental Forms" folder.

Step 2: Printing PDF files

Choose Print from the Adobe Reader File menu. This will open the Print dialog box. In the "Print Range" section of the Print dialog box, select the appropriate print range, then click OK.

Step 3: Filling in PDF files

The PDF files cannot be filled out using your computer. To create your document using one of these files, you must first print it out (see Step 2, above), and then complete it by hand or typewriter.

Files Included on the CD-ROM

The following files are in rich text format (RTF):

File Name	Form Title
Acceptance.rtf	Notice of Conditional Acceptance Based on Credit Report or Other Information
Application.rtf	Rental Application
CheckConsent.rtf	Consent to Contact References and Perform Credit Check
Checklist.rtf	Landlord/Tenant Checklist
Denial.rtf	Notice of Denial Based on Credit Report or Other Information
FixedLease.rtf	Fixed-Term Residential Lease
Mensual.rtf	Month-to-Month Residential Rental Agreement (Spanish Version)
MonthToMonth.rtf	Month-to-Month Residential Rental Agreement
MoveIn.rtf	Move-In Letter
MoveOut.rtf	Move-Out Letter
PlazoFijo.rtf	Fixed-Term Residential Lease (Spanish Version)
References.rtf	Tenant References

The following files are in Adobe Acrobat PDF Format:

File Name	Form/document Title
Application.pdf	Rental Application
leadpdfe.pdf	*Protect Your Family From Lead in Your Home* Pamphlet
leadpdfs.pdf	*Protect Your Family From Lead in Your Home* Pamphlet (Spanish Version)
lesr_eng.pdf	*Disclosure of Information on Lead-Based Paint or Lead-Based Paint Hazards*
MoveNotice.pdf	Tenant's Notice of Intent to Move Out
spanless.pdf	*Disclosure of Information on Lead-Based Paint or Lead-Based Paint Hazards* (Spanish Version)
DiscrimLaw.pdf	Complying With Discrimination Laws (eGuide)

Tear-Out Landlord Rental Forms

Form Name	Chapter
Month-to-Month Residential Rental Agreement	2
Month-to-Month Residential Rental Agreement (Spanish version)	2
Fixed-Term Residential Lease	2
Fixed-Term Residential Lease (Spanish version)	2
Disclosure of Information on Lead-Based Paint or Lead-Based Paint Hazards	2
Disclosure of Information on Lead-Based Paint or Lead-Based Paint Hazards (Spanish version)	2
Protect Your Family From Lead in Your Home Pamphlet	2
Protect Your Family From Lead in Your Home Pamphlet (Spanish version)	2
Rental Application	3
Consent to Contact References and Perform Credit Check	3
Tenant References	3
Notice of Denial Based on Credit Report and Other Information	3
Notice of Conditional Acceptance Based on Credit Report or Other Information	3
Landlord-Tenant Checklist	4
Move-In Letter	4
Tenant's Notice of Intent to Move Out	5
Move-Out Letter	5

Month-to-Month Residential Rental Agreement

Clause 1. Identification of Landlord and Tenant

This Agreement is entered into between _____
_____ [Tenant] and
_____ [Landlord].
Each Tenant is jointly and severally liable for the payment of rent and performance of all other terms of this Agreement.

Clause 2. Identification of Premises

Subject to the terms and conditions in this Agreement, Landlord rents to Tenant, and Tenant rents from Landlord, for residential purposes only, the premises located at _____
_____ [the premises], together with the following furnishings and appliances: _____
_____.

Rental of the premises also includes _____
_____.

Clause 3. Limits on Use and Occupancy

The premises are to be used only as a private residence for Tenant(s) listed in Clause 1 of this Agreement, and their minor children. Occupancy by guests for more than _____ is prohibited without Landlord's written consent and will be considered a breach of this Agreement.

Clause 4. Term of the Tenancy

The rental will begin on _____, and continue on a month-to-month basis. Landlord may terminate the tenancy or modify the terms of this Agreement by giving the Tenant _____ days' written notice. Tenant may terminate the tenancy by giving the Landlord _____ days' written notice.

Clause 5. Payment of Rent

Regular monthly rent

Tenant will pay to Landlord a monthly rent of $_____, payable in advance on the first day of each month, except when that day falls on a weekend or legal holiday, in which case rent is due on the next business day. Rent will be paid in the following manner unless Landlord designates otherwise:

Delivery of payment.

Rent will be paid:

☐ by mail, to _____

☐ in person, at _____

Form of payment.

Landlord will accept payment in these forms:

☐ personal check made payable to _____

☐ cashier's check made payable to _____

☐ credit card

☐ money order

☐ cash

Prorated first month's rent.

For the period from Tenant's move-in date, _____, through the end of the

month, Tenant will pay to Landlord the prorated monthly rent of $_____. This amount will be

paid on or before the date the Tenant moves in.

Clause 6. Late Charges

If Tenant fails to pay the rent in full before the end of the _____ day after it's due, Tenant will pay

Landlord a late charge as follows: _____

_____.

Landlord does not waive the right to insist on payment of the rent in full on the date it is due.

Clause 7. Returned Check and Other Bank Charges

If any check offered by Tenant to Landlord in payment of rent or any other amount due under this Agreement is

returned for lack of sufficient funds, a "stop payment," or any other reason, Tenant will pay Landlord a returned

check charge of $_____.

Clause 8. Security Deposit

On signing this Agreement, Tenant will pay to Landlord the sum of $_____ as a security

deposit. Tenant may not, without Landlord's prior written consent, apply this security deposit to the last

month's rent or to any other sum due under this Agreement. Within _____

after Tenant has vacated the premises, returned keys, and provided Landlord with a forwarding address,

Landlord will return the deposit in full or give Tenant an itemized written statement of the reasons for, and the

dollar amount of, any of the security deposit retained by Landlord, along with a check for any deposit balance.

Clause 9. Utilities

Tenant will pay all utility charges, except for the following, which will be paid by Landlord:

_____

_____.

Clause 10. Assignment and Subletting

Tenant will not sublet any part of the premises or assign this Agreement without the prior written consent of Landlord.

Clause 11. Tenant's Maintenance Responsibilities

Tenant will: (1) keep the premises clean, sanitary, and in good condition and, upon termination of the tenancy, return the premises to Landlord in a condition identical to that which existed when Tenant took occupancy, except for ordinary wear and tear; (2) immediately notify Landlord of any defects or dangerous conditions in and about the premises of which Tenant becomes aware; and (3) reimburse Landlord, on demand by Landlord, for the cost of any repairs to the premises damaged by Tenant or Tenant's guests or business invitees through misuse or neglect.

Tenant has examined the premises, including appliances, fixtures, carpets, drapes, and paint, and has found them to be in good, safe, and clean condition and repair, except as noted in the Landlord-Tenant Checklist.

Clause 12. Repairs and Alterations by Tenant

  a. Except as provided by law, or as authorized by the prior written consent of Landlord, Tenant will not make any repairs or alterations to the premises, including nailing holes in the walls or painting the rental unit.

  b. Tenant will not, without Landlord's prior written consent, alter, rekey, or install any locks to the premises or install or alter any burglar alarm system. Tenant will provide Landlord with a key or keys capable of unlocking all such rekeyed or new locks as well as instructions on how to disarm any altered or new burglar alarm system.

Clause 13. Violating Laws and Causing Disturbances

Tenant is entitled to quiet enjoyment of the premises. Tenant and guests or invitees will not use the premises or adjacent areas in such a way as to: (1) violate any law or ordinance, including laws prohibiting the use, possession, or sale of illegal drugs; (2) commit waste (severe property damage); or (3) create a nuisance by annoying, disturbing, inconveniencing, or interfering with the quiet enjoyment and peace and quiet of any other tenant or nearby resident.

Clause 14. Pets

No animal, bird, or other pet will be kept on the premises, even temporarily, except properly trained service animals needed by blind, deaf, or disabled persons and _____ under the following conditions: _____

_____

_____ .

Clause 15. Landlord's Right to Access

Landlord or Landlord's agents may enter the premises in the event of an emergency, to make repairs or improvements, or to show the premises to prospective buyers or tenants. Landlord may also enter the premises to conduct an annual inspection to check for safety or maintenance problems. Except in cases of emergency, Tenant's abandonment of the premises, court order, or where it is impractical to do so, Landlord shall give Tenant _____ notice before entering.

Clause 16. Extended Absences by Tenant

Tenant will notify Landlord in advance if Tenant will be away from the premises for _____ or more consecutive days. During such absence, Landlord may enter the premises at times reasonably necessary to maintain the property and inspect for needed repairs.

Clause 17. Possession of the Premises

a. *Tenant's failure to take possession.*

If, after signing this Agreement, Tenant fails to take possession of the premises, Tenant will still be responsible for paying rent and complying with all other terms of this Agreement.

b. *Landlord's failure to deliver possession.*

If Landlord is unable to deliver possession of the premises to Tenant for any reason not within Landlord's control, including, but not limited to, partial or complete destruction of the premises, Tenant will have the right to terminate this Agreement upon proper notice as required by law. In such event, Landlord's liability to Tenant will be limited to the return of all sums previously paid by Tenant to Landlord.

Clause 18. Tenant Rules and Regulations

☐ Tenant acknowledges receipt of, and has read a copy of, tenant rules and regulations, which are labeled Attachment A and attached to and incorporated into this Agreement by this reference.

Clause 19. Payment of Court Costs and Attorney Fees in a Lawsuit

In any action or legal proceeding to enforce any part of this Agreement, the prevailing party ☐ shall not / ☐ shall recover reasonable attorney fees and court costs.

Clause 20. Disclosures

Tenant acknowledges that Landlord has made the following disclosures regarding the premises:

☐ Disclosure of Information on Lead-Based Paint and/or Lead-Based Paint Hazards

☐ Other disclosures: _____

_____

_____

_____

_____ .

Clause 21. Authority to Receive Legal Papers

The Landlord, any person managing the premises, and anyone designated by the Landlord are authorized to accept service of process and receive other notices and demands, which may be delivered to:

☐ The Landlord, at the following address: _____

_____ .

☐ The manager, at the following address: _____

_____ .

☐ The following person, at the following address: _____

_____ .

Clause 22. Additional Provisions

Additional provisions are as follows: _____

_____

_____

_____

_____

_____

_____

_____

Clause 23. Validity of Each Part

If any portion of this Agreement is held to be invalid, its invalidity will not affect the validity or enforceability of any other provision of this Agreement.

Clause 24. Grounds for Termination of Tenancy

The failure of Tenant or Tenant's guests or invitees to comply with any term of this Agreement, or the misrepresentation of any material fact on Tenant's Rental Application, is grounds for termination of the tenancy, with appropriate notice to Tenant and procedures as required by law.

Clause 25. Entire Agreement

This document constitutes the entire Agreement between the parties, and no promises or representations, other than those contained here and those implied by law, have been made by Landlord or Tenant. Any modifications to this Agreement must be in writing signed by Landlord and Tenant.

_____

| Date | Landlord or Landlord's Agent | Title |

_____

Street Address

_____

| City | State | Zip Code | Phone |

_____

| Date | Tenant | | Phone |

_____

| Date | Tenant | | Phone |

_____

Contrato Mensual de Arrendamiento

Cláusula 1. Identificación del Arrendador y de los Inquilinos.

Este Contrato se hace _____, entre _____

_____ [Inquilinos] y

_____ [Arrendador]. Cada

Inquilino es conjunta y seriamente responsable del pago de renta y del cumplimiento de todos los demás

términos de este Contrato.

Cláusula 2. Identificación de la Propiedad.

De acuerdo con los términos y condiciones referidas en este Contrato, el Arrendador renta al Inquilino, y éste

renta del Arrendador, sólamente para residir, la propiedad ubicada en _____

_____ , [la propiedad],

junto con el mobiliario y los aparatos electrodomésticos siguientes: _____

_____

La renta de la propiedad también incluye _____

_____ .

Cláusula 3. Límitaciones en el Uso y Ocupación.

La propiedad se utilizará sólo como residencia privada por el Inquilino designado en la Cláusula 1 de este

Contrato y sus hijos menores. Está prohibido que invitados habiten la propiedad por más de

_____, excepto con previo consentimiento por escrito del Arrendador. De lo contrario,

será considerado como una violación a este Contrato.

Cláusula 4. Período de Arrendamiento.

La renta comenzará el día _____ de _____ de _____, y podrá continuarse el

arrendamiento, mediante la renovación por cada mes. El Arrendador puede dar por terminado este Contrato o

modificar sus términos, siempre que notifique por escrito, al Inquilino, con _____

días de anticipación. El Inquilino puede terminar este Contrato, notificándoselo al Arrendador por escrito y con

_____ días de anticipación.

Cláusula 5. Renta y Fechas de Pago.

Renta Regular Mensual.

El Inquilino pagará por adelantado, una renta mensual de $ _____ , el primer día del mes; excepto

cuando éste sea en un fin de semana o en un día feriado oficial, en cuyo caso deberá ser pagada el próximo día

laboral. Si no existe otra decisión por parte del Arrendador, la renta deberá ser pagada de la manera siguiente:

Entrega de pago.

El arriendo será pagado:

☐ Por correo, dirigido a _____

☐ Personalmente, en _____

Forma de Pago.

El Arrendador recibirá los pagos en:

☐ Cheque Personal escrito en favor de _____

☐ Cheque de Caja escrito en favor de _____

☐ Tarjeta de Crédito

☐ Giro Postal

☐ Efectivo

Prorrateo del primer mes de renta.

Para el período comenzando con la fecha en que se mudará el Inquilino, el día _____ de

_____ de _____ , hasta el fin del mes en curso, el Inquilino pagará al

Arrendador la renta mensual prorrateada de $ _____ . Esta suma se pagará antes o en la fecha en

que se mude el Inquilino a la propiedad.

Cláusula 6. Cobros por Mora.

Si el Inquilino falla en el pago total de la renta, antes del final del día siguiente a la fecha de pago, tendrá que

pagar costos por atrasos como se explica a continuación: _____

_____ .

El Arrendador no descartará el derecho de insistir en el pago total de la renta en la fecha debida.

Cláusula 7. Pagos por Cheques Sin Fondo y Recargos Bancarios.

En el caso de cualquier cheque, ofrecido por el Inquilino al Arrendador como pago de renta o cualquier otra

suma debida bajo este Contrato, sea regresado por insuficiencia de fondos, un "paro de pago," o cualquier otra

razón, el Inquilino deberá pagar un recargo por la cantidad de $ _____ .

Cláusula 8. Depósito de Garantía.

Al firmar el presente Contrato, el Inquilino pagará al Arrendador, la cantidad de $ _____ como

depósito de seguridad. Este depósito no puede aplicarse al último mes de renta o a cualquier cantidad

debida bajo este Contrato; excepto con previo consentimiento por escrito del Arrendador. Dentro de

_____ , después de que el Inquilino haya desocupado la propiedad, haya

entregado las llaves y proporcionado la dirección donde contactarse, el Arrendador le entregará el depósito

en su totalidad o le detallará de manera escrita, las razones y la cantidad que es retenida por él, junto con un

cheque por la cantidad de su diferencia.

Cláusula 9. Servicios Públicos.

El Inquilino pagará todos los servicios públicos, exceptuando los siguientes, los cuales serán pagados por el

Arrendador: _____

_____ .

Cláusula 10. Prohibición de Traspaso o Subarrendamiento.

El Inquilino no puede subarrendar cualquier parte de la propiedad o traspasar este Contrato, sin previo

consentimiento por escrito del Arrendador.

Cláusula 11. Responsabilidad del Inquilino de Mantenimiento de la Propiedad.

El Inquilino acepta: (1) mantener la propiedad limpia e higiénica, en buena condición, y cuando el arrendamiento

termine, regresar la propiedad al Arrendador en idéntica condición a la que existía cuando la habitaron,

exceptuando el deterioro causado por el uso; (2) Notificar de inmediato al Arrendador, sobre cualquier defecto

o condición peligrosa que note en o alrededor de la propiedad; y (3) reembolsar al Arrendador, bajo demanda de

éste, los costos de cualquier reparación de daños a la propiedad, ocasionados por uso indebido o negligencia del

Inquilino o sus invitados.

El Inquilino ha revisado la propiedad, incluyendo los aparatos electrodomésticos, accesorios, alfombras,

cortinas, y pintura, y los ha encontrado en buenas condiciones, seguras, y limpias, exceptuando las que están en

la Lista Arrendador-Inquilino.

Cláusula 12. Reparaciones y Modificaciones Hechas por el Inquilino.

a. Exceptuando lo provisto por la ley o con la autorización previa y por escrito del Arrendador, el Inquilino no debe hacer modificaciones o reparaciones en la propiedad, incluído el hacer hoyos en las paredes o pintar el lugar.

b. El Inquilino no debe alterar las cerraduras, ni cambiarlas, ni instalar o modificar el sistema de alarma; excepto que haya recibido del Arrendador, una autorización previa y por escrito. El Inquilino deberá proveer al Arrendador una copia de llave o llaves para abrir cada cerradura modificada o nueva, así como instrucciones de cómo desarmar un sistema de alarma modificado o nuevo.

Cláusula 13. Causar Disturbios y Violaciones a la Ley.

El Inquilino tiene derecho al goce pacífico de la propiedad. Este y sus invitados no deben usar la propiedad o áreas aledañas, de manera que: (1) Viole cualquier ley o reglamento, incluyendo leyes que prohiben el uso, posesión o venta ilegal de drogas; (2) Permite el uso abusivo de la propiedad (daño serio a la propiedad); o (3) Cree un estorbo al molestar, provocar disturbios, provocar inconvenientes, o interferir en el disfrute de paz y tranquilidad de otros inquilinos o vecinos.

Cláusula 14. Mascotas.

No se permite, ni siquiera temporalmente, tener ningún animal, pájaro, u otros animales en la propiedad, excepto animales de servicio _____

y _____ bajo las

condiciones siguientes: _____

_____

_____ .

Cláusula 15. Derecho del Arrendador al Acceso a la Propiedad.

El Arrendador o agentes de éste pueden entrar a la propiedad, en caso de emergencia, para hacer reparaciones o mejoras, o para mostrar la propiedad a potenciales nuevos inquilinos o compradores en perspectiva. También podrá entrar para la inspección anual para revisar la seguridad o chequear problemas de mantenimiento. Excepto en caso de emergencia, por el abandono de la propiedad por parte del Inquilino, orden de la corte, o cuando no sea práctico, el Arrendador deberá notificarle al Inquilino de su intención de entrar a la propiedad con _____ de anticipación.

Cláusula 16. Ausencias Prolongadas del Inquilino.

El Inquilino deberá previamente notificar al Arrendador, si estará ausente de la propiedad por _____ días consecutivos o más. Durante este tiempo, el Arrendador podrá entrar, cuando sea necesario, a la propiedad para inspeccionarla, para mantenimiento o para reparaciones necesarias.

Cláusula 17. Tomar Posesión de la Propiedad.

    a.   Falla del Inquilino en tomar posesión de la propiedad.

        Si después de haber firmado este Contrato, el Inquilino no toma posesión de la propiedad, aún será responsable por pago de la renta y cumplimiento de todos los demás términos de este Contrato.

    b.   Falla del Arrendador en entregar la propiedad.

        Si el Arrendador no puede entregar la posesión de la propiedad al Inquilino, por cualquier razón fuera de su control, incluyendo, pero no limitado a, destrucción parcial o completa de la propiedad, el Inquilino tendrá el derecho de terminar este Contrato, mediante aviso previo y apropiado como lo señala la ley. En tal situación, la responsabilidad del Arrendador hacia el Inquilino, estará limitada a la devolución de todas las cantidades previamente pagadas por el Inquilino al Arrendador.

Cláusula 18. Normas y Regulaciones del Inquilino.

    ☐ El Inquilino reconoce lo recibido y que ha leído una copia de las Normas y Regulaciones del Inquilino; las cuales como referencia, están adjuntas e incorporadas al presente Contrato.

Cláusula 19. Pago del Abogado y Costos de la Corte en Caso de un Juicio.

    En cualquier acción jurídico-legal para hacer cumplir total o parcialmente este Contrato, la parte prevaleciente

    ☐ No deberá / ☐ Deberá recuperar honorarios justos del abogado y costos de la corte.

Cláusula 20. Divulgaciones.

    El Inquilino reconoce que el Arrendador le ha hecho las siguientes divulgaciones con respecto a la propiedad:

    ☐ Distribución de información sobre pintura a base de plomo y/o los peligros de este tipo de pintura.

    ☐ Otras divulgaciones:

    _____

    _____

    _____ .

Cláusula 21. Personal Autorizado para Recibir Documentos Legales.

    El Arrendador, la persona que administre la propiedad, o a quien haya designado el Arrendador, están autorizados para aceptar servicio de proceso, y recibir otras noticias y demandas, las cuales pueden ser entregadas a:

    ☐ El Arrendador, a la siguiente dirección: _____

    _____

    ☐ El Administrador, a la siguiente dirección: _____

    _____

    ☐ A la persona designada, a la siguiente dirección: _____

    _____

Cláusula 22. Disposiciones Adicionales.

Disposiciones adicionales son las siguientes: _____

_____

_____

_____

_____

_____

Cláusula 23. Validez de las Cláusulas de este Contrato.

Si cualquier cláusula de este Contrato es invalidado, ésto no afectará la validez o cumplimiento de las partes restantes de este Contrato.

Cláusula 24. Razones para Cancelar el Contrato de Arrendamiento.

El incumplimiento de cualesquiera de los términos de este Contrato, por parte del Inquilino o sus invitados o la relación Falsa de un hecho esencial en la solicitud del Inquilino, será razón para dar por cancelado el Contrato de arrendamiento, seguido con la debida notificación al Inquilino, de acuerdo con lo requerido por la ley.

Cláusula 25. Contrato Completo.

Este documento constituye el Contrato completo entre las partes, y el Arrendador y el Inquilino no han hecho otro compromiso, a no ser los contenidos en este Contrato o los señalados por la ley. Cualquier modificación al presente documento, debe ser por escrito y firmado por ambas partes.

_____ _____ _____
Fecha   Arrendador o su representante   Título

_____
Número y Nombre de la Calle

_____ _____ _____ _____
Ciudad   Estado   Código Postal Teléfono

_____ _____ _____
Fecha   Nombre del Inquilino   Teléfono

_____ _____ _____
Fecha   Nombre del Inquilino   Teléfono

_____ _____ _____
Fecha   Nombre del Inquilino   Teléfono

Fixed-Term Residential Lease

Clause 1. Identification of Landlord and Tenant

This Agreement is entered into between _____

_____ [Tenant] and

_____ [Landlord].

Each Tenant is jointly and severally liable for the payment of rent and performance of all other terms of this Agreement.

Clause 2. Identification of Premises

Subject to the terms and conditions in this Agreement, Landlord rents to Tenant, and Tenant rents from Landlord, for residential purposes only, the premises located at _____

_____ [the premises],

together with the following furnishings and appliances: _____

_____

_____.

Rental of the premises also includes _____

_____

_____.

Clause 3. Limits on Use and Occupancy

The premises are to be used only as a private residence for Tenant(s) listed in Clause 1 of this Agreement, and their minor children. Occupancy by guests for more than _____

is prohibited without Landlord's written consent and will be considered a breach of this Agreement.

Clause 4. Term of the Tenancy

The term of the rental will begin on _____ , and end on _____

_____ . If Tenant vacates before the term ends, Tenant will be liable for the balance of the rent for the remainder of the term.

Clause 5. Payment of Rent

Regular monthly rent

Tenant will pay to Landlord a monthly rent of $_____ , payable in advance on the first day of each month, except when that day falls on a weekend or legal holiday, in which case rent is due on the next business day. Rent will be paid in the following manner unless Landlord designates otherwise:

Delivery of payment.

Rent will be paid:

☐ by mail, to _____

☐ in person, at _____

Form of payment.

Landlord will accept payment in these forms:

☐ personal check made payable to _____

☐ cashier's check made payable to _____

☐ credit card

☐ money order

☐ cash

Prorated first month's rent.

For the period from Tenant's move-in date, _____, through the end of the

month, Tenant will pay to Landlord the prorated monthly rent of $_____. This amount will be

paid on or before the date the Tenant moves in.

Clause 6. Late Charges

If Tenant fails to pay the rent in full before the end of the _____ day after it's due, Tenant will pay

Landlord a late charge as follows: _____

_____.

Landlord does not waive the right to insist on payment of the rent in full on the date it is due.

Clause 7. Returned Check and Other Bank Charges

If any check offered by Tenant to Landlord in payment of rent or any other amount due under this Agreement is

returned for lack of sufficient funds, a "stop payment," or any other reason, Tenant will pay Landlord a returned

check charge of $_____.

Clause 8. Security Deposit

On signing this Agreement, Tenant will pay to Landlord the sum of $_____ as a security

deposit. Tenant may not, without Landlord's prior written consent, apply this security deposit to the last

month's rent or to any other sum due under this Agreement. Within _____

after Tenant has vacated the premises, returned keys, and provided Landlord with a forwarding address,

Landlord will return the deposit in full or give Tenant an itemized written statement of the reasons for, and the

dollar amount of, any of the security deposit retained by Landlord, along with a check for any deposit balance.

Clause 9. Utilities

Tenant will pay all utility charges, except for the following, which will be paid by Landlord:

_____

_____ .

Clause 10. Assignment and Subletting

Tenant will not sublet any part of the premises or assign this Agreement without the prior written consent of Landlord.

Clause 11. Tenant's Maintenance Responsibilities

Tenant will: (1) keep the premises clean, sanitary, and in good condition and, upon termination of the tenancy, return the premises to Landlord in a condition identical to that which existed when Tenant took occupancy, except for ordinary wear and tear; (2) immediately notify Landlord of any defects or dangerous conditions in and about the premises of which Tenant becomes aware; and (3) reimburse Landlord, on demand by Landlord, for the cost of any repairs to the premises damaged by Tenant or Tenant's guests or business invitees through misuse or neglect.

Tenant has examined the premises, including appliances, fixtures, carpets, drapes, and paint, and has found them to be in good, safe, and clean condition and repair, except as noted in the Landlord-Tenant Checklist.

Clause 12. Repairs and Alterations by Tenant

a. Except as provided by law, or as authorized by the prior written consent of Landlord, Tenant will not make any repairs or alterations to the premises, including nailing holes in the walls or painting the rental unit.

b. Tenant will not, without Landlord's prior written consent, alter, rekey, or install any locks to the premises or install or alter any burglar alarm system. Tenant will provide Landlord with a key or keys capable of unlocking all such rekeyed or new locks as well as instructions on how to disarm any altered or new burglar alarm system.

Clause 13. Violating Laws and Causing Disturbances

Tenant is entitled to quiet enjoyment of the premises. Tenant and guests or invitees will not use the premises or adjacent areas in such a way as to: (1) violate any law or ordinance, including laws prohibiting the use, possession, or sale of illegal drugs; (2) commit waste (severe property damage); or (3) create a nuisance by annoying, disturbing, inconveniencing, or interfering with the quiet enjoyment and peace and quiet of any other tenant or nearby resident.

Clause 14. Pets

No animal, bird, or other pet will be kept on the premises, even temporarily, except properly trained service animals needed by blind, deaf, or disabled persons and _____

under the following conditions: _____

_____

_____

Clause 15. Landlord's Right to Access

Landlord or Landlord's agents may enter the premises in the event of an emergency, to make repairs or improvements, or to show the premises to prospective buyers or tenants. Landlord may also enter the premises to conduct an annual inspection to check for safety or maintenance problems. Except in cases of emergency, Tenant's abandonment of the premises, court order, or where it is impractical to do so, Landlord shall give Tenant _____ notice before entering.

Clause 16. Extended Absences by Tenant

Tenant will notify Landlord in advance if Tenant will be away from the premises for _____ or more consecutive days. During such absence, Landlord may enter the premises at times reasonably necessary to maintain the property and inspect for needed repairs.

Clause 17. Possession of the Premises

a. *Tenant's failure to take possession.*

If, after signing this Agreement, Tenant fails to take possession of the premises, Tenant will still be responsible for paying rent and complying with all other terms of this Agreement.

b. *Landlord's failure to deliver possession.*

If Landlord is unable to deliver possession of the premises to Tenant for any reason not within Landlord's control, including, but not limited to, partial or complete destruction of the premises, Tenant will have the right to terminate this Agreement upon proper notice as required by law. In such event, Landlord's liability to Tenant will be limited to the return of all sums previously paid by Tenant to Landlord.

Clause 18. Tenant Rules and Regulations

☐ Tenant acknowledges receipt of, and has read a copy of, tenant rules and regulations, which are labeled Attachment A and attached to and incorporated into this Agreement by this reference.

Clause 19. Payment of Court Costs and Attorney Fees in a Lawsuit

In any action or legal proceeding to enforce any part of this Agreement, the prevailing party ☐ shall not / ☐ shall recover reasonable attorney fees and court costs.

Clause 20. Disclosures

Tenant acknowledges that Landlord has made the following disclosures regarding the premises:

☐ Disclosure of Information on Lead-Based Paint and/or Lead-Based Paint Hazards

☐ Other disclosures: _____

_____

_____

_____

Clause 21. Authority to Receive Legal Papers

The Landlord, any person managing the premises, and anyone designated by the Landlord are authorized to accept service of process and receive other notices and demands, which may be delivered to:

☐ The Landlord, at the following address: _____

_____

☐ The manager, at the following address: _____

_____

☐ The following person, at the following address: _____

_____

Clause 22. Additional Provisions

Additional provisions are as follows: _____

_____

_____

_____

_____

_____

_____

_____

Clause 23. Validity of Each Part

If any portion of this Agreement is held to be invalid, its invalidity will not affect the validity or enforceability of any other provision of this Agreement.

Clause 24. Grounds for Termination of Tenancy

The failure of Tenant or Tenant's guests or invitees to comply with any term of this Agreement, or the misrepresentation of any material fact on Tenant's Rental Application, is grounds for termination of the tenancy, with appropriate notice to Tenant and procedures as required by law.

Clause 25. Entire Agreement

This document constitutes the entire Agreement between the parties, and no promises or representations, other than those contained here and those implied by law, have been made by Landlord or Tenant. Any modifications to this Agreement must be in writing signed by Landlord and Tenant.

_____   _____   _____
Date   Landlord or Landlord's Agent   Title

_____
Street Address

_____   _____   _____ _____
City   State   Zip Code Phone

_____   _____   _____
Date   Tenant   Phone

_____   _____   _____
Date   Tenant   Phone

_____   _____   _____
Date   Tenant   Phone

Cláusula 1. Identificación del Arrendador y de los Inquilinos.

Este Contrato se hace _____ , entre _____

_____ [Inquilinos] y

_____ [Arrendador]. Cada

Inquilino es conjunta y seriamente responsable del pago de renta y del cumplimiento de todos los demás

términos de este Contrato.

Cláusula 2. Identificación de la Propiedad.

De acuerdo con los términos y condiciones referidas en este Contrato, el Arrendador renta al Inquilino, y éste

renta del Arrendador, sólamente para residir, la propiedad ubicada en _____

_____ , [la propiedad],

junto con el mobiliario y los aparatos electrodomésticos siguientes: _____

_____

_____

La renta de la propiedad también incluye _____

_____ .

Cláusula 3. Límitaciones en el Uso y Ocupación.

La propiedad se utilizará sólo como residencia privada por el Inquilino designado en la Cláusula 1 de este

Contrato y sus hijos menores. Está prohibido que invitados habiten la propiedad por más de

_____ , excepto con previo consentimiento por escrito del Arrendador. De lo contrario,

será considerado como una violación a este Contrato.

Cláusula 4. Período de Arrendamiento.

La renta comenzará el día _____ de _____ de _____ , y concluirá el día

_____ de _____ de _____ . Si el Inquilino desocupa antes del vencimiento

del período de renta, será responsable por la diferencia de la renta que falta por el resto del término.

Cláusula 5. Renta y Fechas de Pago.

Renta Regular Mensual.

El Inquilino pagará por adelantado, una renta mensual de $ _____ , el primer día del mes; excepto

cuando éste sea en un fin de semana o en un día feriado oficial, en cuyo caso deberá ser pagada el próximo día

laboral. Si no existe otra decisión por parte del Arrendador, la renta deberá ser pagada de la manera siguiente:

nolo
NOLO
www.nolo.com
Contrato de Arrendamiento Residencial a Plazo Fijo
Página 1 de 6

Entrega de Pago.

El arriendo será pagado:

☐ Por correo, dirigido a _____

☐ Personalmente, en _____

Forma de Pago.

El Arrendador recibirá los pagos en:

☐ Cheque Personal escrito en favor de _____

☐ Cheque de Caja escrito en favor de _____

☐ Tarjeta de Crédito

☐ Giro Postal

☐ Efectivo

Prorrateo del primer mes de renta.

Para el período comenzando con la fecha en que se mudará el Inquilino, el día _____ de

_____ de _____ , hasta el fin del mes en curso, el Inquilino pagará al

Arrendador la renta mensual prorratada de $ _____. Esta suma se pagará antes o en la fecha en

que se mude el Inquilino a la propiedad.

Cláusula 6. Cobros por Mora.

Si el Inquilino falla en el pago total de la renta, antes del final del día siguiente a la fecha de pago, tendrá que

pagar costos por atrasos como se explica a continuación: _____

_____.

El Arrendador no descartará el derecho de insistir en el pago total de la renta en la fecha debida.

Cláusula 7. Pagos por Cheques Sin Fondo y Recargos Bancarios.

En el caso de cualquier cheque, ofrecido por el Inquilino al Arrendador como pago de renta o cualquier otra

suma debida bajo este Contrato, sea regresado por insuficiencia de fondos, un "paro de pago," o cualquier otra

razón, el Inquilino deberá pagar un recargo por la cantidad de $_____.

Cláusula 8. Depósito de Garantía.

Al firmar el presente Contrato, el Inquilino pagará al Arrendador, la cantidad de $_____ como

depósito de seguridad. Este depósito no puede aplicarse al último mes de renta o a cualquier cantidad

debida bajo este Contrato; excepto con previo consentimiento por escrito del Arrendador. Dentro de

_____ , después de que el Inquilino haya desocupado la propiedad, haya

entregado las llaves y proporcionado la dirección donde contactarse, el Arrendador le entregará el depósito

en su totalidad o le detallará de manera escrita, las razones y la cantidad que es retenida por él, junto con un

cheque por la cantidad de su diferencia.

[Si quiere incluir alguna claúsula opcional, escríbalo aquí]

Cláusula 9. Servicios Públicos.

El Inquilino pagará todos los servicios públicos, exceptuando los siguientes, los cuales serán pagados por el

Arrendador: _____

_____.

Cláusula 10. Prohibición de Traspaso o Subarrendamiento.

El Inquilino no puede subarrendar cualquier parte de la propiedad o traspasar este Contrato, sin previo

consentimiento por escrito del Arrendador.

Cláusula 11. Responsabilidad del Inquilino de Mantenimiento de la Propiedad.

El Inquilino acepta: (1) mantener la propiedad limpia e higiénica, en buena condición, y cuando el arrendamiento

termine, regresar la propiedad al Arrendador en idéntica condición a la que existía cuando la habitaron,

exceptuando el deterioro causado por el uso; (2) Notificar de inmediato al Arrendador, sobre cualquier defecto

o condición peligrosa que note en o alrededor de la propiedad; y (3) reembolsar al Arrendador, bajo demanda de

éste, los costos de cualquier reparación de daños a la propiedad, ocasionados por uso indebido o negligencia del

Inquilino o sus invitados.

El Inquilino ha revisado la propiedad, incluyendo los aparatos electrodomésticos, accesorios, alfombras,

cortinas, y pintura, y los ha encontrado en buenas condiciones, seguras, y limpias, exceptuando las que están en

la Lista Arrendador-Inquilino.

Cláusula 12. Reparaciones y Modificaciones Hechas por el Inquilino.

a. Exceptuando lo provisto por la ley o con la autorización previa y por escrito del Arrendador, el Inquilino no debe hacer modificaciones o reparaciones en la propiedad, incluído el hacer hoyos en las paredes o pintar el lugar.

b. El Inquilino no debe alterar las cerraduras, ni cambiarlas, ni instalar o modificar el sistema de alarma; excepto que haya recibido del Arrendador, una autorización previa y por escrito. El Inquilino deberá proveer al Arrendador una copia de llave o llaves para abrir cada cerradura modificada o nueva, así como instrucciones de cómo desarmar un sistema de alarma modificado o nuevo.

Cláusula 13. Causar Disturbios y Violaciones a la Ley.

El Inquilino tiene derecho al goce pacífico de la propiedad. Este y sus invitados no deben usar la propiedad o áreas aledañas, de manera que: (1) Viole cualquier ley o reglamento, incluyendo leyes que prohiben el uso, posesión o venta ilegal de drogas; (2) Permite el uso abusivo de la propiedad (daño serio a la propiedad); o (3) Cree un estorbo al molestar, provocar disturbios, provocar inconvenientes, o interferir en el disfrute de paz y tranquilidad de otros inquilinos o vecinos.

Cláusula 14. Mascotas.

No se permite, ni siquiera temporalmente, tener ningún animal, pájaro, u otros animales en la propiedad, excepto animales de servicio _____

y _____ bajo las

condiciones siguientes: _____

_____

_____ .

Cláusula 15. Derecho del Arrendador al Acceso a la Propiedad.

El Arrendador o agentes de éste pueden entrar a la propiedad, en caso de emergencia, para hacer reparaciones o mejoras, o para mostrar la propiedad a potenciales nuevos inquilinos o compradores en perspectiva. También podrá entrar para la inspección anual para revisar la seguridad o chequear problemas de mantenimiento. Excepto en caso de emergencia, por el abandono de la propiedad por parte del Inquilino, orden de la corte, o cuando no sea práctico, el Arrendador deberá notificarle al Inquilino de su intención de entrar a la propiedad con _____ de anticipación.

Cláusula 16. Ausencias Prolongadas del Inquilino.

El Inquilino deberá previamente notificar al Arrendador, si estará ausente de la propiedad por _____ días consecutivos o más. Durante este tiempo, el Arrendador podrá entrar, cuando sea necesario, a la propiedad para inspeccionarla, para mantenimiento o para reparaciones necesarias.

Cláusula 17. Tomar Posesión de la Propiedad.

    a.   *Falla del Inquilino en tomar posesión de la propiedad.*

        Si después de haber firmado este Contrato, el Inquilino no toma posesión de la propiedad, aún será responsable por pago de la renta y cumplimiento de todos los demás términos de este Contrato.

    b.   *Falla del Arrendador en entregar la propiedad.*

        Si el Arrendador no puede entregar la posesión de la propiedad al Inquilino, por cualquier razón fuera de su control, incluyendo, pero no limitado a, destrucción parcial o completa de la propiedad, el Inquilino tendrá el derecho de terminar este Contrato, mediante aviso previo y apropiado como lo señala la ley. En tal situación, la responsabilidad del Arrendador hacia el Inquilino, estará limitada a la devolución de todas las cantidades previamente pagadas por el Inquilino al Arrendador.

Cláusula 18. Normas y Regulaciones del Inquilino.

    ☐   El Inquilino reconoce lo recibido y que ha leído una copia de las Normas y Regulaciones del Inquilino; las cuales como referencia, están adjuntas e incorporadas al presente Contrato.

Cláusula 19. Pago del Abogado y Costos de la Corte en Caso de un Juicio.

    En cualquier acción jurídico-legal para hacer cumplir total o parcialmente este Contrato, la parte prevaleciente

    ☐ No deberá / ☐ Deberá recuperar honorarios justos del abogado y costos de la corte.

Cláusula 20. Divulgaciones.

    El Inquilino reconoce que el Arrendador le ha hecho las siguientes divulgaciones con respecto a la propiedad:

    ☐   Distribución de información sobre pintura a base de plomo y/o los peligros de este tipo de pintura.

    ☐   Otras divulgaciones:

    _____

    _____

    _____ .

Cláusula 21. Personal Autorizado para Recibir Documentos Legales.

    El Arrendador, la persona que administre la propiedad, o a quien haya designado el Arrendador, están autorizados para aceptar servicio de proceso, y recibir otras noticias y demandas, las cuales pueden ser entregadas a:

    ☐   El Arrendador, a la siguiente dirección: _____

    _____

    ☐   El Administrador, a la siguiente dirección: _____

    _____

    ☐   A la persona designada, a la siguiente dirección: _____

    _____

Cláusula 22. Disposiciones Adicionales.

Disposiciones adicionales son las siguientes: _____

_____

_____

_____

_____

_____ .

Cláusula 23. Validez de las Cláusulas de este Contrato.

Si cualquier cláusula de este Contrato es invalidado, ésto no afectará la validez o cumplimiento de las partes restantes de este Contrato.

Cláusula 24. Razones para Cancelar el Contrato de Arrendamiento.

El incumplimiento de cualesquiera de los términos de este Contrato, por parte del Inquilino o sus invitados o la relación Falsa de un hecho esencial en la solicitud del Inquilino, será razón para dar por cancelado el Contrato de arrendamiento, seguido con la debida notificación al Inquilino, de acuerdo con lo requerido por la ley.

Cláusula 25. Contrato Completo.

Este documento constituye el Contrato completo entre las partes, y el Arrendador y el Inquilino no han hecho otro compromiso, a no ser los contenidos en este Contrato o los señalados por la ley. Cualquier modificación al presente documento, debe ser por escrito y firmado por ambas partes.

_____ _____ _____
Fecha   Arrendador o su representante   Título

_____
Número y Nombre de la Calle

_____ _____ _____ _____
Ciudad   Estado   Código Postal   Teléfono

_____ _____ _____
Fecha   Nombre del Inquilino   Teléfono

_____ _____ _____
Fecha   Nombre del Inquilino   Teléfono

_____ _____ _____
Fecha   Nombre del Inquilino   Teléfono

Disclosure of Information on Lead-Based Paint and/or Lead-Based Paint Hazards

Lead Warning Statement

Housing built before 1978 may contain lead-based paint. Lead from paint, paint chips, and dust can pose health hazards if not managed properly. Lead exposure is especially harmful to young children and pregnant women. Before renting pre-1978 housing, lessors must disclose the presence of known lead-based paint and/or lead-based paint hazards in the dwelling. Lessees must also receive a federally approved pamphlet on lead poisoning prevention.

Lessor's Disclosure

(a) Presence of lead-based paint and/or lead-based paint hazards (check (i) or (ii) below):

    (i) _____ Known lead-based paint and/or lead-based paint hazards are present in the housing (explain).

    _____

    _____

    (ii) _____ Lessor has no knowledge of lead-based paint and/or lead-based paint hazards in the housing.

(b) Records and reports available to the lessor (check (i) or (ii) below):

    (i) _____ Lessor has provided the lessee with all available records and reports pertaining to lead-based paint and/or lead-based paint hazards in the housing (list documents below).

    _____

    _____

    (ii) _____ Lessor has no reports or records pertaining to lead-based paint and/or lead-based paint hazards in the housing.

Lessee's Acknowledgment (initial)

(c) _____ Lessee has received copies of all information listed above.

(d) _____ Lessee has received the pamphlet *Protect Your Family from Lead in Your Home.*

Agent's Acknowledgment (initial)

(e) _____ Agent has informed the lessor of the lessor's obligations under 42 U.S.C. 4852d and is aware of his/her responsibility to ensure compliance.

Certification of Accuracy

The following parties have reviewed the information above and certify, to the best of their knowledge, that the information they have provided is true and accurate.

Lessor	Date	Lessor	Date
Lessee	Date	Lessee	Date
Agent	Date	Agent	Date

Declaración de Información sobre Pintura a Base de Plomo y/o Peligros de la Pintura a Base de Plomo

Declaración sobre los Peligros del Plomo

Las viviendas construidas antes del año 1978 pueden contener pintura a base de plomo. El plomo de pintura, pedazos de pintura y polvo puede representar peligros para la salud si no se maneja apropiadamente. La exposición al plomo es especialmente dañino para los niños jóvenes y las mujeres embarazadas. Antes de alquilar (rentar) una vivienda construida antes del año 1978, los arrendadores tienen la obligación de informar sobre la presencia de pintura a base de plomo o peligros de pintura a base de plomo conocidos en la vivienda. Los arrendatarios (inquilinos) también deben recibir un folleto aprobado por el Gobierno Federal sobre la prevención del envenenamiento de plomo.

Declaración del Arrendador

(a) Presencia de pintura a base de plomo y/o peligros de pintura a base de plomo (marque (i) ó (ii) abajo):

(i) _____ Confirmado que hay pintura a base de plomo y/o peligro de pintura a base de plomo en la vivienda (explique).

_____

(ii) _____ El arrendador no tiene ningún conocimiento de que haya pintura a base de plomo y/o peligro de pintura a base de plomo en la vivienda.

(b) Archivos e informes disponibles para el vendedor (marque (i) ó (ii) abajo):

(i) _____ El arrendador le ha proporcionado al comprador todos los archivos e informes disponibles relacionados con pintura a base de plomo y/o peligro de pintura a base de plomo en la vivienda (anote los documentos abajo).

_____

(ii) _____ El arrendador no tiene archivos ni informes relacionados con pintura a base de plomo y/o peligro de pintura a base de plomo en la vivienda.

Acuse de Recibo del Arrendatario o Inquilino (inicial)

(c) _____ El arrendatario ha recibido copias de toda la información indicada arriba.

(d) _____ El arrendatario ha recibido el folleto titulado *Proteja a Su Familia del Plomo en Su Casa*.

Acuse de Recibo del Agente (inicial)

(e) _____ El agente le ha informado al arrendador de las obligaciones del arrendador de acuerdo con 42 U.S.C. 4852d y está consciente de su responsabilidad de asegurar su cumplimiento.

Certificación de Exactitud

Las partes siguientes han revisado la información que aparece arriba y certifican que, según su entender, toda la información que han proporcionado es verdadera y exacta.

Arrendador	Fecha	Arrendador	Fecha
Arrendatario	Fecha	Arrendatario	Fecha
Agente	Fecha	Agente	Fecha

Protect Your Family From Lead In Your Home

⊕EPA United States Environmental Protection Agency

United States Consumer Product Safety Commission

United States Department of Housing and Urban Development

Are You Planning To Buy, Rent, or Renovate a Home Built Before 1978?

Many houses and apartments built before 1978 have paint that contains high levels of lead (called lead-based paint). Lead from paint, chips, and dust can pose serious health hazards if not taken care of properly.

OWNERS, BUYERS, and RENTERS are encouraged to check for lead (see page 6) before renting, buying or renovating pre-1978 housing.

Federal law requires that individuals receive certain information before renting, buying, or renovating pre-1978 housing:

LANDLORDS have to disclose known information on lead-based paint and lead-based paint hazards before leases take effect. Leases must include a disclosure about lead-based paint.

SELLERS have to disclose known information on lead-based paint and lead-based paint hazards before selling a house. Sales contracts must include a disclosure about lead-based paint. Buyers have up to 10 days to check for lead.

RENOVATORS disturbing more than 2 square feet of painted surfaces have to give you this pamphlet before starting work.

IMPORTANT!

Lead From Paint, Dust, and Soil Can Be Dangerous If Not Managed Properly

FACT: Lead exposure can harm young children and babies even before they are born.

FACT: Even children who seem healthy can have high levels of lead in their bodies.

FACT: People can get lead in their bodies by breathing or swallowing lead dust, or by eating soil or paint chips containing lead.

FACT: People have many options for reducing lead hazards. In most cases, lead-based paint that is in good condition is not a hazard.

FACT: Removing lead-based paint improperly can increase the danger to your family.

If you think your home might have lead hazards, read this pamphlet to learn some simple steps to protect your family.

Lead Gets in the Body in Many Ways

Childhood lead poisoning remains a major environmental health problem in the U.S.

People can get lead in their body if they:

◆ Breathe in lead dust (especially during renovations that disturb painted surfaces).

◆ Put their hands or other objects covered with lead dust in their mouths.

◆ Eat paint chips or soil that contains lead.

Lead is even more dangerous to children under the age of 6:

◆ At this age children's brains and nervous systems are more sensitive to the damaging effects of lead.

◆ Children's growing bodies absorb more lead.

◆ Babies and young children often put their hands and other objects in their mouths. These objects can have lead dust on them.

Even children who appear healthy can have dangerous levels of lead in their bodies.

Lead is also dangerous to women of childbearing age:

◆ Women with a high lead level in their system prior to pregnancy would expose a fetus to lead through the placenta during fetal development.

Lead's Effects

It is important to know that even exposure to low levels of lead can severely harm children.

In children, lead can cause:

◆ Nervous system and kidney damage.

◆ Learning disabilities, attention deficit disorder, and decreased intelligence.

◆ Speech, language, and behavior problems.

◆ Poor muscle coordination.

◆ Decreased muscle and bone growth.

◆ Hearing damage.

While low-lead exposure is most common, exposure to high levels of lead can have devastating effects on children, including seizures, unconsciousness, and, in some cases, death.

Although children are especially susceptible to lead exposure, lead can be dangerous for adults too.

In adults, lead can cause:

◆ Increased chance of illness during pregnancy.

◆ Harm to a fetus, including brain damage or death.

◆ Fertility problems (in men and women).

◆ High blood pressure.

◆ Digestive problems.

◆ Nerve disorders.

◆ Memory and concentration problems.

◆ Muscle and joint pain.

Brain or Nerve Damage

Hearing Problems

Slowed Growth

Digestive Problems

Reproductive Problems (Adults)

Lead affects the body in many ways.

Where Lead-Based Paint Is Found

In general, the older your home, the more likely it has lead-based paint.

Many homes built before 1978 have lead-based paint. The federal government banned lead-based paint from housing in 1978. Some states stopped its use even earlier. Lead can be found:

◆ In homes in the city, country, or suburbs.

◆ In apartments, single-family homes, and both private and public housing.

◆ Inside and outside of the house.

◆ In soil around a home. (Soil can pick up lead from exterior paint or other sources such as past use of leaded gas in cars.)

Checking Your Family for Lead

Get your children and home tested if you think your home has high levels of lead.

To reduce your child's exposure to lead, get your child checked, have your home tested (especially if your home has paint in poor condition and was built before 1978), and fix any hazards you may have. Children's blood lead levels tend to increase rapidly from 6 to 12 months of age, and tend to peak at 18 to 24 months of age.

Consult your doctor for advice on testing your children. A simple blood test can detect high levels of lead. Blood tests are usually recommended for:

◆ Children at ages 1 and 2.

◆ Children or other family members who have been exposed to high levels of lead.

◆ Children who should be tested under your state or local health screening plan.

Your doctor can explain what the test results mean and if more testing will be needed.

Identifying Lead Hazards

Lead-based paint is usually not a hazard if it is in good condition, and it is not on an impact or friction surface, like a window. It is defined by the federal government as paint with lead levels greater than or equal to 1.0 milligram per square centimeter, or more than 0.5% by weight.

Deteriorating lead-based paint (peeling, chipping, chalking, cracking or damaged) is a hazard and needs immediate attention. It may also be a hazard when found on surfaces that children can chew or that get a lot of wear-and-tear, such as:

◆ Windows and window sills.

◆ Doors and door frames.

◆ Stairs, railings, banisters, and porches.

Lead dust can form when lead-based paint is scraped, sanded, or heated. Dust also forms when painted surfaces bump or rub together. Lead chips and dust can get on surfaces and objects that people touch. Settled lead dust can re-enter the air when people vacuum, sweep, or walk through it. The following two federal standards have been set for lead hazards in dust:

◆ 40 micrograms per square foot ($\mu g/ft^2$) and higher for floors, including carpeted floors.

◆ 250 $\mu g/ft^2$ and higher for interior window sills.

Lead in soil can be a hazard when children play in bare soil or when people bring soil into the house on their shoes. The following two federal standards have been set for lead hazards in residential soil:

◆ 400 parts per million (ppm) and higher in play areas of bare soil.

◆ 1,200 ppm (average) and higher in bare soil in the remainder of the yard.

The only way to find out if paint, dust and soil lead hazards exist is to test for them. The next page describes the most common methods used.

Lead from paint chips, which you can see, and lead dust, which you can't always see, can both be serious hazards.

Checking Your Home for Lead

You can get your home tested for lead in several different ways:

◆ A paint **inspection** tells you whether your home has lead-based paint and where it is located. It won't tell you whether or not your home currently has lead hazards.

◆ A **risk assessment** tells you if your home currently has any lead hazards from lead in paint, dust, or soil. It also tells you what actions to take to address any hazards.

◆ A combination risk assessment and inspection tells you if your home has any lead hazards and if your home has any lead-based paint, and where the lead-based paint is located.

Hire a trained and certified testing professional who will use a range of reliable methods when testing your home.

◆ Visual inspection of paint condition and location.

◆ A portable x-ray fluorescence (XRF) machine.

◆ Lab tests of paint, dust, and soil samples.

There are state and federal programs in place to ensure that testing is done safely, reliably, and effectively. Contact your state or local agency (see bottom of page 11) for more information, or call **1-800-424-LEAD (5323)** for a list of contacts in your area.

Home test kits for lead are available, but may not always be accurate. Consumers should not rely on these kits before doing renovations or to assure safety.

Just knowing that a home has lead-based paint may not tell you if there is a hazard.

What You Can Do Now To Protect Your Family

If you suspect that your house has lead hazards, you can take some immediate steps to reduce your family's risk:

◆ **If you rent, notify your landlord of peeling or chipping paint.**

◆ **Clean up paint chips immediately.**

◆ **Clean floors, window frames, window sills, and other surfaces weekly.** Use a mop or sponge with warm water and a general all-purpose cleaner or a cleaner made specifically for lead. REMEMBER: NEVER MIX AMMONIA AND BLEACH PRODUCTS TOGETHER SINCE THEY CAN FORM A DANGEROUS GAS.

◆ **Thoroughly rinse sponges and mop heads after cleaning dirty or dusty areas.**

◆ **Wash children's hands often, especially before they eat and before nap time and bed time.**

◆ **Keep play areas clean.** Wash bottles, pacifiers, toys, and stuffed animals regularly.

◆ **Keep children from chewing window sills or other painted surfaces.**

◆ **Clean or remove shoes before entering your home to avoid tracking in lead from soil.**

◆ **Make sure children eat nutritious, low-fat meals high in iron and calcium,** such as spinach and dairy products. Children with good diets absorb less lead.

Reducing Lead Hazards In The Home

In addition to day-to-day cleaning and good nutrition:

◆ You can **temporarily** reduce lead hazards by taking actions such as repairing damaged painted surfaces and planting grass to cover soil with high lead levels. These actions (called "interim controls") are not permanent solutions and will need ongoing attention.

◆ To **permanently** remove lead hazards, you should hire a certified lead "abatement" contractor. Abatement (or permanent hazard elimination) methods include removing, sealing, or enclosing lead-based paint with special materials. Just painting over the hazard with regular paint is not permanent removal.

Removing lead improperly can increase the hazard to your family by spreading even more lead dust around the house.

Always use a professional who is trained to remove lead hazards safely.

Always hire a person with special training for correcting lead problems—someone who knows how to do this work safely and has the proper equipment to clean up thoroughly. Certified contractors will employ qualified workers and follow strict safety rules as set by their state or by the federal government.

Once the work is completed, dust cleanup activities must be repeated until testing indicates that lead dust levels are below the following:

◆ 40 micrograms per square foot ($\mu g/ft^2$) for floors, including carpeted floors;

◆ 250 $\mu g/ft^2$ for interior windows sills; and

◆ 400 $\mu g/ft^2$ for window troughs.

Call your state or local agency (see bottom of page 11) for help in locating certified professionals in your area and to see if financial assistance is available.

Other Sources of Lead

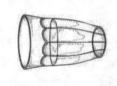

◆ **Drinking water.** Your home might have plumbing with lead or lead solder. Call your local health department or water supplier to find out about testing your water. You cannot see, smell, or taste lead, and boiling your water will not get rid of lead. If you think your plumbing might have lead in it:

- Use only cold water for drinking and cooking.

- Run water for 15 to 30 seconds before drinking it, especially if you have not used your water for a few hours.

While paint, dust, and soil are the most common sources of lead, other lead sources also exist.

◆ **The job.** If you work with lead, you could bring it home on your hands or clothes. Shower and change clothes before coming home. Launder your work clothes separately from the rest of your family's clothes.

◆ Old painted **toys** and **furniture.**

◆ Food and liquids stored in **lead crystal** or **lead-glazed pottery or porcelain.**

◆ **Lead smelters** or other industries that release lead into the air.

◆ **Hobbies** that use lead, such as making pottery or stained glass, or refinishing furniture.

◆ **Folk remedies** that contain lead, such as "greta" and "azarcon" used to treat an upset stomach.

Remodeling or Renovating a Home With Lead-Based Paint

Take precautions before your contractor or you begin remodeling or renovating anything that disturbs painted surfaces (such as scraping off paint or tearing out walls):

◆ **Have the area tested for lead-based paint.**

◆ **Do not use a belt-sander, propane torch, high temperature heat gun, dry scraper, or dry sandpaper** to remove lead-based paint. These actions create large amounts of lead dust and fumes. Lead dust can remain in your home long after the work is done.

◆ **Temporarily move your family** (especially children and pregnant women) out of the apartment or house until the work is done and the area is properly cleaned. If you can't move your family, at least completely seal off the work area.

◆ **Follow other safety measures to reduce lead hazards.** You can find out about other safety measures by calling 1-800-424-LEAD. Ask for the brochure "Reducing Lead Hazards When Remodeling Your Home." This brochure explains what to do before, during, and after renovations.

If you have already completed renovations or remodeling that could have released lead-based paint or dust, get your young children tested and follow the steps outlined on page 7 of this brochure.

If not conducted properly, certain types of renovations can release lead from paint and dust into the air.

For More Information

The National Lead Information Center

Call **1-800-424-LEAD (424-5323)** to learn how to protect children from lead poisoning and for other information on lead hazards.

To access lead information via the web, visit **www.epa.gov/lead** and **www.hud.gov/offices/lead/**.

EPA's Safe Drinking Water Hotline

Call **1-800-426-4791** for information about lead in drinking water.

Consumer Product Safety Commission (CPSC) Hotline

To request information on lead in consumer products, or to report an unsafe consumer product or a product-related injury call **1-800-638-2772**, or visit CPSC's Web site at: **www.cpsc.gov.**

Health and Environmental Agencies

Some cities, states, and tribes have their own rules for lead-based paint activities. Check with your local agency to see which laws apply to you. Most agencies can also provide information on finding a lead abatement firm in your area, and on possible sources of financial aid for reducing lead hazards. Receive up-to-date address and phone information for your local contacts on the Internet at **www.epa.gov/lead** or contact the National Lead Information Center at **1-800-424-LEAD.**

For the hearing impaired, call the Federal Information Relay Service at **1-800-877-8339** to access any of the phone numbers in this brochure.

11

EPA Regional Offices

Your Regional EPA Office can provide further information regarding regulations and lead protection programs.

EPA Regional Offices

Region 1 (Connecticut, Massachusetts, Maine, New Hampshire, Rhode Island, Vermont)

Regional Lead Contact
U.S. EPA Region 1
Suite 1100 (CPT)
One Congress Street
Boston, MA 02114-2023
1 (888) 372-7341

Region 2 (New Jersey, New York, Puerto Rico, Virgin Islands)

Regional Lead Contact
U.S. EPA Region 2
2890 Woodbridge Avenue
Building 209, Mail Stop 225
Edison, NJ 08837-3679
(732) 321-6671

Region 3 (Delaware, Maryland, Pennsylvania, Virginia, Washington DC, West Virginia)

Regional Lead Contact
U.S. EPA Region 3 (3WC33)
1650 Arch Street
Philadelphia, PA 19103
(215) 814-5000

Region 4 (Alabama, Florida, Georgia, Kentucky, Mississippi, North Carolina, South Carolina, Tennessee)

Regional Lead Contact
U.S. EPA Region 4
61 Forsyth Street, SW
Atlanta, GA 30303
(404) 562-8998

Region 5 (Illinois, Indiana, Michigan, Minnesota, Ohio, Wisconsin)

Regional Lead Contact
U.S. EPA Region 5 (DT-8J)
77 West Jackson Boulevard
Chicago, IL 60604-3666
(312) 886-6003

Region 6 (Arkansas, Louisiana, New Mexico, Oklahoma, Texas)

Regional Lead Contact
U.S. EPA Region 6
1445 Ross Avenue, 12th Floor
Dallas, TX 75202-2733
(214) 665-7577

Region 7 (Iowa, Kansas, Missouri, Nebraska)

Regional Lead Contact
U.S. EPA Region 7
(ARTD-RALI)
901 N. 5th Street
Kansas City, KS 66101
(913) 551-7020

Region 8 (Colorado, Montana, North Dakota, South Dakota, Utah, Wyoming)

Regional Lead Contact
U.S. EPA Region 8
999 18th Street, Suite 500
Denver, CO 80202-2466
(303) 312-6021

Region 9 (Arizona, California, Hawaii, Nevada)

Regional Lead Contact
U.S. EPA Region 9
75 Hawthorne Street
San Francisco, CA 94105
(415) 947-4164

Region 10 (Alaska, Idaho, Oregon, Washington)

Regional Lead Contact
U.S. EPA Region 10
Toxics Section WCM-128
1200 Sixth Avenue
Seattle, WA 98101-1128
(206) 553-1985

12

Simple Steps To Protect Your Family From Lead Hazards

If you think your home has high levels of lead:

◆ Get your young children tested for lead, even if they seem healthy.

◆ Wash children's hands, bottles, pacifiers, and toys often.

◆ Make sure children eat healthy, low-fat foods.

◆ Get your home checked for lead hazards.

◆ Regularly clean floors, window sills, and other surfaces.

◆ Wipe soil off shoes before entering house.

◆ Talk to your landlord about fixing surfaces with peeling or chipping paint.

◆ Take precautions to avoid exposure to lead dust when remodeling or renovating (call 1-800-424-LEAD for guidelines).

◆ Don't use a belt-sander, propane torch, high temperature heat gun, scraper, or sandpaper on painted surfaces that may contain lead.

◆ Don't try to remove lead-based paint yourself.

CPSC Regional Offices

Your Regional CPSC Office can provide further information regarding regulations and consumer product safety.

Eastern Regional Center
Consumer Product Safety Commission
201 Varick Street, Room 903
New York, NY 10014
(212) 620-4120

Western Regional Center
Consumer Product Safety Commission
1301 Clay Street, Suite 610-N
Oakland, CA 94612
(510) 637-4050

Central Regional Center
Consumer Product Safety Commission
230 South Dearborn Street, Room 2944
Chicago, IL 60604
(312) 353-8260

HUD Lead Office

Please contact HUD's Office of Healthy Homes and Lead Hazard Control for information on lead regulations, outreach efforts, and lead hazard control and research grant programs.

U.S. Department of Housing and Urban Development
Office of Healthy Homes and Lead Hazard Control
451 Seventh Street, SW, P-3206
Washington, DC 20410
(202) 755-1785

This document is in the public domain. It may be reproduced by an individual or organization without permission. Information provided in this booklet is based upon current scientific and technical understanding of the issues presented and is reflective of the jurisdictional boundaries established by the statutes governing the co-authoring agencies. Following the advice given will not necessarily provide complete protection in all situations or against all health hazards that can be caused by lead exposure.

U.S. EPA Washington DC 20460
U.S. CPSC Washington DC 20207
U.S. HUD Washington DC 20410

EPA747-K-99-001
June 2003

¿Está planeando comprar, alquilar o renovar una casa que se construyó antes de 1978?

Muchas casas y apartamentos construidos antes de 1978 tienen pintura que contiene altos niveles de plomo (llamada pintura con base de plomo). El plomo en la pintura, las partículas y el polvo puede ser un riesgo grave para la salud si no se atiende apropiadamente.

La ley federal requiere que las personas reciban cierta información antes de alquilar, comprar o renovar viviendas construidas antes de 1978:

LOS PROPIETARIOS tienen que revelar la información que posean acerca de la pintura con base de plomo y los riesgos relacionados con la misma antes de realizar el alquiler. Los contratos de alquiler deben incluir un formulario de divulgación acerca de la pintura con base de plomo.

LOS VENDEDORES tienen que divulgar la información que posean acerca de la pintura con base de plomo y los riesgos relacionados con la misma antes de vender una casa. Los contratos de venta deben incluir un formulario de información acerca de la pintura con base de plomo. Los compradores tienen un plazo de 10 días para revisar si existen riesgos relacionados con el plomo.

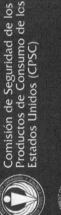

LOS RENOVADORES tienen que darle este folleto antes de comenzar el trabajo.

SI DESEA MÁS INFORMACIÓN

acerca de estos requisitos, llame a la National Lead Information Center (Centro Nacional de Distribución de Información sobre Plomo) al **1-800-424-LEAD (424-5323)**.

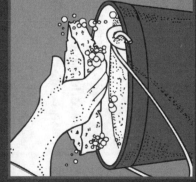

Este documento es del dominio público. Las personas u organizaciones pueden reproducir o sin permiso. La información proporcionada en este folleto está basada en el entendimiento actual científico y técnico de los asuntos presentados y refleja los límites de jurisdicción establecidos por los estatutos que gobiernan a las agencias coautoras. Seguir los consejos que se ofrecen no proporcionará necesariamente una protección completa en todas las situaciones o contra todos los riesgos de salud que puede causar la exposición al plomo.

Proteja a Su Familia en Contra del Plomo en Su Casa

EPA Agencia de Protección Ambiental de los Estados Unidos (EPA)

Comisión de Seguridad de los Productos de Consumo de los Estados Unidos (CPSC)

Departamento de Desarrollo Urbano y de la Vivienda de los Estados Unidos (HUD)

EPA747-K-01-001
November 2001

U.S. EPA Washington DC 20460
U.S. CPSC Washington DC 20207
U.S. HUD Washington DC 20410

El plomo entra al organismo de muchas maneras

El envene-namiento infantil con plomo continúa siendo un gran problema de salud ambiental en los Estados Unidos.

Aun los niños que parecen sanos pueden tener niveles peligrosos de plomo en sus organismos.

El plomo puede entrar en el organismo si:

◆ Inhalan el polvo de plomo (especialmente durante las renovaciones que alteran las superficies pintadas).

◆ Se llevan a la boca las manos u otros objetos cubiertos con polvo de plomo.

◆ Comen partículas de pintura o tierra que contiene plomo.

El plomo es aún más peligroso para los niños que para los adultos ya que:

◆ El cerebro y el sistema nervioso de los niños son más sensibles a los efectos dañinos del plomo.

◆ El cuerpo en crecimiento de los niños absorbe más plomo.

◆ Los bebés y los niños pequeños se llevan las manos y otros objetos a la boca con frecuencia. Dichos objetos pueden estar cubiertos de polvo que contiene plomo.

¡IMPORTANTE!

El plomo de la pintura, del polvo y de la tierra puede ser peligroso si no se atiende apropiadamente

ES CIERTO QUE: La exposición al plomo puede hacerle daño a los niños pequeños y a los bebés aun antes del nacimiento.

ES CIERTO QUE: Aun los niños que parecen sanos pueden tener altos niveles de plomo en sus organismos.

ES CIERTO QUE: El plomo puede entrar en el organismo al inhalar o tragar polvo de plomo, o al comer tierra o partículas de pintura que contengan plomo.

ES CIERTO QUE: Las personas tienen muchas opciones para reducir los riesgos relacionados con el plomo. En la mayoría de los casos, la pintura con base de plomo que esté en buenas condiciones no es peligrosa.

ES CIERTO QUE: Remover incorrectamente la pintura con base de plomo puede aumentar los riesgos para su familia.

Si cree que su casa podría tener algún riesgo relacionado con el plomo, lea este folleto para aprender algunos pasos sencillos para proteger a su familia.

Los efectos del plomo

Si no se detectan pronto, los niños que tienen niveles altos de plomo en sus organismos pueden sufrir:

- Daños al cerebro y al sistema nervioso
- Problemas de conducta y aprendizaje (tal como hiperactividad)
- Crecimiento retrasado
- Problemas de audición
- Dolores de cabeza.

El plomo también es dañino para los adultos. Éstos pueden padecer:

- Dificultades durante el embarazo
- Otros problemas del sistema reproductor (tanto los hombres como las mujeres)
- Presión alta
- Problemas digestivos
- Padecimientos nerviosos
- Problemas con la memoria y la concentración
- Dolores musculares y de las articulaciones.

Problemas de audición

Daño nervioso o cerebral

Crecimiento retrasado

Problemas digestivos

Problemas del sistema de reproducción (adultos)

El plomo afecta al organismo de muchas maneras.

Dónde se encuentra la pintura con base de plomo

Muchas viviendas construidas antes de 1978 tienen pintura con base de plomo. El gobierno federal prohibió la pintura con base de plomo en las viviendas en 1978. Algunos estados dejaron de usarla aun antes. El plomo puede encontrarse en:

- Casas en la ciudad, el campo o los suburbios.
- En apartamentos, casas y viviendas privadas o públicas.
- Dentro y fuera de la casa.
- En la tierra alrededor de la casa. (La tierra puede recoger plomo de la pintura exterior u otras fuentes tales como la gasolina con plomo que se usaba en el pasado, en los automóviles.)

Generalmente, entre más vieja sea su casa, la posibilidad de que tenga pintura con base de plomo será mayor.

Para realizarle exámenes de plomo a su familia

Haga que examinen a sus niños y su casa si cree que ésta tiene niveles altos de plomo.

Para reducir la exposición de sus niños al plomo, realícele un examen a su niño y a su casa (especialmente si la pintura de su casa está en malas condiciones y se construyó antes de 1978), y arregle los riesgos que puedan existir. El nivel de plomo en la sangre de los niños tiende a incrementarse con rapidez entre los 6 y 12 meses de edad; y tiende a llegar al nivel más alto entre los 18 y 24 meses de edad.

Consulte a su médico para que le aconseje cómo examinar a sus niños. Un sencillo análisis de sangre puede detectar el nivel alto de plomo. Los análisis de sangre se recomiendan generalmente a:

- Los niños de 1 y 2 años de edad.
- Los niños u otros miembros de la familia que hayan estado expuestos a niveles altos de plomo.
- Los niños que deben examinarse bajo el plan local o estatal de exámenes médicos.

Su médico puede explicarle los resultados de las pruebas y decirle si es necesario realizar más análisis.

Identificando los peligros del plomo

La pintura con base de plomo generalmente no es peligrosa si está en buenas condiciones, y no lo es si no es en una superficie de impacto o fricción, como una ventana. El gobierno federal lo define como la pintura con niveles de plomo superiores o iguales a 1.0 miligramos por centímetro cuadrado, o más de 0.5% de peso.

La pintura con base de plomo deteriorada (descascarándose, picándose, pulverizándose o partiéndose) es un riesgo y necesita atención inmediata. También puede ser un riesgo si se encuentra en superficies que los niños puedan morder o que reciban mucho desgaste. Estas áreas incluyen:

◆ Ventanas y marcos.

◆ Puertas y marcos.

◆ Escaleras, pasamanos, barandas y patios.

El **polvo de plomo** puede formarse al lijar o raspar en seco o al calentar la pintura con base de plomo. También puede formarse el polvo cuando las superficies pintadas se golpean o frotan entre sí. Las partículas y el polvo que contienen plomo pueden acumularse en superficies y objetos que las personas tocan. El polvo de plomo que se ha posado puede volver a mezclarse con el aire cuando las personas aspiran, barren o caminan sobre el mismo. Se han establecido las siguientes dos normas federales para los riesgos de plomo en el polvo:

◆ 40 microgramos por pie cuadrado (μg/pie²) y más alto en los pisos, incluyendo los pisos alfombrados.

◆ 250 μg/pie² y más alto en las repisas de las ventanas.

El **plomo en la tierra** puede ser un riesgo al jugar los niños en tierra descubierta o cuando las personas meten tierra en la casa con los zapatos. Las siguientes dos normas federales se han establecido para los riesgos de plomo en la tierra de las residencias:

◆ 400 partes por millón (ppm) y más alto en las áreas de juego de tierra descubierta.

◆ 1,200 ppm (promedio) y más alto en la tierra descubierta del resto del jardín.

La única forma de descubrir si existen riesgos de plomo en la pintura, el polvo y la tierra es realizando pruebas. La página siguiente describe los métodos más comúnmente usados.

Tanto el plomo de las partículas de pintura que se pueden ver, como el polvo de plomo, el cual no siempre se puede ver, pueden ser un grave peligro.

Para revisar si su casa tiene plomo

Usted puede hacer que examinen si hay algún riesgo relacionado con el plomo en su casa de una de dos maneras, o de ambas maneras:

◆ Una **inspección** de la pintura le dará el contenido de plomo de cada tipo diferente de superficie pintada en su casa. No le dirá si la pintura es un riesgo o cómo deberá atenderla.

◆ Una **evaluación de riesgo** le dirá si existe alguna fuente grave de exposición al plomo (tal como pinturas descascarándose y polvo que contiene plomo). También le dirá qué acciones debe realizar para atacar estos riesgos.

Contrate a un profesional certificado, bien capacitado que usará una variedad de métodos confiables al examinar su casa, tales como.

◆ Inspección visual de las condiciones y la ubicación de la pintura.

◆ Una máquina portátil de fluorescencia por rayos X (XRF).

◆ Pruebas de laboratorio de las muestras de la pintura, el polvo y la tierra.

Existen normas establecidas para garantizar que el trabajo se realice de modo seguro, confiable y con eficacia. Comuníquese con el programa estatal para la prevención del envenenamiento con plomo para obtener más información. Llame al **1-800-424-LEAD** para obtener una lista de contactos en su área.

Los estuches caseros para pruebas de plomo están disponibles, pero puede ser que no siempre sean precisos. Los consumidores no deben atenerse a estas pruebas antes de hacer renovaciones o para garantizar la seguridad.

Saber que su casa tiene pintura con base de plomo no decirle si hay peligro.

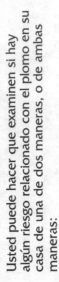

Lista de Verificación

Cómo reducir los riesgos relacionados con el plomo en el hogar

Además de la limpieza diaria y la buena nutrición:

◆ Usted puede reducir **temporalmente** los riesgos relacionados con el plomo tomando medidas como la reparación de las superficies pintadas que estén dañadas y plantar césped para cubrir la tierra que tiene niveles altos de plomo. Estas medidas (llamadas "controles provisionales") no son soluciones permanentes y necesitarán atención continua.

◆ Para remover **permanentemente** los riesgos relacionados con el plomo, usted debe contratar a un contratista certificado para que "remueva" el plomo. Los métodos para remover (o eliminar permanentemente el peligro) incluyen la eliminación, el sellado o revestimiento de la pintura con base de plomo con materiales especiales. El pintar simplemente sobre el riesgo con una pintura común no lo remueve permanentemente.

Remover incorrectamente la pintura con plomo puede aumentar el riesgo para su familia ya que esparce aún más el polvo de plomo en la casa.

Siempre use los servicios de un profesional que esté capacitado para remover plomo de modo seguro.

Siempre contrate a una persona con capacitación especial en la corrección de los problemas con plomo—alguien que sepa cómo realizar este trabajo en forma segura y que tenga el equipo apropiado para limpiar minuciosamente. Los contratistas certificados contratarán trabajadores calificados y seguirán reglas estrictas de seguridad según lo dicta el estado o el gobierno federal.

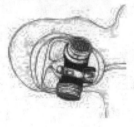

Una vez que se termine el trabajo, deben repetirse las actividades de limpieza del polvo hasta que las pruebas indiquen que los niveles de plomo están por debajo de:

◆ 40 microgramos por pie cuadrado (μg/pie^2) en los pisos, incluyendo los pisos alfombrados;

◆ 250 μg/pie^2 y más alto en las repisas de las ventanas y

◆ 400 μg/pie^2 en los canales de la ventana.

Llame a su agencia local (vea la página 11) para obtener ayuda para localizar contratistas certificados en su localidad y para enterarse si hay ayuda financiera disponible.

8

Lo que puede hacer ahora para proteger a su familia

Si sospecha que su casa tiene algún riesgo relacionado con el plomo, puede tomar algunas medidas inmediatas para reducir el riesgo a su familia:

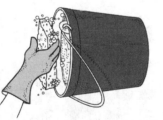

◆ **Si alquila la casa, infórmele al propietario si hay pintura descascarándose o picándose.**

◆ **Limpie inmediatamente las partículas de pintura.**

◆ **Limpie semanalmente los pisos, los marcos de ventanas, los alféizares y las demás superficies.** Use un trapeador o una esponja con agua tibia y un limpiador para usos múltiples o uno hecho específicamente para plomo. RECUERDE: NUNCA MEZCLE PRODUCTOS DE AMONÍACO CON BLANQUEADORES YA QUE PUEDEN FORMAR GASES PELIGROSOS.

◆ **Enjuague completamente las esponjas y los trapeadores después de limpiar áreas sucias o con polvo.**

◆ **Lávele con frecuencia las manos a los niños, especialmente antes de que coman, antes de las siestas y antes de irse a dormir.**

◆ **Mantenga limpias las áreas de juego.** Lave con regularidad los biberones, chupones, juguetes y animales de peluche.

◆ **No permita que los niños muerdan los marcos de las ventanas ni las demás superficies pintadas.**

◆ **Límpiese o quítese los zapatos antes de entrar a la casa para evitar meter el plomo de la tierra.**

◆ **Asegúrese de que los niños coman alimentos nutritivos, bajos en grasa y altos en hierro y calcio,** tales como las espinacas y los productos lácteos. Los niños con una dieta buena absorben menos plomo.

7

Otras fuentes de plomo

◆ **El agua potable.** Su casa podría tener tuberías de plomo o con soldadura de plomo. Llame al departamento local de salud o al proveedor de agua para averiguar cómo examinar el agua. El plomo no puede verse, olerse ni tiene sabor, y el hervir el agua no eliminará el plomo. Si cree que sus tuberías tienen plomo:

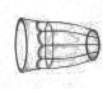

Aunque la pintura, el polvo y la tierra tienen los riesgos relacionados con plomo más comunes, existen también otras fuentes de plomo.

- Use agua fría para beber y cocinar.

- Deje correr el agua durante 15 a 30 segundos antes de beberla, especialmente si no se ha usado el agua durante algunas horas.

◆ **El trabajo.** Si trabaja con plomo, podría traerlo a su casa en las manos o en la ropa. Báñese y cámbiese la ropa antes de volver a casa. Lave la ropa de su trabajo por separado del resto de la ropa de la familia.

◆ **Los juguetes y muebles** viejos pintados.

◆ Alimentos y líquidos almacenados en **cristal de plomo** o **cerámica** o **porcelana con esmalte de plomo.**

◆ **Los hornos de fundición de plomo** u otras industrias que emiten plomo al aire.

◆ **Los pasatiempos** que usan plomo, tales como los cacharros, cerámicas, pinturas y tintes, pintar en vidrio o refinar muebles.

◆ **Los remedios** caseros que contengan plomo, tales como "greta" y "azarcón" que se usan para tratar padecimientos estomacales.

Remodelación o renovación de una casa que tiene pintura con base de plomo

Tome medidas de precaución antes de que el contratista o usted comience la remodelación o cualquier renovación que alterará las superficies pintadas (tales como el raspado de la pintura o la demolición de paredes):

◆ **Haga que examinen el área por si hay pintura con base de plomo.**

◆ **No use una lijadora de correa, un soplete de gas propano, una pistola de calor, un raspador seco o papel para lijar en seco** para remover la pintura con base de plomo. Estas acciones pueden crear grandes cantidades de gases y polvo que contiene plomo. El polvo que contiene plomo puede permanecer en su hogar mucho tiempo después de finalizar el trabajo.

◆ **Mude temporalmente a su familia** (especialmente los niños y las mujeres embarazadas) a otro sitio fuera del apartamento o la casa hasta que se termine el trabajo y el área se limpie correctamente. Si no puede cambiar de lugar a su familia, por lo menos selle completamente el área de trabajo.

◆ **Siga otras medidas de seguridad para reducir el riesgo relacionado con el plomo.** Usted puede encontrar información acerca de otras medidas de seguridad llamando al 1-800-424-LEAD. Pida el folleto "Reducing Lead Hazards When Remodeling Your Home (Reducción de los riesgos relacionados con el plomo al remodelar su casa)". Este folleto le explica qué hacer antes, durante y después de las renovaciones.

Si no se realizan correctamente, ciertos tipos de renovación pueden liberar el plomo de la pintura y el polvo al aire.

Si ya terminó las renovaciones o la remodelación de su casa y existe la posibilidad de que se haya emitido pintura o polvo con base de plomo, haga que examinen a sus niños pequeños y siga los pasos que se indican en la página 7 de este folleto.

Para obtener más información

Centro Nacional de Información Sobre el Plomo

Llame al **1-800-424-LEAD (424-5323)** para averiguar cómo proteger a los niños del envenenamiento por plomo y para otra información sobre los riesgos relacionados con el plomo. Para acceder a información acerca del plomo mediante la red mundial de Internet, visite **www.epa.gov/lead y www.hud.gov/offices/lead.**

Para las personas con impedimentos auditivos, llame al Servicio Federal de Retransmisión de Información al **1-800-877-8339** y pida el Centro Nacional de Información sobre el Plomo al **1-800-424-LEAD.**

Línea directa de agua potable segura de EPA

Llame al **1-800-426-4791** para obtener información acerca del agua potable.

Línea directa de la Comisión de seguridad de los productos de consumo (CPSC)

Para pedir información relacionada con el plomo en los productos de consumo, o para denunciar un producto de consumo inseguro o una lesión relacionada con un producto llame al **1-800-638-2772** o visite el sitio de Internet de CPSC: **www.cpsc.gov.**

Agencias del Medio Ambiente y de Salud

Algunas ciudades, estados y tribus tienen sus propias reglas para las actividades relacionadas con pintura con base de plomo. Consulte con su agencia estatal para ver si existen leyes estatales o locales que le correspondan. La mayoría de las agencias estatales también pueden proporcionarle información para conseguir una compañía para remover la pintura con plomo en su área, y para conseguir posibles fuentes de ayuda financiera para la reducción de los riesgos relacionados con el plomo. Reciba la última información en direcciones y números telefónicos de contactos locales o estatales por Internet en **www.epa.gov/lead** o comuníquese con el Centro Nacional de Información sobre el Plomo al **1-800-424-LEAD.**

11

Oficinas Regionales de la Agencia de Protección Ambiental (EPA)

Su oficina regional de EPA puede proporcionarle más información relacionada con las regulaciones y los programas de protección contra el plomo.

Oficinas Regionales de EPA

Región 1 (Connecticut, Massachusetts, Maine, New Hampshire, Rhode Island, Vermont)

Contacto regional para el plomo
U.S. EPA Region 1
Suite 1100 (CPT)
One Congress Street
Boston, MA 02114-2023
1 (800) 372-7341

Región 2 (New Jersey, New York, Puerto Rico, Virgin Islands)

Contacto regional para el plomo
U.S. EPA Region 2
2890 Woodbridge Avenue
Building 209, Mail Stop 225
Edison, NJ 08837-3679
(732) 321-6671

Región 3 (Delaware, Maryland, Pennsylvania, Virginia, Washington DC, West Virginia)

Contacto regional para el plomo
U.S. EPA Region 3 (3WC33)
1650 Arch Street
Philadelphia, PA 19103
(215) 814-5000

Región 4 (Alabama, Florida, Georgia, Kentucky, Mississippi, North Carolina, South Carolina, Tennessee)

Contacto regional para el plomo
U.S. EPA Region 4
61 Forsyth Street, SW
Atlanta, GA 30303
(404) 562-8998

Región 5 (Illinois, Indiana, Michigan, Minnesota, Ohio, Wisconsin)

Contacto regional para el plomo
U.S. EPA Region 5 (DT-8)
77 West Jackson Boulevard
Chicago, IL 60604-3666
(312) 886-6003

Región 6 (Arkansas, Louisiana, New Mexico, Oklahoma, Texas)

Contacto regional para el plomo
U.S. EPA Region 6
1445 Ross Avenue, 12th Floor
Dallas, TX 75202-2733
(214) 665-7577

Región 7 (Iowa, Kansas, Missouri, Nebraska)

Contacto regional para el plomo
U.S. EPA Region 7
(ARTD-RALI)
901 N. 5th Street
Kansas City, KS 66101
(913) 551-7020

Región 8 (Colorado, Montana, North Dakota, South Dakota, Utah, Wyoming)

Contacto regional para el plomo
U.S. EPA Region 8
999 18th Street, Suite 500
Denver, CO 80202-2466
(303) 312-6021

Región 9 (Arizona, California, Hawaii, Nevada)

Contacto regional para el plomo
U.S. EPA Region 9
75 Hawthorne Street
San Francisco, CA 94105
(415) 947-4164

Región 10 (Alaska, Idaho, Oregon, Washington)

Contacto regional para el plomo
U.S. EPA Region 10
Toxics Section WCM-128
1200 Sixth Avenue
Seattle, WA 98101-1128
(206) 553-1985

12

Pasos sencillos para proteger a su familia en contra de los riesgos relacionados con el plomo

Si cree que su casa tiene niveles altos de plomo:

◆ Haga que examinen a sus niños pequeños para determinar el nivel de plomo, incluso si parecen estar saludables.

◆ Lávele con frecuencia las manos a los niños, los biberones, los chupones y los juguetes.

◆ Asegúrese de que los niños coman alimentos nutritivos y bajos en grasa.

◆ Haga que examinen su casa para descubrir riesgos relacionados con el plomo.

◆ Limpie con regularidad los pisos, los marcos de las ventanas y las demás superficies.

◆ Limpie la tierra de los zapatos antes de entrar en su casa.

◆ Hable con el propietario para que le arregle las superficies con pintura descascarada o picada.

◆ Tome medidas para evitar la exposición al polvo que contiene plomo al remodelar o renovar su casa (llame al 1-800-424-LEAD para obtener consejo).

◆ No use lijadoras de banda, sopletes de gas propano, pistolas de calor, raspadores en seco ni lijas de papel en seco en las superficies pintadas que pudieran tener plomo.

◆ No trate de remover usted mismo la pintura con base de plomo.

Oficinas Regionales de CPSC

Su oficina regional de CPSC puede proporcionarle más información relacionada con los reglamentos y la seguridad de los productos de consumo.

Centro Regional del Este
Consumer Product Safety Commission
201 Varick Street, Room 903
New York, NY 10014
(212) 620-4120

Centro Regional del Oeste
Consumer Product Safety Commission
1301 Clay Street, Suite 610-N
Oakland, CA 94612
(510) 637-4050

Centro Regional Central
Consumer Product Safety Commission
230 South Dearborn Street, Room 2944
Chicago, IL 60604
(312) 353-8260

Oficina de Asuntos Relacionados Con el Plomo de HUD

Comuníquese con la Oficina de control de riesgos relacionados con el plomo y hogares saludables para obtener más información acerca de los reglamentos relacionados con el plomo, esfuerzos de alcance comunitario y los programas de control de los riesgos relacionados con el plomo y estipendios para investigación.

Departamento de Desarrollo Urbano y de la Vivienda de los Estados Unidos (HUD)
U.S. Department of Housing and Urban Development
Office of Healthy Homes and Lead Hazard Control
451 Seventh Street, SW, P-3206
Washington, DC 20410
(202) 755-1785

Rental Application

Separate application required from each applicant age 18 or older.

Date and time received by landlord _____

Credit check fee _____ Received _____

THIS SECTION TO BE COMPLETED BY LANDLORD

Address of Property to Be Rented: _____

Rental Term: ☐ month-to-month ☐ lease from _____ to _____

Amounts Due Prior to Occupancy

First month's rent .... $_____

Security deposit .... $_____

Other (specify): _____ $_____

TOTAL.. $_____

Applicant

Full Name—include all names you use(d): _____

Home Phone: (_____) _____ Work Phone: (_____)_____

Social Security Number:_____ Driver's License Number/State: _____

Other Identifying Information: _____

Vehicle Make: _____ Model: _____ Color: _____ Year: _____

License Plate Number/State: _____

Additional Occupants

List everyone, including children, who will live with you:

<u>Full Name</u>   Relationship to Applicant

_____

_____

_____

Rental History
FIRST-TIME RENTERS: ATTACH A DESCRIPTION OF YOUR HOUSING SITUATION FOR THE PAST FIVE YEARS.

Current Address: _____

Dates Lived at Address: _____ Rent $_____ Security Deposit $_____

Landlord/Manager: _____ Landlord/Manager's Phone: (_____)_____

Reason for Leaving: _____

Previous Address: _____

Dates Lived at Address: _____ Rent $ _____ Security Deposit $ _____

Landlord/Manager: _____ Landlord/Manager's Phone: ( ) _____

Reason for Leaving: _____

Previous Address: _____

Dates Lived at Address: _____ Rent $ _____ Security Deposit $ _____

Landlord/Manager: _____ Landlord/Manager's Phone: ( ) _____

Reason for Leaving: _____

Employment History

SELF-EMPLOYED APPLICANTS: ATTACH TAX RETURNS FOR THE PAST TWO YEARS

Name and Address of Current Employer: _____

_____ Phone: ( ) _____

Name of Supervisor: _____ Supervisor's Phone: ( ) _____

Dates Employed at This Job: _____ Position or Title: _____

Name and Address of Previous Employer: _____

_____ Phone: ( ) _____

Name of Supervisor: _____ Supervisor's Phone: ( ) _____

Dates Employed at This Job: _____ Position or Title: _____

ATTACH PAY STUBS FOR THE PAST TWO YEARS, FROM THIS EMPLOYER OR PRIOR EMPLOYERS.

Income

1. Your gross monthly employment income (before deductions): $_____

2. Average monthly amounts of other income (specify sources): $_____

   _____ $_____

   _____ $_____

                                    TOTAL: $_____

Bank/Financial Accounts

	Account Number	Bank/Institution	Branch	
Savings Account:				
Checking Account:				
Money Market or Similar Account:				

_____

_____

_____

Credit Card Accounts

Major Credit Card: ☐ VISA ☐ MC ☐ Discover Card ☐ Am Ex ☐ Other: _____

Issuer: _____ Account No. _____

Balance $_____ Average Monthly Payment: $ _____

Major Credit Card: ☐ VISA ☐ MC ☐ Discover Card ☐ Am Ex ☐ Other: _____

Issuer: _____ Account No. _____

Balance $_____ Average Monthly Payment: $ _____

Loans

Type of Loan (mortgage, car, student loan, etc.)	Name of Creditor	Account Number	Amount Owed	Monthly Payment

Other Major Obligations

Type	Payee	Amount Owed	Monthly Payment

Miscellaneous

Describe the number and type of pets you want to have in the rental property: _____

Describe water-filled furniture you want to have in the rental property: _____

Do you smoke? ☐ yes ☐ no

Have you ever:
Filed for bankruptcy?	☐ yes ☐ no	How many times _____
Been sued?	☐ yes ☐ no	How many times _____
Sued someone else?	☐ yes ☐ no	How many times _____
Been evicted?	☐ yes ☐ no	
Been convicted of a crime?	☐ yes ☐ no	How many times _____

Explain any "yes" listed above: _____

_____

_____

_____

References and Emergency Contact

Personal Reference: _____ Relationship: _____

Address: _____

_____ Phone: (___) _____

Personal Reference: _____ Relationship: _____

Address: _____

_____ Phone: (___) _____

Contact in Emergency: _____ Relationship: _____

Address: _____

_____ Phone: (___) _____

Source

Where did you learn of this vacancy? _____

_____

I certify that all the information given above is true and correct and understand that my lease or rental agreement may be terminated if I have made any material false or incomplete statements in this application. I authorize verification of the information provided in this application from my credit sources, credit bureaus, current and previous landlords and employers, and personal references. This permission will survive the expiration of my tenancy.

_____   _____

Applicant   Date

Notes (Landlord/Manager): _____

_____

_____

_____

_____

_____

_____

_____

_____

_____

_____

_____

_____

Consent to Contact References and Perform Credit Check

I authorize _____ to
obtain information about me from my credit sources, current and previous landlords, employers, and personal
references, to enable _____ to evaluate my
rental application.

I give permission for the landlord or its agent to obtain a consumer report about me for the purpose of this
application, to ensure that I continue to meet the terms of the tenancy, for the collection and recovery of any
financial obligations relating to my tenancy, or for any other permissible purpose.

_____
Applicant signature

_____
Printed name

_____
Address

_____
Phone Number

_____
Date

Tenant References

Name of Applicant: _____

Address of Rental Unit: _____

Previous Landlord or Manager

Contact (name, property owner or manager, address of rental unit): _____

_____

Date: _____

Questions

When did tenant rent from you (move-in and move-out dates)? _____

What was the monthly rent? _____ Did tenant pay rent on time? ☐ Yes ☐ No

If rent was not paid on time, did you have to give tenant a legal notice demanding the rent? ☐ Yes ☐ No

If rent was not paid on time, provide details _____

_____

Did you give tenant notice of any lease violation for other than nonpayment of rent? ☐ Yes ☐ No

If you gave a lease violation notice, what was the outcome? _____

Was tenant considerate of neighbors—that is, no loud parties and fair, careful use of common areas?

_____

_____

Did tenant have any pets? ☐ Yes ☐ No If so, were there any problems? _____

_____

Did tenant make any unreasonable demands or complaints? ☐ Yes ☐ No If so, explain: _____

_____

Why did tenant leave? _____

_____

Did tenant give the proper amount of notice before leaving? ☐ Yes ☐ No

Did tenant leave the place in good condition? Did you need to use the security deposit to cover damage?

_____

Any particular problems you'd like to mention? _____

_____

Would you rent to this person again? _____

_____

Other comments: _____

_____

_____

Previous Landlord or Manager

Contact (name, property owner or manager, address of rental unit): _____

_____

Date: _____

Questions

When did tenant rent from you (move-in and move-out dates)? _____

What was the monthly rent? _____   Did tenant pay rent on time? ☐ Yes ☐ No

If rent was not paid on time, did you give have to tenant a legal notice demanding the rent? ☐ Yes ☐ No

If rent was not paid on time, provide details _____

_____

Did you give tenant notice of any lease violation for other than nonpayment of rent? ☐ Yes ☐ No

If you gave a lease violation notice, what was the outcome? _____

Was tenant considerate of neighbors—that is, no loud parties and fair, careful use of common areas?

_____

_____

Did tenant have any pets? ☐ Yes ☐ No   If so, were there any problems? _____

_____

Did tenant make any unreasonable demands or complaints? ☐ Yes ☐ No   If so, explain: _____

_____

Why did tenant leave? _____

_____

Did tenant give the proper amount of notice before leaving? ☐ Yes ☐ No

Did tenant leave the place in good condition? Did you need to use the security deposit to cover damage?

_____

Any particular problems you'd like to mention? _____

_____

Would you rent to this person again? _____

_____

Other comments: _____

_____

_____

_____

_____

_____

Employment Verification

Contact (name, company, position): _____

Date: _____ Salary: $ _____

Dates of Employment: _____

Comments: _____

_____

_____

_____

_____

_____

_____

_____

Personal Reference

Contact (name and relationship to applicant): _____

Date: _____ How long have you known the applicant? _____

Would you recommend this person as a prospective tenant? _____

Comments: _____

_____

_____

_____

_____

_____

_____

_____

Credit and Financial Information

_____

_____

_____

_____

_____

Notes, Including Reasons for Rejecting Applicant

_____

_____

_____

_____

_____

Notice of Denial Based on Credit Report or Other Information

To: _____

Applicant

_____

Street Address

_____

City, State, and Zip Code

Your rights under the Fair Credit Reporting Act and Fair and Accurate Credit Transactions (FACT) Act of 2003. (15 U.S.C. §§ 1681 and following.)

THIS NOTICE is to inform you that your application to rent the property at _____

_____

[rental property address] has been denied because of [*check all that apply*]:

☐ Insufficient information in the credit report provided by:

    Credit reporting agency: _____

    Address, phone number, URL: _____

☐ Negative information in the credit report provided by:

    Credit reporting agency: _____

    Address, phone number, URL: _____

☐ The consumer credit reporting agency noted above did not make the decision not to offer you this rental. It only provided information about your credit history. You have the right to obtain a free copy of your credit report from the consumer credit reporting agency named above, if your request is made within 60 days of this notice or if you have not requested a free copy within the past year. You also have the right to dispute the accuracy or completeness of your credit report. The agency must reinvestigate within a reasonable time, free of charge, and remove or modify inaccurate information. If the reinvestigation does not resolve the dispute to your satisfaction, you may add your own "consumer statement" (up to 100 words) to the report, which must be included (or a clear summary) in future reports.

☐ Information supplied by a third party other than a credit reporting agency or you and gathered by someone other than myself or any employee. You have the right to learn of the nature of the information if you ask me in writing within 60 days of the date of this notice.

_____   _____

Landlord/Manager   Date

Notice of Conditional Acceptance Based on Credit Report or Other Information

To: _____

Applicant

_____

Street Address

_____

City, State, and Zip Code

Your application to rent the property at _____

_____ [rental property address] has been accepted, conditioned on your

willingness and ability to: _____

_____

Your rights under the Fair Credit Reporting Act and Fair and Accurate Credit Transactions (FACT) Act of 2003. (15 U.S.C. §§ 1681 and following.)

Source of information prompting conditional acceptance

My decision to conditionally accept your application was prompted in whole or in part by:

☐ Insufficient information in the credit report provided by

Credit reporting agency: _____

Address, phone number, URL: _____

_____

☐ Negative information in the credit report provided by :

Credit reporting agency: _____

Address, phone number, URL: _____

_____

☐ The consumer credit reporting agency noted above did not make the decision to offer you this conditional acceptance. It only provided information about your credit history. You have the right to obtain a free copy of your credit report from the consumer credit reporting agency named above, if your request is made within 60 days of this notice or if you have not requested a free copy within the past year. You also have the right to dispute the accuracy or completeness of your credit report. The agency must reinvestigate within a reasonable time, free of charge, and remove or modify inaccurate information. If the reinvestigation does not resolve the dispute to your satisfaction, you may add your own "consumer statement" (up to 100 words) to the report, which must be included (or a clear summary) in future reports.

☐ Information supplied by a third party other than a credit reporting agency or you and gathered by someone other than myself or any employee. You have the right to learn of the nature of the information if you ask me in writing within 60 days of the date of this notice.

_____   _____
Landlord/Manager   Date

Landlord-Tenant Checklist

GENERAL CONDITION OF RENTAL UNIT AND PREMISES

Street Address   Unit No.   City

	Condition on Arrival	Condition on Departure	Estimated Cost of Repair/ Replacement
Living Room			
Floors & Floor Coverings			
Drapes & Window Coverings			
Walls & Ceilings			
Light Fixtures			
Windows, Screens, & Doors			
Front Door & Locks			
Fireplace			
Other			
Other			
Kitchen			
Floors & Floor Coverings			
Walls & Ceilings			
Light Fixtures			
Cabinets			
Counters			
Stove/Oven			
Refrigerator			
Dishwasher			
Garbage Disposal			
Sink & Plumbing			
Windows, Screens, & Doors			
Other			
Other			
Dining Room			
Floors & Floor Covering			
Walls & Ceilings			
Light Fixtures			
Windows, Screens, & Doors			
Other			

	Condition on Arrival			Condition on Departure			Estimated Cost of Repair/ Replacement
Bathroom(s)	Bath #1	Bath #2		Bath #1	Bath #2		
Floors & Floor Coverings							
Walls & Ceilings							
Windows, Screens, & Doors							
Light Fixtures							
Bathtub/Shower							
Sink & Counters							
Toilet							
Other							
Other							
Bedroom(s)	Bdrm #1	Bdrm #2	Bdrm #3	Bdrm #1	Bdrm #2	Bdrm #3	
Floors & Floor Coverings							
Windows, Screens, & Doors							
Walls & Ceilings							
Light Fixtures							
Other							
Other							
Other							
Other							
Other Areas							
Heating System							
Air Conditioning							
Lawn/Garden							
Stairs and Hallway							
Patio, Terrace, Deck, etc.							
Basement							
Parking Area							
Other							
Other							
Other							
Other							
Other							

☐ Tenants acknowledge that all smoke detectors and fire extinguishers were tested in their presence and found to be in working order, and that the testing procedure was explained to them. Tenants agree to test all detectors at least once a month and to report any problems to Landlord/Manager in writing. Tenants agree to replace all smoke detector batteries as necessary.

FURNISHED PROPERTY

	Condition on Arrival		Condition on Departure		Estimated Cost of Repair/ Replacement
Living Room					
Coffee Table					
End Tables					
Lamps					
Chairs					
Sofa					
Other					
Other					
Kitchen					
Broiler Pan					
Ice Trays					
Other					
Other					
Dining Room					
Chairs					
Stools					
Table					
Other					
Other					
Bathroom(s)	Bath #1	Bath #2	Bath #1	Bath #2	
Mirrors					
Shower Curtain					
Hamper					
Other					
Bedroom(s)	Bdrm #1	Bdrm #2	Bdrm #3	Bdrm #1	Bdrm #2	Bdrm #3	
Beds (single)							
Beds (double)							
Chairs							
Chests							
Dressing Tables							
Lamps							
Mirrors							
Night Tables							

	Condition on Arrival	Condition on Departure	Estimated Cost of Repair/ Replacement
Other			
Other			
Other Areas			
Bookcases			
Desks			
Pictures			
Other			
Other			

Use this space to provide any additional explanation:

_____

_____

_____

_____

_____

_____

_____

_____

Landlord-Tenant Checklist completed on moving in on _____ and approved by:

_____ and _____
Landlord/Manager   Tenant

_____
Tenant

_____
Tenant

Landlord-Tenant Checklist completed on moving out on _____ and approved by:

_____ and _____
Landlord/Manager   Tenant

_____
Tenant

Move-In Letter

Date _____

Tenant _____

Street Address _____

City and State _____

Dear _____,
                     Tenant

Welcome to _____

(address of rental unit). We hope you will enjoy living here.

This letter is to explain what you can expect from the management and what we'll be looking for from you.

1. Rent: _____
_____
_____.

2. New Roommates: _____
_____
_____
_____.

3. Notice to End Tenancy: _____
_____
_____
_____.

4. Deposits: _____
_____
_____.

5. Manager: _____
_____
_____.

6. Landlord-Tenant Checklist: _____
_____
_____
_____
_____.

7. Maintenance/Repair Problems: _____
_____
_____
_____
_____
_____
_____.

8. Semiannual Safety and Maintenance Update: _____
_____
_____
_____.

9. Annual Safety Inspection: _____
_____
_____
_____
_____.

10. Insurance: _____
_____
_____
_____
_____
_____
_____.

11. Moving Out: _____
_____
_____
_____
_____
_____.

12. Telephone Number Changes: _____
_____.

Please let us know if you have any questions.

Sincerely,

_____   _____
Landlord/Manager   Date

I have read and received a copy of this statement.

_____   _____
Tenant   Date

Tenant's Notice of Intent to Move Out

Date _____

Tenant _____

Street Address _____

City and State _____

Dear _____ ,
                    Landlord

This is to notify you that the undersigned tenants, _____

_____ , will be moving from

_____ ,

on _____ , _____ from today. This

provides at least _____ written notice as required in our rental

agreement.

Sincerely,

_____

Tenant

_____

Tenant

_____

Tenant

Move-Out Letter

Date _____

Tenant _____

Street Address _____

City and State _____

Dear _____ ,

                                     Tenant

We hope you have enjoyed living here. In order that we may mutually end our relationship on a positive note, this move-out letter describes how we expect your unit to be left and what our procedures are for returning your security deposit.

Basically, we expect you to leave your rental unit in the same condition it was when you moved in, except for normal wear and tear. To refresh your memory on the condition of the unit when you moved in, I've attached a copy of the Landlord-Tenant Checklist you signed at the beginning of your tenancy. I'll be using this same form to inspect your unit when you leave.

Specifically, here's a list of items you should thoroughly clean before vacating:

- ☐ Floors
    - ☐ sweep wood floors
    - ☐ vacuum carpets and rugs (shampoo if necessary)
    - ☐ mop kitchen and bathroom floors
- ☐ Walls, baseboards, ceilings, and built-in shelves
- ☐ Kitchen cabinets, countertops and sink, stove and oven—inside and out
- ☐ Refrigerator—clean inside and out, empty it of food, and turn it off, with the door left open
- ☐ Bathtubs, showers, toilets, and plumbing fixtures
- ☐ Doors, windows, and window coverings
- ☐ Other

_____

_____

_____

_____

If you have any questions as to the type of cleaning we expect, please let me know.

Please don't leave anything behind—that includes bags of garbage, clothes, food, newspapers, furniture, appliances, dishes, plants, cleaning supplies, or other items that belong to you.

Please be sure you have disconnected phone and utility services, canceled all newspaper subscriptions, and sent the post office a change of address form.

Once you have cleaned your unit and removed all your belongings, please call me at _____ to arrange for a walk-through inspection and to return all keys. Please be prepared to give me your forwarding address where we may mail your security deposit.

It's our policy to return all deposits either in person or at an address you provide within _____ _____ after you move out. If any deductions are made—for past due rent or because the unit is damaged or not sufficiently clean—they will be explained in writing.

If you have any questions, please contact me at _____.

Sincerely,

_____

Landlord/Manager

Index

A

Absences (extended) by tenant, clause in
    agreement, 35
Access
    landlord's right to, 33–34
    state laws, 126–29
Additional provisions clause, 41–42
Advertising rental property, 52–54
Alterations by tenants
    clause in agreement, 29–30
    disabled tenants and, 30, 67
Amending agreements and leases, 90–91
    state notice laws, 109–11
Americans with Disabilities Act (ADA), business
    activities on rental property, 13
Antennas, 30
Asbestos disclosure, 41
Assignment, defined, 26
Assignment and subletting clause, 25–26
Association of rental property owners, 5
Attachment pages
    Florida Attachment about security deposits, 125
    preparing, 10
Attorney fees, payment clause, 37–38
Automatic debit, for rent payments, 17–18

B

Bad checks, 20–21
Bank account information, verifying, 65
Bank charges clause, 20–21
Burglar alarm, 29
Business activities on rental property, 13

C

California
    child care home business, 13
    move-out inspections, 104
    See also State laws
Cash, accepting for rent payments, 17–18
CD-ROM
    installing the form files, 132
    list of files included, 135–36
    PDF files, 135
    word processing files, 133–34
Child care home business, 13
Commercial property, 2
Conditional acceptance of applicant, 71–73
Consent form, contact references and perform
    credit check, 60
Constructive eviction, 98
Controlled substances releases disclosure, 39, 40
Cosigners, 44
Cotenants, defined, 26
Court costs, payment clause, 37–38
Court records, of prospective tenant, 66
Craigslist, 52
Credit cards, for rent payments, 17
Credit report
    conditional acceptance based on, 71–73
    denial based on, 69–70
    obtaining, 64–65

D

Disclosure clauses, 38–41
Discrimination. *See* Illegal discrimination

Disposing of credit reports, 65, 85

Disturbances caused by tenant, 31

Drug labs, controlled substances releases
   disclosure, 39, 40

Duty to mitigate loss, 102–3

E

Employment verification, 61, 64

Ending a month-to-month tenancy. *See*
   Termination of month-to-month tenancy

Entire agreement clause, 43

Entry of premises, 33–34, 126–29

Equifax, 64

Excise tax number disclosure, 40

Exculpatory clauses, 42

Experian, 64

Expiration of lease, 98–103

Extended absences by tenant
   clause in agreement, 35
   value of clause, 100

F

Fair and Accurate Credit Transactions Act,
   Disposal Rule for credit reports, 65, 85

Fair Housing Act
   disabled tenants and alterations, 30
   housing discrimination resources, 68
   occupancy standards, 16
   rights of disabled tenants, 67

Families with children, discrimination against, 14,
   16

Fees
   attorney fees and court costs, 37–38
   credit reports, 64–65

Fixed-term lease. *See* Lease

Flood disclosure, 40

Florida
   Attachment about security deposits, 125
   See also State laws

Form I-9 (Employment Eligibility Verification),
   55

Forms CD-ROM, 132–36

G

Guests of tenant, tenant's responsibility for, 42

Guide dogs, 33

H

Hidden defects, disclosures, 41

Hold harmless clauses, 42

Home businesses on rental property, 13

I

Illegal discrimination
   avoiding, 67–68
   families with children, 14, 16
   termination of tenancy and, 92

Illegal tenant activity, 31–32

Immigration status, on rental application, 55

Income verification, 61, 64

Individual Taxpayer Identification Number
   (ITIN), on rental application, 55

Inspections
   move-in inspections, 76–82
   move-out inspections, 103–4

Insurance
   business activities on rental property, 13
   renter's insurance, 29

Interest paid on security deposits, 22, 24, 123–24

IRS Schedule E, 86–87

ITIN, on rental application, 55

L

Landlord, identification clause, 11
Landlord's right to access
  clause about, 33–34
  state laws about, 126–29
Landlord-tenant checklist
  move-in inspection, 76–82
  move-out inspections, 103–4
"Last month's rent," 23–24, 95
Late charges clause, 19–20
Lawsuits
  advertising and, 54
  payment of costs clause, 37–38
  tenant breaks lease, 103
Lead disclosures, 38–39
Lease
  amending, 90
  duty to mitigate loss, 102–3
  expiration of, 98–103
  military service and termination, 93
  overview, 8–9
  preparing, 10–43
  signing of, 43–44
  tenant leaves early, 100–101
  tenant remains after expiration, 100
Legal papers, authority to receive clause, 41

M

Maintenance and repair by landlord, 28
Maintenance responsibilities of tenant, clause in
  agreement, 27–29
Managers
  property management companies, 74
  tenant-managers, 73
Megan's Law. See Sexual offender database
Military noise disclosure, 39
Military ordnance disclosure, 39
Military service, and termination of tenancy, 93

Mitigating losses when tenant breaks lease, 102–3
Mobile homes, 2
Mold disclosure, 39, 40
Month-to-month agreement. See Rental agreement
Move-in inspection, 76–82
Move-in letter, 82–84
Move-out inspections, 103–4
Move-out letter, 95, 96–97

N

National Apartment Association, 5
National Fair Housing Advocate, 68
National Multi-Housing Council, 5
New York
  child care home business, 13
  Roommate Law, 14, 16
  See also State laws
Nonrefundable security deposits and fees, 22
Notice of Conditional Acceptance Based on Credit
  Report or Other Information, 71–73
Notice of Denial Based on Credit Report or Other
  Information, 69–70
Notice of expiration of lease, 98
Notice of termination of tenancy
  state laws, 109–11
  by tenant, 92–94
  to tenant, 91
  tenant fails to give notice, 95
Notice to quit, 98
Nuisance, 31

O

Occupancy
  limits clause, 14
  standards for, 16
Online apartment listing services, 52
Open Door program, 33

P

Parents for Megan's Law, 66
PDF files, 135
Pets clause, 32–33
Photograph the rental unit, move-in inspection, 82
Possession of premises, clause in agreement, 35–36
Premises
  identification clause, 11–13
  possession clause, 35–36
Previous landlords, contacting, 61
Proof of identity, on rental application, 55
Property management companies, 74
Prorated first month's rent, 18

Q

Quiet enjoyment, 31

R

README file, 132
Records
  income and expenses for tax reporting, 86–87
  organizing, 85–86
Reference checking, 60–61
  sample form for, 62–63
Rejecting an applicant, 69–70
Rekeying locks, clause forbidding, 29
Rent
  accepting after 30-day notice, 95
  cashing tenant's first check for, 85
  payment clause, 17–19
  state laws, 112–13
  See also Amending agreements and leases
Rental agreement
  amending, 90–91
  military service and termination, 93
  overview, 8

  preparing, 10–43
  sample agreement, 45–50
  signing of, 43–44
  termination of tenancy, 91–98
Rental applications, 54–60
Rent control
  late fees, 19
  ordinances and regulations, 19
  termination of tenancy, 92
  terms of tenancy, 17
Renter's insurance, clause requiring, 29
"Repair and deduct" procedure, 30
Repairs and alterations by tenant, clause in agreement, 29–30
Retaliation, termination of tenancy and, 92
Returned check clause, 20–21
Roommates, defined, 26
RTF file, 133–34

S

San Francisco SPCA, 33
Satellite dishes, 30
Savings clause, 42
Security deposits
  cashing tenant's check for, 85
  clause in agreement, 21–24
  Florida Attachment, 125
  how much to charge, 23
  interest paid on, 22, 24, 123–24
  penalties for violations, 105
  for pets, 33
  returning, 103–5
  state rules, 114–19
  state rules on disclosures, 120–22
Service dogs, 33
Service of process, authority to receive clause, 41
Sexual offender database
  disclosure about, 40
  prospective tenants and, 66

Shared utilities, disclosing, 25, 39, 40
Signal dogs, 33
Smoke detectors, move-in inspection, 81
Social Security number, on rental application, 55
State laws
  access to rental property, 126–29
  interest paid on security deposits, 123–24
  landlord-tenant checklist, 76
  locating, 107
  move-out inspections, 104
  notice to change or terminate tenancy, 109–11
  rent rules, 112–13
  security deposit disclosures, 120–22
  security deposits, 114–19
  statutes, 108
Subletting and assignment clause, 25–26
Subsidized housing, 2
Subtenant, defined, 26

T

Tenant
  defined, 26
  identification clause, 11
Tenant-managers, 73
Tenant rules and regulations clause, 36–37
Termination of month-to-month tenancy
  military service and, 93
  notice by tenant, 92–94
  notice to tenant, 91
  restrictions on, 92
  state notice laws, 109–11

Termination of tenancy, grounds clause, 42
Term of tenancy clause, 14–15
Tips for successful landlords, 4
Title X lead disclosures, 38–39
Townhouses, 2
Translation of agreement, 43–44
TransUnion, 64

U

Use, limits clause, 14
Utilities clause, 24–25

V

Validity of each part clause, 42
Violating laws and causing disturbances, clause in
  agreement, 31–32

W

War and National Defense Servicemembers Civil
  Relief Act, 93
Waste, 31
Wireless antennas, 30
Word processing files, 133–34

Get the Latest in the Law

Nolo's Legal Updater
We'll send you an email whenever a new edition of your book is published!
Sign up at **www.nolo.com/legalupdater**.

Updates at Nolo.com
Check **www.nolo.com/update** to find recent changes in the law that
affect the current edition of your book.

Nolo Customer Service
To make sure that this edition of the book is the most recent one, call us at
800-728-3555 and ask one of our friendly customer service representatives
(7:00 am to 6:00 pm PST, weekdays only). Or find out at **www.nolo.com**.

Complete the Registration & Comment Card ...
... and we'll do the work for you! Just indicate your preferences below:

- -

Registration & Comment Card

NAME _____ DATE _____

ADDRESS _____

CITY _____ STATE _____ ZIP _____

PHONE _____ EMAIL _____

COMMENTS _____

WAS THIS BOOK EASY TO USE?   (VERY EASY)   5   4   3   2   1   (VERY DIFFICULT)

☐ Yes, you can quote me in future Nolo promotional materials. *Please include phone number above.*

☐ Yes, send me **Nolo's Legal Updater** via email when a new edition of this book is available.

Yes, I want to sign up for the following email newsletters:

   ☐ **NoloBriefs** (monthly)
   ☐ **Nolo's Special Offer** (monthly)
   ☐ **Nolo's BizBriefs** (monthly)
   ☐ **Every Landlord's Quarterly** (four times a year)

☐ Yes, you can give my contact info to carefully selected
partners whose products may be of interest to me.

NOLO ⚖

LEAR7

Nolo
950 Parker Street
Berkeley, CA 94710-9867
www.nolo.com

YOUR LEGAL COMPANION